PELICAN BOOKS

A833

MATHEMATICS IN MANAGEMENT

Albert Battersby was born in 1917 and graduated as a chemist in 1939. However, he spent most of the war on operational air-crew duties with the Royal Air Force. Since the war he has been the manager of factories in Brazil, India, and the United Kingdom. He has been interested in modern methods of management, including operational research and work study, and was responsible for one of the earliest applications of electronic computers to production control.

Albert Battersby was a senior lecturer at the College of Aeronautics, Cranfield, before being elected a Fellow of Balliol in 1966, and he has an international reputation as a consultant, lecturer, and broadcaster on management. He is the author of *A Guide to Stock Control* (1962) and *Network Analysis* (1964). Both books have been translated into other languages and a fourth book, on sales forecasting, is being written.

Albert Battersby

Mathematics in Management

Penguin Books
BALTIMORE · MARYLAND

Penguin Books Ltd, Harmondsworth, Middlesex, England
Penguin Books Inc., 3300 Clipper Mill Road, Baltimore 11, Md, U.S.A.
Penguin Books Australia Ltd, Ringwood, Victoria, Australia

—

First Published 1966

—

—

Made and printed in Great Britain by
Hazell Watson & Viney Ltd, Aylesbury, Bucks
Set in Monotype Imprint

TO RUTH

ERRATA

page 65 Exercise 3.7, line 3: For x read y

68 PLANES AND PAYMENTS, line 22: For (3.15) read (3.15a)

69 line 5: For (3.15) read (3.15a)

90 ALGEBRAIC STATEMENT OF THE PROBLEM, line 15: For (1.17) read (3.14)

97 THE VALUE OF OVERTIME, line 13: delete (4.34)

99 THE PRICE OF BOOKCASES, line 7: delete (4.38)

110 Table, *Boozle Oil:* For Viscosity 40 read Viscosity 44

112 Equation 5.7: For $x_1 + x_2 + x_6 = 50$ read $x_1 - x_2 + x_6 = 50$

113 Exercise 5.6: For x_4 read x_5 in both instances

116 Exercise 5.7, line 2: For sulphur read viscosity

126 Third Tableau, quantity 30, column x_6: For $+\frac{3}{5}$ read $-\frac{3}{5}$

131 Exercise 5. Fig. 4: For See Figure S.12 read See Figure 5.12

132 Exercise 5.6: For x_4 read x_5 throughout
Exercise 5.8 (b): For S.13 read 5.13

148 line 31 should read: gives Table 6.12, from which the optimum solution is reached by a third iteration.

151 Heading for Table 6.12: For *Optimum Solution* read *Result of Second Iteration*

Contents

Acknowledgements

I AM indebted to Jonathan Cape Ltd for permission to reproduce the poem 'Business Men' by Louis MacNeice in the heading of Chapter 1. Parts of Chapters 4 and 7 appeared originally in *The Accountant* and *The Manager* respectively, and I am grateful to the editors and publishers of these journals for permission to use this material. The diagram from *Industrial Dynamics* by Jay Forrester in Chapter 7 is reproduced by permission of the publishers, John Wiley and the M.I.T. Press, and the author. The computing for Chapter 8 was done by the service bureau of De La Rue Bull Machines Ltd, and my thanks are due not only to that company as a whole but also to Ian McNaught-Davis, Michael Nichols and Charles Kehela for their personal interest. Frank Houseman and Trevor Russell did most of the hard work behind the case example in Chapter 2, with the willing cooperation of the Department of Flight at Cranfield. Practically every member of the staff of Cranfield Work Study School has helped in some way, especially John Johnson and Myra Ellis. The typing was done with patience and good humour by my wife and Ann Smith. My friend and colleague John O'Shaughnessy read the drafts of the manuscript and gave me much helpful advice.

Above all, I have to thank Warwick Sawyer, whose skilful criticism as the consultant editor was combined with a most human and friendly approach.

I

The Innumerate Nation

The two men talking business
So easily in the train
Project themselves upon me
Just as the window pane

Reflects their faces, and I
Find myself in a trance
To hear two strangers talking
The same language for once.

LOUIS MACNEICE, *Business Men*

THE AGE OF COMPLEXITY

THE big business organization as we know it today did not exist in the early nineteenth century. A hundred years ago even the largest companies were directed in all but their most trivial aspects by a single owner-manager. The weaving-shed with a hundred looms differed from that with five only in size, and not at all in the complexity of its operations. The owner could handle it all comfortably – buying, processing and selling – and there was an abundant supply of cheap labour. The incentive of threatened hunger took the place of factory canteens, welfare services and bonus schemes; National Insurance and P.A.Y.E. still lay in the future. Wages were paid in cash, so administration was simple. These very conditions contained the seeds of their own abolition, but while they prevailed the fundamental simplicity of the one-man controller remained.

Rates of change were also slow. The Victorian mill-owner would install an extra machine in the confident knowledge that it would remain as a lifelong asset to be passed on to his sons; the prudent director of the nineteen-thirties would write off its value over twenty years; the modern manager is considering its rapid obsolescence even as he decides to buy.

In science, the day of the gifted amateur was just past its zenith. Sir Humphrey Davy could isolate sodium with labour and materials supplied entirely from his own resources; his pupil Faraday generated the first currents of electricity with a few simple wires and magnets; Marie Curie wrestled single-handed with her tons of pitchblende in a Parisian backyard.

In such circumstances, the idea of a 'science of management' would have surprised both managers and scientists alike. The notion that so simple and sordid a process as the buying, weaving and selling of cotton could interest a Faraday or a Davy would have seemed ludicrous. The machines themselves, yes, but the *management* – absurd! A few lone voices were raised, Adam Smith and Robert Owen among them, and a few experiments were made, but in the main management remained as a traditional skill, unrecognized as a potential field for scientific investigation.

Now, in the technological explosion of the twentieth century, we see the team predominant. A Henry Ford could no more run his business single-handed in today's conditions than a Madame Curie could build a nuclear reactor unaided. Businesses have grown into organizations of such complexity that the largest of them spread around the planet and spend more each year than many a sovereign state. Specialist managers abound – purchasing officers, financial advisers, market researchers, production controllers, sales administrators, personnel directors – all experts in some branch of management *as such*, distinct from the physics or chemistry or engineering of the processes they control. Management is a study in its own right.

This is the Age of Complexity, when the twelve thousand million cells of the single unaided human brain cannot hope to handle the operations of that mysterious artefact, the Organization. Indeed, there are those who fear that the Organization itself has become the controller of the individual. The paradox is obvious; since no single brain can control the Organization, then it must associate with others to do so – but the association itself is the Organization. The cry of 'Physician, heal thyself!' has become 'Organization, control thyself!'

In the face of this complexity, we are impelled into a search for counterpoising simplicity. Where can we find the means to reduce our problems to manageable size – to strip them of all superfluities so that their essential nature is revealed in stark clarity? How can we then bring them to successful solution?

The answer lies in mathematics, a discipline for handling

pure abstractions which yet provides a versatile and objective implement for solving problems in the real world. The clarity and succinctness of its symbols, the precision and unambiguity of its grammar, make it the ideal language in which to describe these problems. Indeed, the skilful rendering of a physical problem into mathematical terms will often provide its general solution without further effort: this will be so if its formulation fits one of the many standard patterns and methods of solution now available for industrial use.

The use of mathematical language in this way is already desirable and will soon become inevitable. Without its help the further growth of business with its attendant complexity of organization will be retarded and perhaps halted. In the science of management, as in other sciences, mathematics has become a 'condition of progress':

> There is a condition of progress which, in Britain at least, is of the first importance – the recognition of an adequate scale and quality of mathematical teaching as a necessary condition of effective scientific education. . . . The would-be student, quite early in his progress, comes to a gate through which he must pass if he is to emerge as a fully qualified scientist, armed at all points.
>
> On the gate is an inscription in every human tongue: 'MATHEMATICS SPOKEN. ICI ON PARLE MATHEMATIQUE. HIER SPRICHT MAN MATHEMATIK'.[1]

Some tentative approaches to mathematics in management were made in the first quarter of the twentieth century, but the big advance did not begin until the late nineteen-forties, when two main stimuli arose. The first was the success of mathematical thinking about military operations in the war of 1939–45; the second was the invention of the electronic computer. Military operational research proved the value of mathematics in a special sort of management and gave a broad hint of its potentiality in the industrial field; computers by their speed and relative cheapness raised the upper limit of economically feasible calculation by several orders of magnitude. Indeed, the full power of electronic computation in business has not yet been released, because of the lack of widespread mathematical competence. These wonderful machines have characteristics quite different from those of the brain, yet all too often they are programmed to reproduce only the most elementary mental processes. Their prodigious capacity for arithmetic is frittered away on simple price extensions and tax calculations. If computers had emotions, then surely frustration would be the first.

There has, of course, been a very real advance in the application of computing machinery and of mathematics in general during the last ten years. To see how this is so, one has only to go back to 1954, when a writer on 'Mathematics in Industry' was able to say:

> The applications of mathematics to industry so far discussed provide justification for the employment of the mathematician as a specialist. Whatever title he or his department is given, his use in enabling industrial problems to be solved on a logical basis is so obvious that the only reason for *his present lack of employment* can be lack of mathematical knowledge by industrialists. This state of affairs should be remedied in time . . . but until it is, the mathematician will remain largely outside the industrial sphere, where his knowledge should be one of those things we cannot afford to be without.[2]

MATHEMATICIANS AND MONEY

Such an apologetic approach already looks old-fashioned in the context of today's scarcity. The demand for industrial mathematicians not only exceeds their present availability but, as Carter and Williams point out:

> the attraction of industry has certainly denuded the school-teaching profession of good scientists and mathematicians, and has threatened the future supply.[3]

The 'attraction' to which they refer is not entirely money, but it must be one of the principal factors. A dedicated teacher will certainly accept a substantially lower salary than his commercial colleagues, balancing other advantages against the difference, but when industry is paying twice as much, it takes a strong-minded idealist to resist the temptation.

There is a conventional hypocrisy amongst scientists which demands that money should never be advanced as the main factor which moves a man into one job rather than another. 'Lack of research facilities' is usually put at the head of the list but this argument is particularly thin in mathematics where so much can be achieved with no more research equipment than a pencil and some paper. Even so unworldly a person as G. N. Hardy ranks, alongside intellectual curiosity and professional pride,

> . . . ambition, desire for reputation, and the position, even the power or the money, which it brings. It may be fine to feel, when you have done your work, that you have added to the happiness or alleviated the sufferings of others, but that will not be why you did it. So if a mathematician, or a chemist, or even a physiologist, were to tell me that the driving force in his work had been the desire to benefit humanity, then I should not believe him (nor should I think the better of him if I did). His dominant motives have been those which I have stated, and in which surely, there is nothing of which any decent man need be ashamed.[4]

Why should there be such a big discrepancy between salaries in industry and teaching? Commercial managements will argue that their salary rates are dictated by the inexorable law of supply and demand; does the nation as a whole, the taxpayers and ratepayers, begrudge the money which would provide a counter-attraction towards teaching? Galbraith says of a similar situation in the U.S.A.:

> The investment in the refinery is an unmitigated good. It adds to our stock of wealth. It is a categorical achievement. But the training of the scientists and engineers who will run the refinery, improve its economic efficiency, and possibly in the end replace it with something better is not a categorical good. The money so invested is not regarded with approval. On the contrary, it is widely regarded as a burden.[5]

MATHEMATICIANS AS A SCARCE RESOURCE

As a nation, we are squandering our meagre capital of mathematical talent, harvesting the crop without sowing new seed. The wider and more effective use of mathematics in management needs not only an adequate supply of specialist mathematicians but also a higher average level of mathematical education in managers themselves and in the population as a whole.

The Normanbrooke report on British business schools takes account of the second need when it describes two sorts of student, post-graduate and post-experience. In these schools, whose teaching is bound to include the new mathematics of business, the post-experience student will be the developing or mature manager; his purpose in attending the school's ten-week or twenty-week course will be to acquire the knowledge which will enable him to create a suitable climate of opinion for the eager young post-graduates. A very high proportion of this knowledge will be mathematical, and yet another demand for teachers will have been created.

As the Robbins report has said:

> ... some permanent increase in the proportion of able graduates who become teachers ... will be especially needed in mathematics, where it is also essential that the output of graduates should grow more rapidly than in most other subjects.[6]

We have here a problem of allocating scarce resources, and in any such problem there are two complementary approaches.

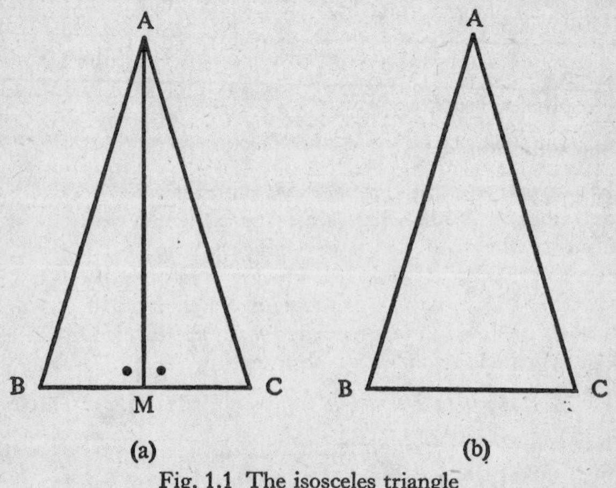

Fig. 1.1 The isosceles triangle

$$
\begin{aligned}
AB &= AC \\
AC &= AB \\
BAC &= CAB \\
\therefore \quad \triangle ABC &\equiv \triangle ACB \\
\therefore \quad A\hat{B}C &= A\hat{C}B
\end{aligned}
$$

The first, and more obvious, is to create more resources – to attract more people into careers as mathematicians, to increase the number of university chairs, to create departments of applied as well as pure mathematics, to persuade industry to help, to encourage mathematicians to immigrate into Britain and make it less attractive for them to emigrate, and so on.

The second approach is that of the work study practitioner – to make better use of such resources as are available. So much of our present mathematics teaching is not merely wasted, but actually retards the progress of mathematics. This practical, beautiful and easy subject is dragged down to a depressing dullness which begins with learning multiplication tables by rote and continues as a course of systematic memory-stuffing. Norbert Wiener once said that merely repetitive mental work degrades a human being to the level of a machine as surely as purely physical labour turns him into a beast of burden, yet this is exactly what we do in teaching mathematics to our children. We programme them like electronic computers, to produce the appropriate permutations of a limited input when the 'examination' button is pressed. Perhaps we do even worse, suppressing the creative instincts of our children at the same time as researchers try to imitate them with machines. A computer is said to have applied a problem-solving programme to the proposition that the base angles of an isosceles triangle are equal.[7] Instead of the Euclidean proof which proves the

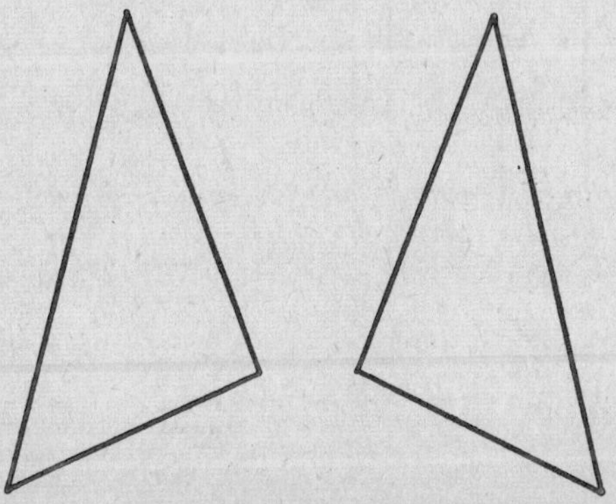

Fig. 1.2 Congruent or not?

two right-angled triangles in Figure 1.1(a) to be congruent, the computer produced a more elegant proof from the simpler construction in Figure 1.1(b).

The conventional working must have been taught to millions of children: we may reasonably ask why none of them, apparently, have discovered this simple new proof for themselves. Is it because they have merely been *taught* the proof, and not encouraged to *think* about it? Children have shown so often that their unsophisticated minds are supremely logical. It is more likely that the questioning child has been told firmly that the former proof is 'what the examiners expect'. This rock-crushing argument may well be used to suppress a bright boy who asks how the triangles in Figure 1.2 could be proved congruent by superimposition without the postulate of a third dimension so that one may be turned over. It would have been better to give him Wells's 'Plattner Experiment', Abbott's 'Flatland' and a pair of left- and right-handed quartz crystals to study (Figure 1.3).

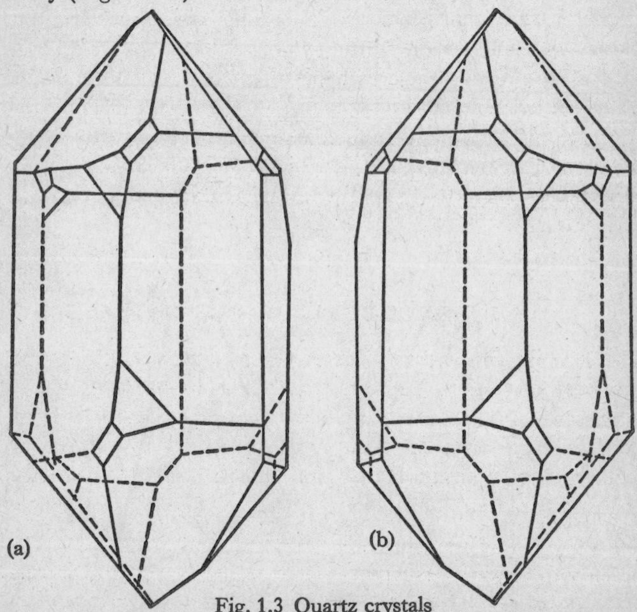

Fig. 1.3 Quartz crystals

The harassed teacher may well reply with some spirit that he and the pupil together *do* in fact have to satisfy the examiners, and perhaps it is the examiners we ought to examine. There are signs of revolt in the ranks of those most closely associated with the pupils, not only in mathematics but across the whole gamut of science in schools, and ranging from the schoolmaster himself to the Minister for Science:

> The school curriculum tends to become a lumber room, to which things are added, but from which they are seldom taken away.... There can be no doubt that the revision of science (and mathematics) curricula along modern lines is both highly desirable in itself and would clear the way for all pupils to study science at school in reasonable depth.[8]

The School Mathematics Project and the Midlands Mathematics Experiment are practical expressions of this dissatisfaction, but they are still minority movements largely sustained by the voluntary work of already hard-pressed teachers.

> ... not a single penny comes, or under existing procedures can come, from central government sources even though our work receives, as far as it is possible to judge, the firm approval of the Ministry of Education.[9]

The same report tells us that a similar group in the U.S.A., the School Mathematics Study Group at Stamford University, is supported by the American Government to the tune of over a million dollars a year.

THE SNOBBERY OF PURITY

The second shadow across our teaching of mathematics is the snobbery of purity. Gauss is said to have remarked that if mathematics is the queen of the sciences, then the theory of numbers is, because of its supreme uselessness, the queen of mathematics (although Hardy has questioned the authenticity of this attribution), and

> one of the greatest representatives of number theory in the nineteenth century, Kummer, is said to have remarked on one occasion that of all his discoveries he appreciated ideal numbers

most because they had not soiled themselves as yet with any practical applications.[10]

The identification of purity with uselessness can be challenged – indeed, Hardy himself does so:

> It is quite natural to suppose that there is a great difference in utility between 'pure' and 'applied' mathematics. This is a delusion: there is a sharp distinction between the two kinds of mathematics . . . but it hardly affects their utility.[11]

He goes on to describe useful mathematics as 'dull and elementary'. Such snobbery has a parallel in the arts, where the academic classicist will applaud the study of torture, massacre and rape, provided it is in Latin or Greek (which subjects he has quaintly christened 'humanities'), and argue vigorously that a technical paper in Russian cannot possibly exercise the mind so effectively.

This Olympian detachment from the rough-and-tumble of business may be on the wane, but it dies hard. The motto 'Keep it abstract! Eschew the practical!' can be admirable in research mathematicians, but is not likely to earn much money in industrial management. This is not an attack on research, but only on the arrogant assumption of its universal supremacy. Practical problems can give the mind as much intellectual exercise as abstract ones – indeed they may even give more. The practical investigator must always begin his work in an open system and one of the most important parts of his work is to set boundaries to his problem: he needs the exploratory approach as much as his colleague in research. Granted that the latter may break out of his immediate field of study into a whole countryside of a new branch of mathematics, such achievement is still rare.

NEGATIVE EDUCATION

Whatever the cause may be – shortage of teachers, fossilization of syllabuses or academic snobbery – the average product of the British educational system (and, I suspect, of many others) emerges with inadequate mathematics. (The Russian mathematician Kantorovich has said that Soviet economists had been inspired by a fear of mathematics that left the Soviet Union far behind the United States in the application of mathematics to economic problems, when it could have been a decade ahead.)

Indeed, the achievement of our schools is often negative, in that their students are left not just with indifference to mathematical symbolism, but with a fear of it. Their attitude to even the simplest mathematical equations reflects the primitive tribesman's approach to his ju-ju rather than a civilized curiosity about a rich field of human knowledge. I have little doubt that many potential readers of this book put it down hastily when a flip of its pages revealed some terrifying monster such as

$$ax^2 + bx + c = 0.$$

Hence we find ourselves in the company of astute and intelligent businessmen, men of culture whose conversation may range from the paintings of Kokoschka to the intricacies of international finance, but whose minds have been closed to the stimulating challenge of mathematics. Yet here is a subject which stretches from the metaphysical extremes of pure philosophy to the hard facts of costing on the shop floor – the only subject in which a man may graduate as either a Bachelor of Arts or a Bachelor of Science.

The conscientious manager is thus led into a dilemma: on the one hand, he lacks confidence in his ability to understand the language of mathematics; on the other, he may see around him an ever-growing array of monetary benefits from it. The result is bewilderment – in extreme cases, subconscious guilt. The situation is not helped by the disdainful attitude of some mathematicians, who not only regard anyone unfamiliar with their language as a moron, but take little pains to conceal their views.

In the face of such bad manners, I once heard a senior manager of a large company make the comment, 'I have been in this job for twenty-five years, and you tell me I have not been doing it as well as I might. This I am prepared to accept. You go on to say that your knowledge of mathematics alone guarantees that you will do better. This I am inclined to doubt.'

The Franks report[12] speaks of the belief held by many business men that the universities 'are prone to despise applied knowledge and competence. And there is excuse for this in the way some professors talk.'

Nigel Balchin comments on this pharisaical attitude in describing the statistician Till, who

> divided people into statisticians, people who know about statistics, and people who didn't. He liked the middle group best. He didn't like real statisticians much because they argued with him, and he thought the people who didn't know any statistics were just animal life.[13]

Till is a fictional character, but many will recognize, if not the man, at least the type. Arrogance of this sort is confined to a minority of the mathematical profession. Nevertheless, it is substantial enough for us to ask what it is based on, at least when directed towards the problems of business. If the mathematician were asked what quality would distinguish his investigation of a practical problem from that of lesser men, he would probably reply, 'Objectivity'. This is a fallacy.

Leaving aside the argument that the pure mathematician's choice of axioms and logical rules may itself introduce an element of subjectivity, let us examine the claim that a mathematical model of an industrial problem is objective. The model will embody certain variables and their functional relationships which purport to represent measurements and rules of behaviour in the real world, but the link between abstract symbolism and reality must be forged subjectively. The operational research worker who says 'Let C be the cost of running out of stock' assumes that there *is* such a cost and that it can be isolated and measured; the statistician who claims that the diameters of steel bars are Normally distributed necessarily implies a small but finite probability that bars of negative length could exist. However precise the mathematical treatment may be in itself, as a representation of the real world it must be empirical and approximate. The statistician must modify his claim and say rather that the diameters behave *as if* they obeyed the Normal distribution law – that the model embodied in his quality control chart is adequate rather than absolute. If the cost of running out of stock cannot be measured, then the operations on its symbol may have to be restricted or even dispensed with altogether, by a complete re-formulation of the problem.

NUMERACY

The problem is surely one of communication. If we were not universally literate in the industrial countries, we could not rely on the effectiveness of written messages. The word 'numeracy' was coined in the Crowther report to describe a corresponding familiarity with the language of figures, and the concept is of such overwhelming importance that the appropriate paragraph is quoted here in full:

> Literacy has long been important, and its value is as great as ever. Just as by 'literacy', in this context, we mean much more than its dictionary sense of the ability to read and write, so by 'numeracy' we mean more than mere ability to manipulate the rule of three. When we say that a scientist is 'illiterate', we mean that he is not well enough read to be able to communicate effectively with those who have had a literary education. When we say that a historian or a linguist is 'innumerate' we mean that he cannot even begin to understand what scientists and mathematicians are talking about. The aim of a good Sixth Form should be to send out into the world men and women who are both literate and numerate.
>
> It is perhaps possible to distinguish two different aspects of numeracy that should concern the Sixth Former. On the one hand is an understanding of the scientific approach to the study of phenomena–observation, hypothesis, experiment, verification. On the other hand, there is the need in the modern world to think quantitatively, to realize how far our problems are problems of degree even when they appear as problems of kind. Statistical ignorance and statistical fallacies are quite as widespread and quite as dangerous as the logical fallacies which come under the heading of illiteracy. The man who is innumerate is cut off from understanding some of the relatively new ways in which the human mind is now most busily at work. Numeracy has come to be an indispensable tool to the understanding and mastery of all phenomena, and not only of those in the relatively close field of the traditional natural sciences. The way in which we think, marshal our evidence and formulate our arguments in

every field today is influenced by techniques first applied in science. The educated man, therefore, needs to be numerate as well as literate. Side by side with this need for understanding a new and essential approach to knowledge, the educated man also requires a general acquaintance with the directions in which science is most rapidly advancing and with the nature of the new knowledge that is being acquired. Neither the understanding of scientific method nor this general scientific knowledge is possible unless a sound foundation has been laid in the main school by thorough mathematical and scientific teaching. However able a boy may be, he cannot reach a Sixth Form level of numeracy except on the foundation of a Fifth Form level; but, if his numeracy has stopped short at the usual Fifth Form level, he is in danger of relapsing into innumeracy. It is now one of the most important tasks of the Sixth Form to ensure that no boy or girl leaves school as innumerate as most have done in the past, and as far too many do even today. The boys' schools at least can no longer be criticized for providing an inadequate proportion of science specialists. The task that boys' no less than girls' schools have little more than begun is that of seeing that the Sixth Former who is not going to be a scientist or a technologist is given enough understanding of the scientific side of human knowledge to be able to hold his or her own in an increasingly scientific and technological world. By whatever means this problem is tackled in the schools, it will make heavy demands on really good teachers. But we believe that it must be done, and that the fruits will amply repay the labour.[14]

Numeracy now vies in importance with literacy as a necessary part of man's mental equipment in an industrial world. It cannot be denied that the general level of numeracy is probably rising, but is it rising fast enough? The gap between need and knowledge may even now be widening, and will certainly grow greater in the future unless more vigorous measures are taken to close it. As a nation we are innumerate.

Although the number of specialist mathematicians in industry needs to be increased, we must also take care that this vanguard does not get too far ahead from the main army of industry, including its managers. If it does, the lines of communication – already stretched too far – may snap entirely. The need for numeracy must be taken as much for granted as that for literacy; the company director who boasts of his mathematical inadequacy is fast becoming an anachronism. The modern politician should be as ashamed of his mathematical deficiencies as he would be of an inability to read.

QUANTITIES AND JUDGEMENTS

On the other hand, the mathematician's deficiency is equally deplorable – the failure to understand the technicalities of the manager's job – especially insofar as it includes *responsibility*. Sir Charles (now Lord) Snow put this point well in speaking of operational research in the Second World War:

> The lesson to the scientists was that the prerequisite of sound military advice is that the giver must convince himself that, if he were responsible for action, he would himself act so. It is a difficult lesson to learn.[15]

Again, the manager is more likely to be aware of the *people* in the problem, who collectively make up the biggest immeasurable factor. Human emotions and aesthetic values cannot be quantified. An industrial problem may be analysed, then, into two main groups of components as shown in Figure 1.4.

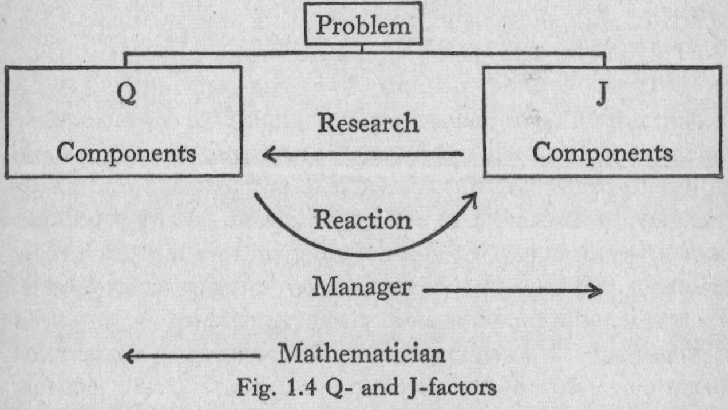

Fig. 1.4 Q- and J-factors

The 'Q (for Quantity) Components' box contains everything that can be measured, the 'J (for Judgement) Components' everything else. The 'Research' arrow indicates the attempts to transfer components from J to Q, as in intelligence tests, measurement of mental load, skill-and-effort rating, and merit rating. Leonard Bernstein even tells us that:

When I was at Harvard, Professor Birkhoff had just published a system of aesthetic *measure* – actually trying to evolve a mathematical system whereby any object of art could be awarded a beauty-rating on a given continuum of aesthetic work.[16]

A pointer to the future may be discerned in the development of new theories of sociology and industrial organization. Rashevsky, speaking of developments in this field of study, says:

Many significant areas of these disciplines have already been removed by the advances of the past two decades beyond the reach of anyone who does not know mathematics.[17]

There is always, of course, the corresponding reaction shown in Figure 1.4 as tending to undo the effects of research. It ranges from the true scepticism of the scientist to the stubborn resistance exemplified by 'Don't confuse me with facts – my mind is already made up'. At its worst, reaction takes on a spurious appearance of reasonableness, as when the manager says firmly, 'In this business, you simply *can't* forecast', before continuing with his production schedules for the next six months.

Figure 1.4 shows the manager and the mathematician centrally between the two boxes, at what should be their point of contact. The mathematician must concern himself mainly with Q, while remaining aware of the need for the manager's judgement. The manager must be prepared to sacrifice the clutter of routine figure-work and to accept that more of his job may be reducible to mathematical procedures than his pride cares to admit. In doing so, he will free himself for the better exercise of his judgement on more worthy targets. Boole's demolition of a similar argument a century ago, if applied to the broader framework of management rather than to pure logic, is still topical.

If, through the advancing power of scientific methods, we find that the pursuits on which we were once engaged, afford no longer a sufficiently ample field for intellectual effort, the remedy is, to proceed to higher inquiries, and, in new tracks, to seek for difficulties yet unsubdued. And such is, indeed, the actual law of scientific progress.[18]

COMMUNICATION

Thus we arrive at the purpose of this book: it aims to bring about better communication between the layman – in particular the manager – and the mathematician. If they are to cooperate, there must be a constant interchange of ideas between them, a continuous sharing and examination of the *Q* and *J* components. The manager who says, 'Solve this problem for me', is abdicating his responsibility – in any case, his real meaning is often, 'Get out some figures to prove I'm right'. Likewise the mathematician who takes a quick look at the physical realities of the situation, retires to formulate, compute, and produce a 'final' solution with the flourish of a conjurer pulling a rabbit out of a hat, will fail to convince. He must be prepared to explain, as best he can, the concepts and reasoning behind each *Q* step, checking against the manager's judgement as he goes. The mathematician must remind himself that he is bilingual in English and Number, whereas the manager usually is not. The manager in turn must try to acquire at least a rudimentary vocabulary of the mathematical language and its 'dialects' if he is to use its methods as a practical aid.

The aim of this book is to help build a bridge between the applied mathematician and the everyday world of industry and commerce. Its theme is the use of mathematics to solve problems of physical reality and it is entirely concerned with practical applications: every method described in it has been used by someone, somewhere, to help solve a problem in management. Case studies are used as illustrations, simplified in many cases so that their essential mathematical content emerges uncluttered by the purely local details.

It is not easy to draw a dividing line between management and other industrial applications of mathematics, and the distinction is most easily seen by comparing management applications with others such as process and design studies. Such a comparison is given in Table 1.1: it is neither complete nor representative, but it does serve to show that management is, generally speaking, concerned with the provision and deployment of resources, be they men, machines, or materials. Alternatively, this field of application of mathematics has been defined as 'systems analysis', which considers the thing-being-managed as a system subject to control and operating within an environment with which it interacts. A system may be represented by a model, the analysis of which can lead to conclusions about its counterpart in the real world.

In the chapters which follow, the proportion of plain English to mathematical symbolism is high; the physical equivalent of abstract variables and operators is continually kept in mind. The reader is assumed to have retained the more memorable parts of his earlier education in arithmetic, algebra, and geometry, but a good deal of revisionary work is included. Exercises punctuate the text, and the solution of each is given in full: they will help the reader to assimilate the subject matter step by step.

TABLE 1.1

Technique	*Management Applications*	*Other Industrial Applications*
Matrix Algebra	Programme of expansion for a steelworks	Aerodynamic studies in aircraft design
Laplace Transforms	Stock control	Study of electrical circuits
Differential Calculus	Size of a fleet of vehicles	Trajectories of projectiles
Theory of Graphs	Organization structures	Design of printed circuits
Theory of Communication	Study of managerial decisions	Design of transoceanic telephone cables
Statistics	Inventory budgets	Design of atomic piles

It is not intended to be an exhaustive survey, but rather as a shop-window of mathematical technique which may tempt the customer to come in and survey the whole stock more closely.

Chapter 2 deals with project management by network analysis, a technique which needs no more than simple arithmetic and logical thinking, at least in its elementary applications. Chapter 3 introduces algebraic notation for the first time, and shows the wide range of uses of the equation of a straight line. It also introduces the notion of inequalities, which is extended in Chapter 4 to a simple algebraic explanation of linear programming. Chapter 5 retraces the ground covered in Chapter 4, but in geometric terms. The geometric approach will lead to a better understanding among those who are natural visualizers, whereas algebra may have greater appeal to the abstract reasoners[19,20]. Chapter 6 reverts to straightforward arithmetic in describing a particular type of linear programming – the transportation method – which has been applied to problems of distribution.

All these mathematical procedures are illustrated by small examples, but their use in practical situations may call for large amounts of repetitive calculations and hence generate a need for an electronic computer. Chapter 7 underlines this need in describing how the operations of a business may be simulated by a set of logical rules. Accordingly, Chapter 8 introduces the computer by explaining how the manager who wants to use one should go about it, using the network from Chapter 2 as an illustration. Chapter 9 brings us back to algebra with an outline of the uses to which curved lines may be put; finally, Chapter 10 deals briefly with some of the other areas of application of mathematics in management.

The mathematical development has been kept at a fairly elementary level. This has been done not only to make the book understandable, but also because a few relatively simple tools can be usefully applied to a wide variety of problems. Furthermore, greater mathematical sophistication does not always add a new *concept*.

Above all, it is an attempt to break down the widespread fear of mathematics as something beyond the grasp of ordinary men – the idea that only a favoured few possess the right sort of brain to comprehend it. Our mathematical heritage is as great a treasure as our literary one – the fourth centenary of Newton should be as much of a public celebration as that of

Shakespeare. Indeed, one may argue that it is even greater, the language of mathematics being universal.

NOTES AND REFERENCES

1 Hailsham, Lord (now Hogg, Q.), *Science and Politics* (Faber & Faber, 1963), pp. 40–41.
2 Fox, N. W., *Penguin Science News* No. 34 (1954), p. 114 (my italics – A.B.)
3 Carter, C. F. and Williams, B. R., *Science in Industry: Policy for Progress* (O.U.P., 1959), p. 126.
4 Hardy, G. N., *A Mathematician's Apology* (C.U.P., 1941), p. 19.
5 Galbraith, J. K., *The Affluent Society* (Penguin Books, edn 1958), chap. 19, p. 223.
6 Robbins, *Higher Education*, Appendix Three, (Cmnd. 2154 – III, 1963), Part IV, Section 3, Para. 30.
7 Good, I. J. (ed.), *The Scientist Speculates* (Heinemann, 1962), p. 192.
8 Thwaites, B., and others, *On Teaching Mathematics* (*Southampton Mathematical Conference*) (Pergamon Press, 1961), chap. IV.
9 Thwaites, B., *The School Mathematics Project. Directors' Report* 1962–3 (University of Southampton, 1964), p. 9.
10 Uspensky, J. V., and Heaslet, M. A., *Elementary Number Theory* (McGraw-Hill, 1939), 1st edn, p. 20.
11 Hardy, G. N., *A Mathematician's Apology* (Cambridge University Press, 1940), footnote on p. 60.
12 Franks, *British Business Schools* (B.I.M., 1963), para. 17.
13 Balchin, N., *The Small Back Room* (Collins, 1943).
14 Crowther, G., 15–18. *A Report of the Central Advisory Council for Education, Vol. I* (Ministry of Education, H.M.S.O., 1963), pp. 270–71.
15 Snow, C. P., *Science and Government* (O.U.P., 1960), p. 29.
16 Bernstein, L., *The Joy of Music* (Weidenfeld & Nicolson, 1954), p. 12.
17 Rubenstein, A. H. and Haberstroh, C., *Some Theories of Organization* (Dorsey Press & Richard Irwin, Illinois, 1960), p. 14.
18 Boole, G., *The Mathematical Analysis of Logic* (Blackwell, 1847), p. 9.
19 Gray Walter, W., *The Living Brain* (Duckworth, 1953), chap. 8.
20 Pearson, E. S., *Journal of the Royal Statistical Society* (1956), Series A, vol. 119, Part II, pp. 125–49.

Similar arguments to those expressed in this chapter may also be found in

Yates, I. and Healy, M. J. R., *Journal of the Royal Statistical Society* (1964), Series A, vol. 127, Part 2, pp. 199–210, and Discussion, pp. 221–33.

2
Plans, Projects and Programmes

Turn their kind faces from us
And our projects under construction,
Look only in one direction,
Fix their gaze on our completed work.
Pile-driver, concrete-mixer,
Crane and pickaxe wait to be used again,
But how can we repeat this?

W. H. AUDEN, *Nones*

IN this chapter, we shall see how a *project* is subdivided into the individual jobs which contribute to its achievement, and how a study of their logical sequence can give results of immense value to the man in charge of it. By 'project' we mean a scheme to utilize certain resources – usually men, machinery, and materials – in order to reach a defined objective. This may be the completion of a new chemical works or housing estate, the overhaul of a diesel locomotive, the first flight of a new aeroplane, the installation of a better accounting system, or the marketing of a new product. The new technique of 'network analysis' has been successfully applied to all these projects as well as many others; it is a method of allocating priorities to individual jobs, so that a criterion is available for dealing with them in the most effective order. Although the technique is less than ten years old, it has had a great and growing impact on both sides of the Atlantic, and its range of application is spreading.

For the purpose of illustration we shall take the overhaul of an aircraft as our project. The work to be described was actually performed in the hangars of the College of Aeronautics at Cranfield and was a 'Check III' inspection of a D.H. 'Dove' aircraft; the objective to be achieved was 'Inspection completed and aircraft serviceable', and the main resources employed were fitters and inspectors. The whole project may be represented by a single arrow, as in Figure 2.1, which shows the nature of the work and its direction in time. The head of the arrow is the end of the project, which obviously cannot precede its start.

The circles in Figure 2.1, which are called 'nodes', represent the states of the aircraft before and after the inspection. They

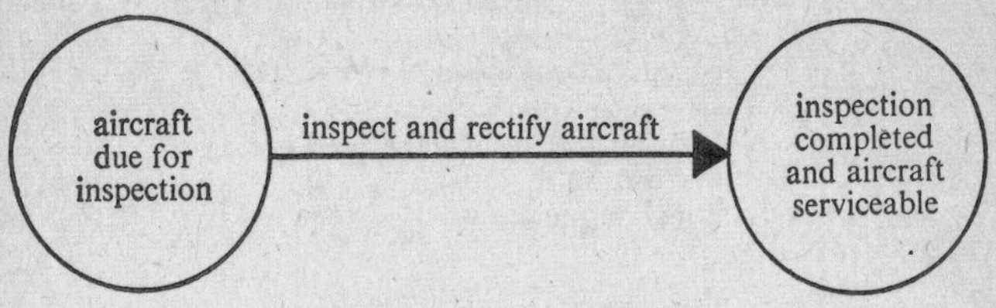

Fig. 2.1 Arrow and nodes

are, so to speak, 'snapshots' taken at a moment in time, and therefore the states (of which the nodes are a pictorial representation) are called 'events'.

We can now start to analyse the project, and Figure 2.2 shows the first stages. In (a), the analysis is as simple as

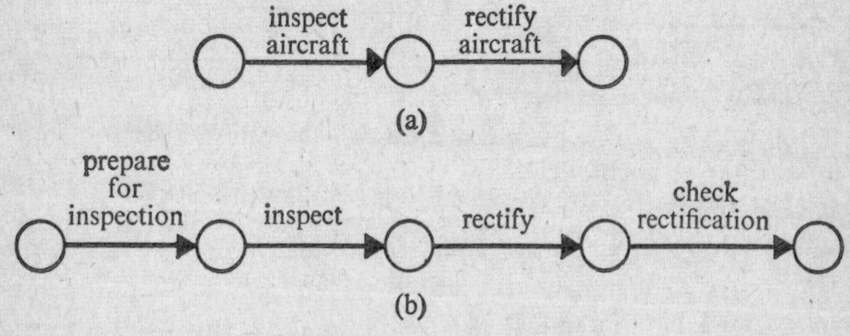

Fig. 2.2 Division of project into jobs

possible: it shows a breakdown into two jobs only. They are drawn as successive arrows because rectification must *of necessity* follow inspection: we cannot put things right until we know where they are wrong. Figure 2.2(b) shows the analysis carried a stage further; again, the jobs follow a logical sequence represented by the chain of nodes and arrows. It is important to note that the sequence is dictated by the logic of the situation rather than by restrictions on resources.

Exercise 2.1

Describe the 'event' which the middle node in Figure 2.2(a) represents.

Exercise 2.2

Suppose that instead of choosing the division in Figure 2.2(a), we had chosen two other jobs

Inspect and rectify engines
Inspect and rectify airframe

What is the logical sequence, if any, of these two jobs?

Exercise 2.3

When I take my car to a service station, the attendant first fills the petrol tank and then checks the oil. Is this sequence of jobs logically necessary?

Exercise 2.4

The attendant opens the bonnet before he checks the oil. Is this a logical sequence?

So far, we have considered only simple chains of jobs, but more complicated relationships are possible when concurrent as well as successive jobs are taken into account. Figure 2.3 shows how the network is developed by separating airframe, undercarriage, and engines so that the jobs on these go on at the

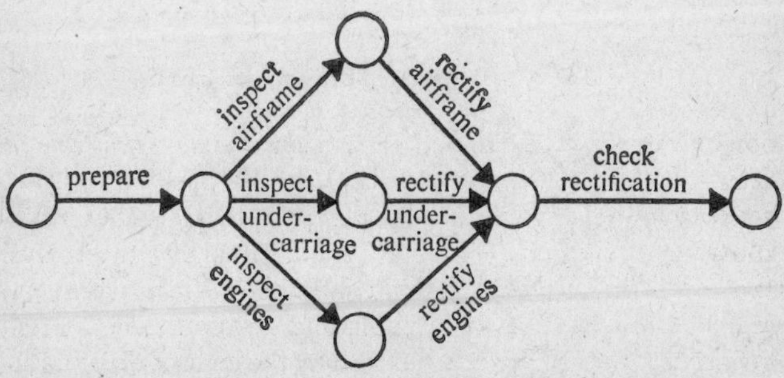

Fig. 2.3 Development of network

same time. This network tells us that none of the three inspections can begin until the preparation has been concluded, and that the rectifications cannot be finally checked until all three groups have been dealt with.

Exercise 2.5

Suppose that the single job 'prepare' in Figure 2.3 were separated into the following three jobs:

Position and jack up aircraft
Clean undercarriage and remove wheels
Unpanel and clean engines

Draw a revised network incorporating these modifications.

We can carry the analysis further for each of the three groups. Work on the undercarriage, for instance, is detailed as:

Clean undercarriage and remove wheels
Inspect main wheels
Inspect nose wheel
Rectify and replace main wheels
Rectify and replace nose wheels
Test retraction mechanism
Rectify retraction mechanism.

The wheels cannot be inspected until they have been removed, and the retraction test cannot be done until they have been replaced. This part of the network will therefore be as shown in Figure 2.4.

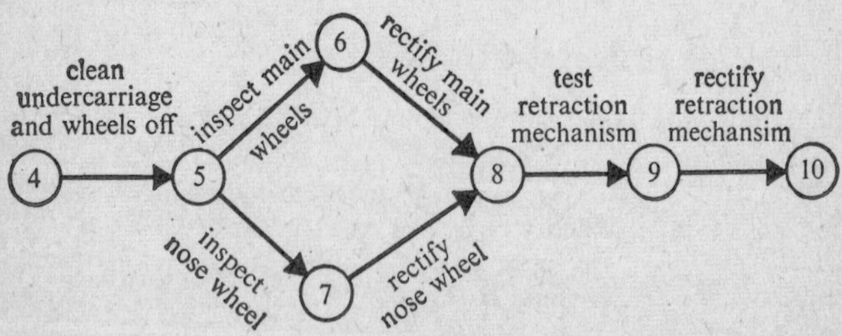

Fig. 2.4 Details of work on undercarriage

NUMBERING AND EVENTS

Drawing a network for a project can be a rewarding occupation in itself, because it forces the compiler to think right through the project in detail; the possibility of vital steps being overlooked is much reduced. The full value of a network is not realized, however, until certain calculations have been carried out, and these calculations make it necessary to number the events in a systematic way.

There are several methods of numbering, of which the commonest and most useful is the so-called '*i j*' system. Any job has an initial and a final event – the number of the initial event is *i* and that of the final event, *j*; the rule for numbering events is that *j* must be greater than *i* in every case. The network in Figure 2.4 has been numbered in this way. Any number may be used for the initial event, and 4 has been taken in this case. For a complete network, it is usual to start with either 0 or 1.

Exercise 2.6

Number the network from Exercise 2.5 in accordance with the *i j* system, beginning with 1.

When a network has been numbered, each job on it can be identified by its *i j* numbers. In Figure 2.4, 'Test retraction mechanism' is job 5, 6. If the jobs are to be distinguished in this way, each must have a unique pair of numbers.

DUMMIES

The following jobs occur during the overhaul of the undercarriage:

Test retraction mechanism
Rectify retraction mechanism
Recharge emergency system
General check

Both the rectification and recharging must precede the general check, and neither can begin until after the retraction test. The network for this might therefore be drawn as in Figure 2.5(a). In this 'job 9, 10' could mean either 'rectify' or 'recharge'. In order to avoid ambiguity, a device called a 'dummy activity' is used, as indicated by the dotted arrow in Figure 2.5(b). This is an activity which consumes no resources

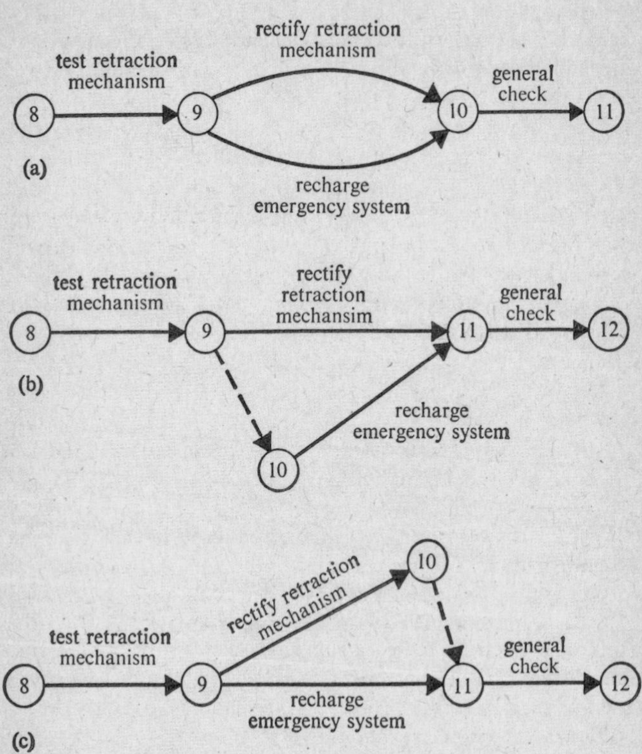

Fig. 2.5 Use of dummies in numbering

and takes no time at all: it merely preserves a logical sequence, and enables us to distinguish the two jobs by their $i\,j$ numbers. Another possible way of using the dummy is shown in Figure 2.5(c).

Dummies may also be used to preserve a logical sequence even though no numbering problem exists. In the aircraft overhaul, the fire extinguishers may be checked at the same time as the engines, but work on them cannot begin until both engines have been cleaned. The logical sequence can only be drawn with the aid of dummies as shown in Figure 2.6.

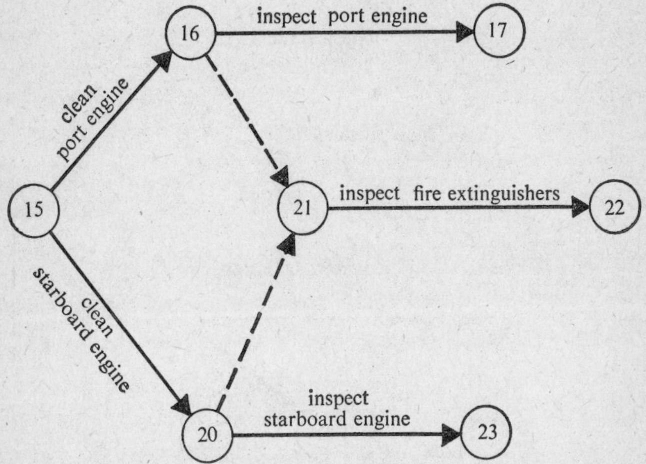

Fig. 2.6 Use of dummies to show logical sequence

Dummies whose only purpose is to preserve the numbering system are sometimes called 'identity dummies'. This distinguishes them from so-called 'logical dummies', which play an essential part in the construction of an arrow diagram even though no numbering problem may exist.

Figure 2.6 gives an example. The single job 'Inspect fire extinguishers' cannot be done until both engines have been cleaned. The logical dummy 16, 21 shows that 'Inspect fire extinguishers' must follow the cleaning of the port engine and 20, 21 does the same for the starboard engine. This is the only way of showing the relationship. Otherwise, you may find that incorrect sequences are creeping in, such as the inspection of the starboard engine following the cleaning of the port engine.

Exercise 2.7

Draw a network of the following jobs in attending to a motor car at a service station.

Driver arrives
Driver selects brands of oil and petrol
Fill petrol tank
Prepare bill
Receive payment
Wash windscreen
Polish windscreen
Check tyre pressures
Inflate tyres
Open bonnet
Check oil requirement
Add oil
Add distilled water to battery
Fill radiator
Close bonnet
Driver departs

Assume that all the jobs must be done. Number the network, using the *ij* rule.

THE COMPLETE NETWORK

Figure 2.7 shows the complete network for the aircraft overhaul, in which many of the features already mentioned may be recognized. A further important point is that the network has only one starting point, event 1, and one end point, event 31: there are no loose ends within the network. This is assured by having a single job (or event) which precedes all the others, as well as one which succeeds them all. There are two such jobs, which are respectively 'Prepare for inspection' and 'General check'.

The network has been numbered by the *ij* rule, but gaps have deliberately been left in the series of numbers used. If it should become necessary to modify the network, extensive renumbering will be avoided if some numbers have been kept in reserve (as will be shown later).

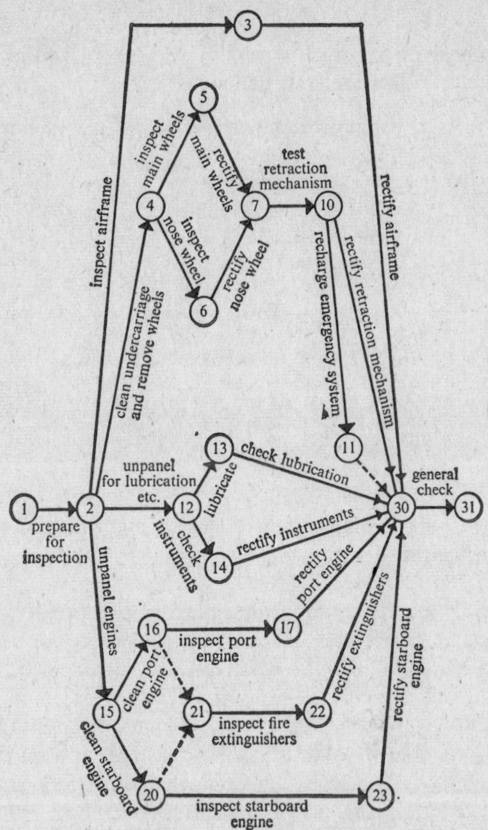

Fig. 2.7 Aircraft overhaul – complete network

The next stage is to estimate the durations of the individual jobs and find out how long the overhaul will take. The practical difficulties of estimation are considerable, but they will not be dwelt on here; we shall assume that discussions between the engineers and work study men have produced a set of values, in hours, as shown in Figure 2.8.

THE CRITICAL PATH

One sequence of jobs in Figure 2.8 has been picked out with heavier arrows than the rest, that is:

Job			
Job	1, 2	Prepare for inspection	1 hour
	2, 15	Unpanel engines	3 hours
	15, 16	Clean port engine	1 hour
	16, 17	Inspect port engine	24 hours
	17, 30	Rectify port engine	36 hours
	30, 31	General check	1 hour
		Total	66 hours

These jobs make up the *longest path* through the network, and therefore determine the total duration of the project as 66 hours. For this reason, they are called *critical jobs* and the path along which they lie is called the critical path.

Exercise 2.8

Find the path through the network in Figure 2.8 which has the *second longest* duration.

Of the 26 jobs (excluding dummies) in this project, only 6 are critical, in that a delay in completing any one of them would delay the completion of the whole project. On the other hand, there is some latitude in the times for all the other jobs. Finding the critical path enables us to concentrate our attention on a relatively small proportion of the jobs, with a view to shortening the planned project by reducing their durations and subsequently fulfilling the plan by selective control.

FINDING THE CRITICAL PATH

There are only 11 different paths through the network in Figure 2.8, which makes it easy to find the critical path by trial and error. In practice, networks used on large projects may contain hundreds or even thousands of individual jobs, with a correspondingly high number of alternative paths. A systematic and rapid method of finding the critical path is therefore

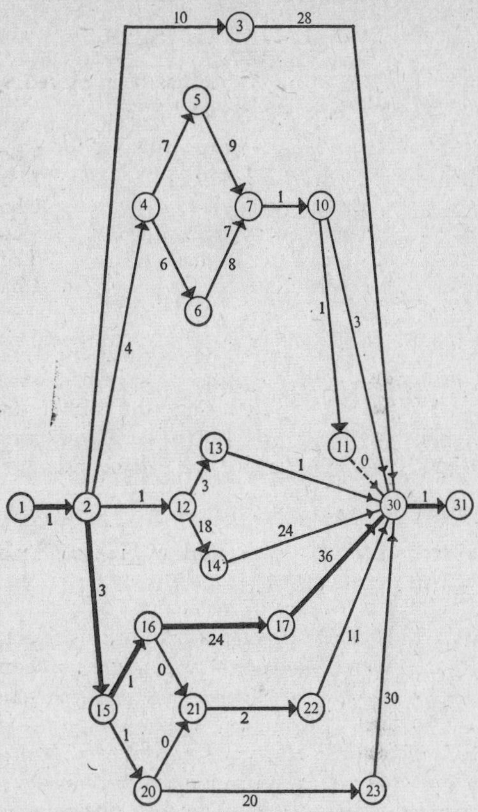

Fig. 2.8 Aircraft overhaul – critical path

needed. The most common method begins by ascribing an earliest and latest time to each event by working forward from the first to the last events through the successive numbers, and then returning.

At this stage the difference between jobs and events must again be emphasized. A job *endures* in time and we shall refer to its *duration* in hours. The word *time* will be used exclusively for events, which are instantaneous, and to avoid confusion we shall refer to times as *o'clock*. Then job i, j may begin with

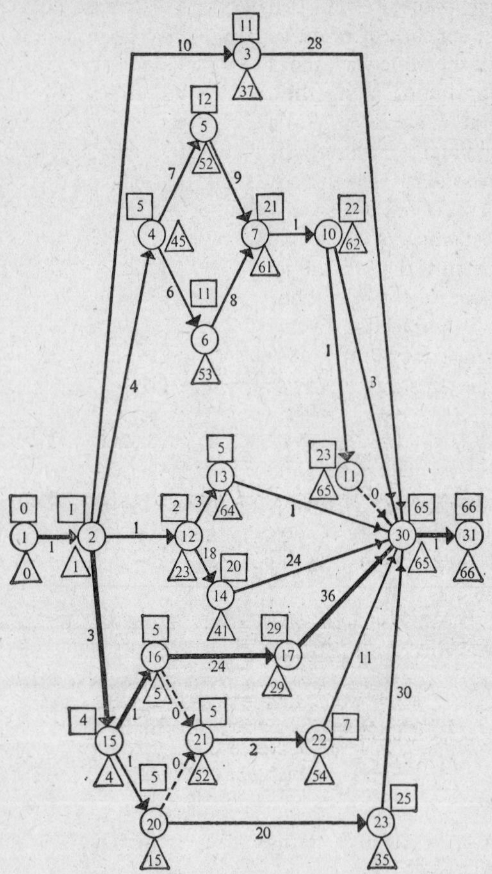

Fig. 2.9 Aircraft overhaul – earliest and latest event times

event *i* at time 3 o'clock, have a duration of 5 hours and finish with event *j* at 8 o'clock. We shall also preserve simplicity by using times such as '100 o'clock' rather than introducing days.

Let us begin by assuming that the project begins at some time which we shall call zero o'clock. This is then the *earliest event time* for event No. 1, and is shown surrounded by a square in Figure 2.9. Job 1, 2 is completed one hour later, and all the jobs which precede event 2 have now been completed: consequently, its earliest event time is 1 o'clock, also shown in a square. In the same way, the earliest time for event 3 is 1 + 10 = 11. Continuing along the same path, we should arrive at event 30 at 11 + 28 = 39 o'clock, if job 3, 30 were the only one preceding it. Obviously, it is not, so we must calculate the event times along the other paths first. This is where the virtues of the *ij* numbering system become evident; if we calculate the earliest times of the events in their numerical order, then we can be sure that all the jobs preceding an event will have been taken into consideration.

Event 7 is preceded by two jobs, 5, 7 and 6, 7. Since the earliest time for event 5 is at 12 o'clock and the duration of job 5, 7 is 9 hours, the time at which event 7 would be reached is 12 + 9 = 21 o'clock. On the other hand, event 6 at 11 o'clock plus job 6, 7 at 8 hours gives 11 + 8 = 19 o'clock for the time at event 7. Which figure should we take as the earliest event time, 21 or 19? Remembering that job 7, 10 cannot begin until *all* the jobs preceding it have been completed, we find that we must take the greater figure, 21 o'clock, as the earliest event time.

Event 30 is preceded by 7 jobs and a dummy (of zero duration) which must also be included, so we have

Preceding Event	*Earliest Event Time*	*Preceding Job*	*Job Duration*	*Earliest Finish*
3	11	3, 30	28	39
10	22	10, 30	3	25
11	23	11, 30	0	23
13	5	13, 30	1	6
14	20	14, 30	24	44
17	29	17, 30	36	65
22	7	22, 30	11	18
23	25	23, 30	30	55

The greatest figure in the last column is the earliest time for event 30; it is 65 hours and arises from job 17, 30: in this case it also follows that job 17, 30 will be on the critical path.

Finally, at event 31, we find the earliest time to be 66 o'clock, which also tells us that 66 hours is the minimum possible duration for the entire project. This is conventionally taken as the latest finishing time and we work backwards from it to find the latest event times, in much the same way as before. The latest time for event 23, for example, is 65 — 30 = 35 o'clock. Event 16 is succeeded by two jobs, so one arrives at it through two paths when working backwards: the latest time for event 21 is 52 o'clock, and job 16, 21 has zero duration (as all dummies do) giving 52 — 0 = 52 o'clock; from event 17 we have 29 — 24 = 5 o'clock, and this smaller figure gives the latest event time for event 6. It may seem paradoxical to call the *earlier* of the two times the *latest* event times, but the common sense of the matter may be seen when we remember that the project is not to be delayed, and ask what would happen to the overall time if event 16 were not reached until 52 o'clock. The latest event times are shown enclosed in triangles in Figure 2.9.

Exercise 2.9

Event 2 is succeeded by four jobs. Calculate their latest starting times and deduce the earliest time for this event.

Exercise 2.10

The durations of the jobs in Exercise 2.7, in seconds, are

Driver arrives		30
Driver selects brands of oil and petrol		10
Fill petrol tank	(average)	120
Prepare bill		45
Receive payment		25
Wash windscreen		20
Polish windscreen		15
Check tyre pressures		80
Inflate tyres		100
Open bonnet		15
Check oil requirement		60
Add oil		25
Add distilled water to battery		30
Fill radiator		50
Close bonnet		5
Driver departs		10

Calculate the earliest and latest event times, and the overall project time (assuming that an unlimited number of men is available).

TOTAL FLOAT

We have already seen that some latitude in event times and job durations may be permissible without delaying the project: this is measured by the 'float' of a job. Take for example job 12, 14. The earliest time for event 12 is at 2 o'clock: if the job were begun then, it would end at 2 + 18 = 20 o'clock, the earliest finish time. The latest time for event 14 being 41 o'clock, it follows that a delay of up to 21 hours in this job would have no effect upon the overall project time. Conversely, to reach event 14 by the latest time, 41 o'clock, the job need not start until 41 − 18 = 23 o'clock. This latest start time is 21 hours after its earliest start time, and this 21 hours is called the *total float* of job 12, 14. In other words,

Total Float of job i, j
= Latest time of event j −
Earliest time of event i −
Duration of job i, j (2.1)

Exercise 2.II

Calculate the total floats of the following jobs in Figure 2.9.

14, 30
6, 7
16, 17
20, 23

The float defined by equation (2.1) is called the 'total float'. The reason for this nomenclature is best explained by considering two successive jobs in an unbranched chain. Figure 2.10 reproduces two of the jobs from Figure 2.9, each of which has a total float of 26 hours. It should be obvious that this float can only be used once: it belongs to the path rather than to the individual job. If job 2, 3 were delayed by 26 hours, job 3, 30 would be left with no float at all. Any delay in job 3, 20 would then delay the whole project – in other words, it would have become critical. It follows that all the jobs on the critical path (or paths) have zero float; it is this property which enables us to identify the critical path.

FREE FLOAT

It would be useful to have some type of float which could be allocated to specific jobs rather than to the paths on which they lie. Some systems of analysis apportion the total float according to some arbitrary rule – for example, in proportion to the duration of each job. These 'allocated floats' would then be:

For job 2, 3 $\qquad \dfrac{10}{10 + 28} \times 26 = 7$ hours

For job 3, 30 $\qquad \dfrac{28}{10 + 28} \times 26 = 19$ hours

Total Float = 26 hours

The more common practice is to assign float preferentially, as far as possible, to the job at the end of a path. This leads to the concept of 'free float' defined by equation (2.2).

Free Float of job i, j
= Earliest time of event j –
Earliest time of event i –
Duration of job i, j (2.2)

Figure 2.10 shows how this method assigns all the float preferentially to the second job.

Exercise 2.12

Calculate the total and free floats of jobs 21, 22 and 22, 30 in Figure 2.9.

Exercise 2.13

Calculate the total and free floats of the network in Exercises 2.7 and 2.10, and find the critical path through it.

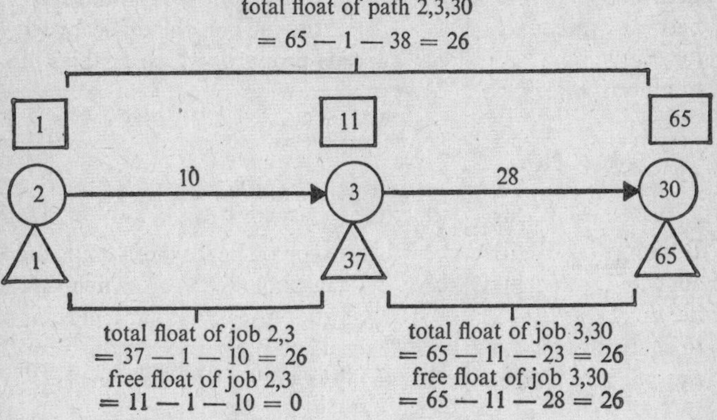

Fig. 2.10 Total and free floats

THE COMPLETE SCHEDULE

Table 2.1 shows the complete schedule for the aircraft overhaul, summarizing all the calculations described so far. The jobs have also been sorted into the order of their total float, so that the critical ones appear at the head of the list. Jobs having the same float have also been sorted into the order of their earliest event times. Other systems of sorting are possible – by

TABLE 2.1

Schedule for Aircraft Overhaul

JOB			*Duration*	JOB TIMES				FLOAT		
				EARLIEST		LATEST				
i	*j*	*Description*		*Start*	*End*	*Start*	*End*	*Total*	*Free*	*Crit.*
1	2	Prepare for Insp.	1	0	1	0	1	0	0	*
2	15	Unpanel Engines	3	1	4	1	4	0	0	*
15	16	Clean Port Engine	1	4	5	4	5	0	0	*
16	17	Inspect Port Engine	24	5	29	5	29	0	0	*

TABLE 2.1—*continued*

JOB			*Duration*	JOB TIMES				FLOAT		
				EARLIEST		LATEST				
i	*j*	*Description*		*Start*	*End*	*Start*	*End*	*Total*	*Free*	*Crit.*
17	30	Rectify Port Engine	36	29	65	29	65	0	0	*
30	31	General Check	1	65	66	65	66	0	0	*
15	20	Clean Starboard Engine	1	4	5	14	15	10	0	S
20	23	Inspect Starboard Engine	20	5	25	15	35	10	0	S
23	30	Rectify Starboard Engine	30	25	55	35	65	10	10	S
2	12	Unpanel for Lubrication etc.	1	1	2	22	23	21	0	
12	14	Check Instruments	18	2	20	23	41	21	0	
14	30	Rectify Instruments	24	20	44	41	65	21	21	
2	3	Inspect Airframe	10	1	11	27	37	26	0	
3	30	Rectify Airframe	28	11	39	37	65	26	26	
2	4	Clean, Remove Wheels	4	1	5	41	45	40	0	
4	5	Inspect Main Wheels	7	5	12	45	52	40	0	
5	7	Rectify Main Wheels	9	12	21	52	61	40	0	
7	10	Test Retraction	1	21	22	61	62	40	0	
10	30	Rectify Retraction	3	22	25	62	65	40	40	
4	6	Inspect Nose Wheel	6	5	11	47	53	42	0	
6	7	Rectify Nose Wheel	8	11	19	53	61	42	2	
10	11	Recharge Emergency System	1	22	23	64	65	42	42	*See Note*
21	22	Inspect Fire Extinguisher	2	5	7	52	54	47	0	
22	30	Rectify Fire Extinguisher	11	7	18	54	65	47	47	
12	13	Lubricate	3	2	5	61	64	59	0	
13	30	Check Lubrication	1	5	6	64	65	59	59	

Note: For the purpose of calculating free float, jobs 10, 11 and 11, 30 are combined. All times are in hours.

event numbers, durations or (with the aid of a suitable code) departments and cost centres.

The critical jobs are indicated by asterisks, and three jobs have also been marked 'S', meaning 'sub-critical'. This rather imprecise term means that their float is relatively low; in this case all jobs with a float of less than 12 hours have been ranked as sub-critical – in other words, as jobs which a relatively short delay could render critical.

REVISING THE PLAN

The plan as it stands calls for 66 hours work to complete the schedule. It can now be used as a basis from which alternative plans may be generated and presented to the manager for decision and action. If we want to speed up the aircraft overhaul,

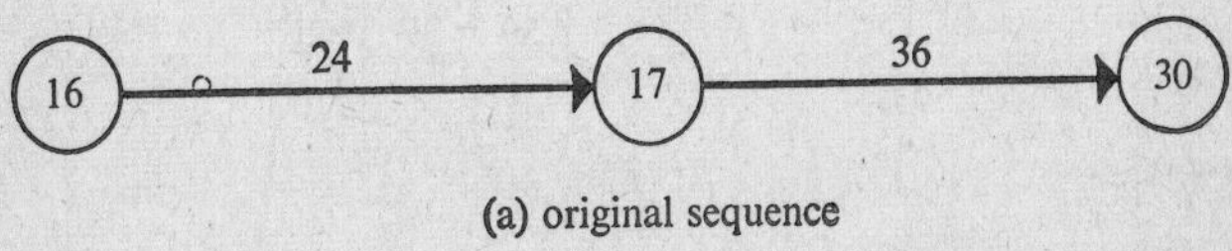

(a) original sequence

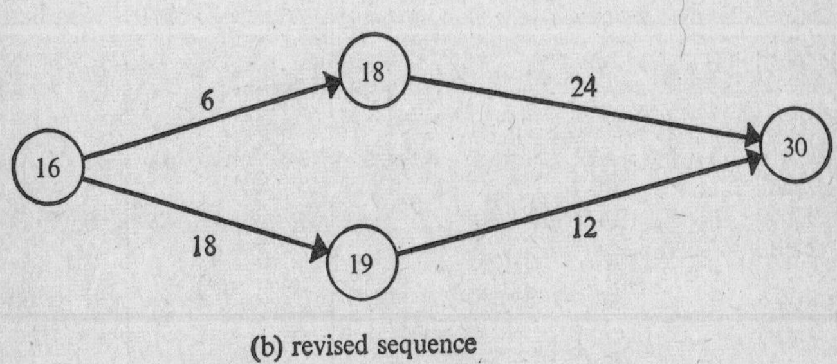

(b) revised sequence

Fig. 2.11 Revision of plan – port engine

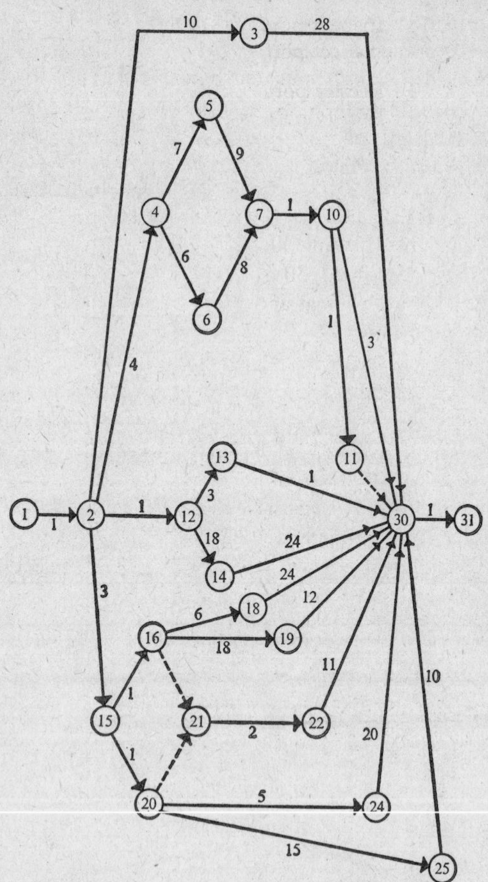

Fig. 2.12 Aircraft overhaul – revised network

we should be well advised to direct our attention in the first place towards the critical jobs in Figure 2.9. Take the inspection and rectification of the port engine, for example. The estimates of their durations were made on the assumption that only one man would work on the engine. With two men working, the jobs could be separated into two concurrent sets. Then the old jobs 16, 17 and 17, 30 would become

16, 18	Inspect port engine (A)	6 hours
16, 19	Inspect port engine (B)	18 hours
18, 30	Rectify port engine (A)	24 hours
19, 30	Rectify port engine (B)	12 hours

The original sequence between events 16 and 30 had an overall duration of 60 hours. The new one, shown in Figure 2.11, takes only 30 hours. However, the project itself will not be shortened by the full 30 hours: this is because the sub-critical path 15, 20, 23, 30 becomes the new critical path, losing its 10 hours of float and shortening the overall duration by this amount only.

We can now sub-divide the jobs on the starboard engine in a similar way, and the network becomes as shown in Figure 2.12; the critical jobs are now concerned with the instruments rather than the engines, and the overall duration is reduced to 45 hours. Other variations of the network are possible, but the three versions already discussed suffice to illustrate the factors which affect the manager's decision, as in Figure 2.13. To allocate extra resources will penalize him in some way, either

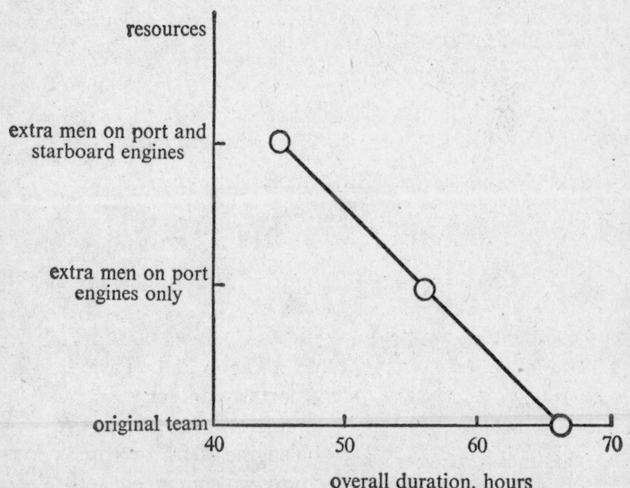

Fig. 2.13 Aircraft overhaul – resources against duration

by increased direct costs or by delay on some other work, and he must balance these costs against the advantages of a shorter duration.

When this principle is extended to cover the bigger networks which occur in practice, which may involve a dozen or more skilled trades as well as special machinery, the problem of allocating resources becomes very complex. Work in this field is still going on – some successful empirical decision rules have been devised and are being regularly applied. There is also a close relationship between this problem and the family of allocation problems discussed in Chapters 4 and 5: this line of research is being pursued.

Meanwhile, the use of network analysis for controlling large projects is expanding at an explosive rate throughout the world. It is less than a decade since the first successful trials were made, but the essential simplicity of the method has already established it firmly in the toolkit of the modern progressive manager.

2
Solutions to Exercises

Exercise 2.1

'Aircraft inspected but not yet rectified.'

Exercise 2.2

There is no reason why either job should follow the other; they could run concurrently.

Exercise 2.3

No. It is dictated by a restriction on resources, in that there is only one attendant. With two attendants, the petrol and oil could be dealt with simultaneously.

Exercise 2.4

Yes. The job 'check oil' cannot possibly be done before the job 'open bonnet', no matter how many attendants are available.

Exercise 2.5

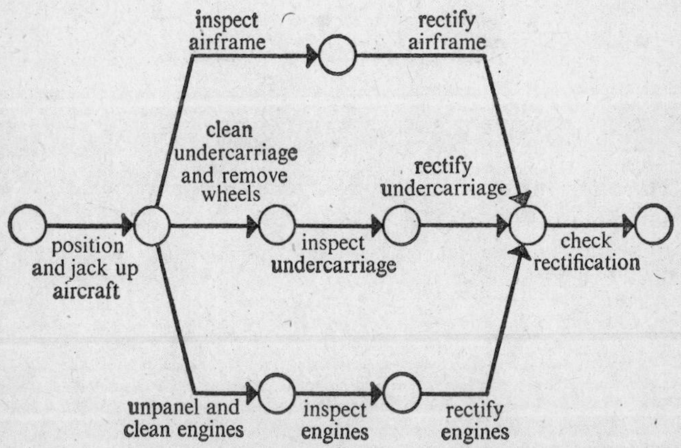

Exercise 2.6

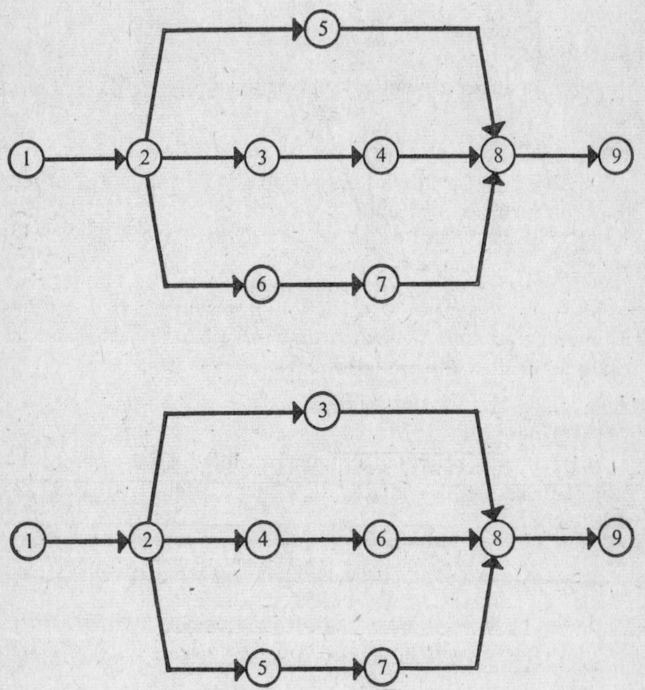

These are two possible solutions under the *ij* system: there are others.

Exercise 2.7

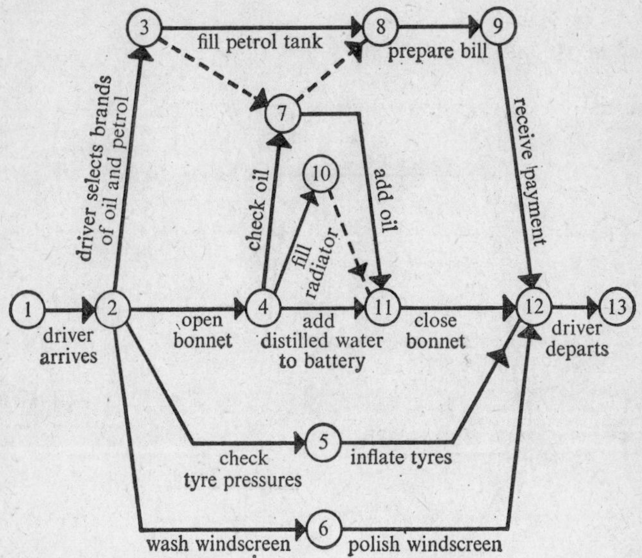

Exercise 2.8

Job 1, 2	1 hour
2, 15	3 hours
15, 20	1 hour
20, 23	20 hours
23, 30	30 hours
30, 31	1 hour
Total	56 hours

Exercise 2.9

Succeeding Event	*Latest Event Time*	*Succeeding Job*	*Job Duration*	*Latest Start*
15	4	2, 15	3	1
12	23	2, 12	1	22
4	45	2, 4	4	41
3	37	2, 3	10	27

The smallest number in the last column gives the latest time for event 2 as *1 o'clock.*

Exercise 2.10

See Figure 2.4.

Overall project time *240 seconds.*

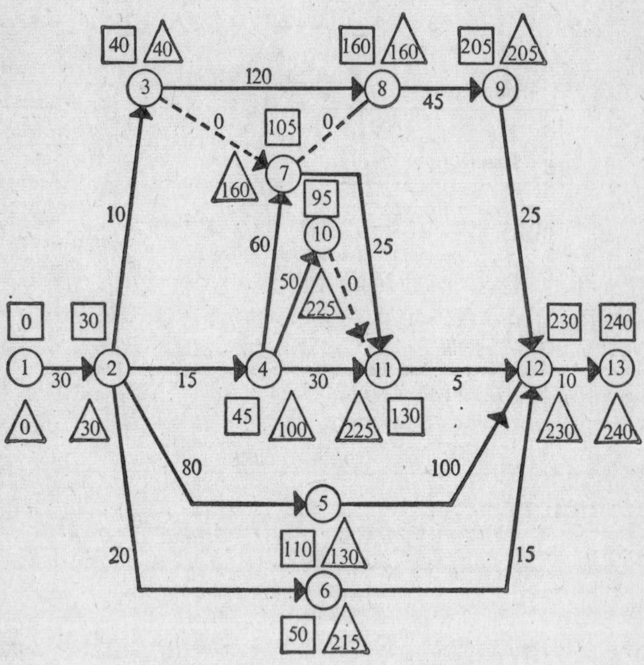

Exercise 2.11

Job i, j	*Latest Time, Event j*	*Earliest Time, Event i*	*Difference*	*Duration*	*Total Float*
14, 30	65	20	45	24	21
6, 7	61	11	50	8	42
16, 17	29	5	24	24	0
20, 23	35	5	30	20	10

Exercise 2.12

Job	*Total Float (hours)*	*Free Float (hours)*
21, 22	54 – 5 – 2 = 47	7 – 5 – 2 = 0
22, 30	65 – 7 – 11 = 47	65 – 7 – 11 = 47

Exercise 2.13

i	*j*	*Job Description*	*Float (seconds) Total*	*Free*	*Critical Jobs*
1	2	Driver arrives	0	0	*
2	3	Driver selects brands	0	0	*
2	4	Open bonnet	55	0	
2	5	Check tyre pressures	20	0	
2	6	Wash windscreen	165	0	
3	8	Fill petrol tank	0	0	*
4	7	Check oil requirement	55	0	
4	10	Fill radiator	130	0 (see note)	
4	11	Add d.w. to battery	150	55	
5	12	Inflate tyres	20	20	
6	12	Polish windscreen	165	165	
7	11	Add oil	100	0	
8	9	Prepare bill	0	0	*
9	12	Receive payment	0	0	*
11	12	Close bonnet	95	95	
12	13	Driver departs	0	0	*

The critical path is 1, 2, 3, 8, 9, 12, 13. Note that free float which apparently belongs to dummies may often be transferred back to real jobs. Thus the free float of 35 seconds on dummy (10, 11) can be assigned to job (4, 10).

NOTES AND REFERENCES

22 Battersby, A., *Network Analysis for Planning and Scheduling* (Macmillan, 1964).

23 Lockyer, K., *Critical Path Analysis* (Pitman, 1964).

24 Anon., *DOD & NASA Guide to PERT/COST* (1962), Office of the Secretary of Defense; National Aeronautics and Space Administration, Washington, U.S.A.

3
Graphs and Gradients

How slow Progressive Points protract the Line,
As pendant spiders spin the filmy twine;

FRERE, CANNING *and* ELLIS, *The Loves of the Triangles*

ONE link between the abstract reasoners and the visualizers – between the algebraists and the geometers, is provided by algebraic geometry, devised by Descartes in 1650 and variously known as coordinate geometry and analytical geometry. The system of rectangular coordinates on which it is based is called 'Cartesian' in honour of the great French philosopher, and closely resembles the latitude and longitude on a Mercator projection, as shown in Figure 3.1. In both those systems, the position of a point on a graph is defined by two coordinates.

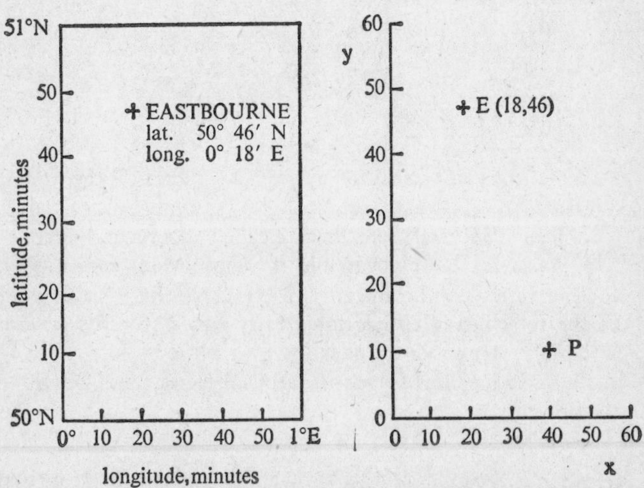

Fig. 3.1 (a) Latitude and longitude of Eastbourne and rectangular (or Cartesian) coordinates of point E

Thus Eastbourne is shown in relation to a reference point at which the 50°N parallel of latitude intersects the Greenwich meridian (0°). Any such reference point is called an *origin.* Eastbourne is 18 minutes east of it and 46 minutes north, as shown by point E in Figure 3.1(b); we can describe its relation to the origin as E (18, 46). In a more general way, we can call the distance east of the origin 'x' and the distance north of the origin 'y'. For E, $x = 18$ and $y = 46$.

The general expression $P(x, y)$ can denote any point in Figure 3.1(b), where x is the distance along the horizontal line (called the x-axis) and y is the distance along the vertical line (y-axis).

Exercise 3.1

What are the values of x and y for point P in Figure 3.1?

Exercise 3.2

Draw a graph similar to Figure 3.1(b) showing the points

Q (10, 20)
R (20, 10)
S (0, 30)
T (40, 0)
U (25, 25)

and label the origin, the x-axis and the y-axis.

One of the great virtues of analytical geometry is that it may be used to illustrate relationships between two variables graphically. Such relationships are called 'algebraic functions'.

Suppose we have a variable y, whose value depends on another variable x: for instance, y (the *dependent* variable) may be the total hiring charge for a lorry and x (the *independent* variable) the number of miles for which it is hired.

This relationship is a particularly simple one and is written algebraically as

$$y = mx \tag{3.1}$$

where m is the mileage rate, say 2 shillings per mile. Note that y is a *total* payment while m is a *rate*. In this case, the value of m does not vary, but is always the same; it is therefore referred to technically as a 'constant', whereas x and y are called 'variables'. We may also write

$$m = \frac{y}{x} \tag{3.2}$$

Knowing the value of m, we are now able to deduce the value of y corresponding to a particular value of x.

The equation becomes, when $m = 2$,

$$y = 2x \tag{3.3}$$

and if x is 50 miles, y is 100 shillings. The algebraic equation takes no account of the units which are associated with the numerical values, but merely deals with the values as pure numbers. We must be careful, when dealing with practical situations, to make sure that the units of measurement are the same throughout.

Exercise 3.3

(a) If $x = 75$, what is y?
(b) If $y = 200$, what is x?
(c) If $x = 0$, what is y?
(d) Where is the point $P(0, 0)$?

Exercise 3.4

What do we know about the set of points described by the general expression $P(x, 0)$?

(If you find this problem difficult, pick a few values of x at random and plot the corresponding points on a graph.)

Now let us look at the graphical representation of this simple relationship, using two axes at right angles to represent x and y (Figure 3.2). Each pair of values (x, y) is represented by a point on the graph, and all the points lie on a straight line. The function $y = mx$ is called a 'linear function' for this reason, and m is called the 'slope' or 'gradient' of the curve. (Mathematicians use the word 'curve' in a general sense for any line which represents a function, even though it may be a straight line.)

Since the origin of the graph is the point at which both x and y have zero value, the curve of the function $y = mx$ passes

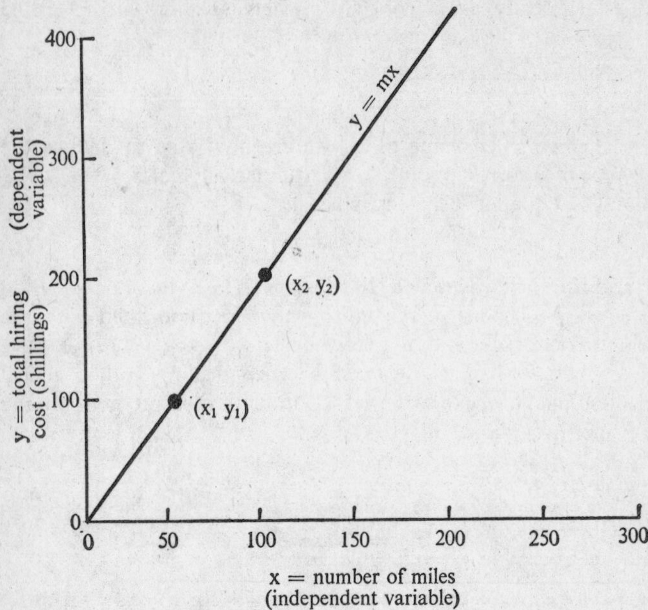

Fig. 3.2 Cost of hiring a lorry

through it. This is not necessarily true of all linear functions: if we were running our own lorry instead of hiring one, the cost would include a fixed weekly sum – call it '*c*' – for hire purchase instalments, tax and insurance as well as the mileage rate *m*. We now have two cases to consider:

(a) hiring lorries with no fixed cost but a high mileage rate

(b) owning lorries with a fixed cost but a lower mileage rate.

The two cases are shown in Figure 3.3. The curve labelled 'Hired lorry' is the same as that in Figure 3.2; the 'Owned lorry' curve is one for which a fixed cost of £10 (200 shillings) is accompanied by a mileage rate of 1 shilling per mile. Its algebraic equation is

$$y = x + 200 \tag{3.4}$$

which may be written in more general terms as

$$y = mx + c \tag{3.5}$$

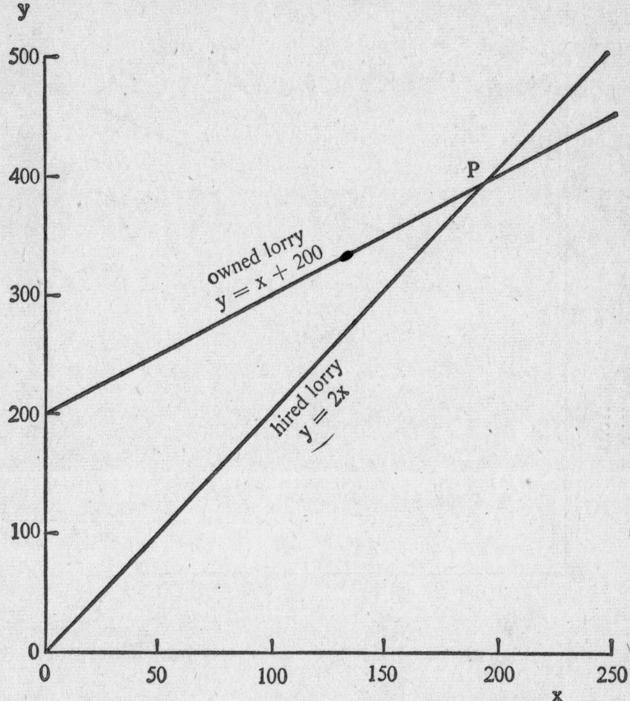

Fig. 3.3 Comparison of two rates of mileage costs

The gradient, *m*, is 1 shilling per mile and the constant value, *c*, is 200 shillings in the special case of equation (3.4); *c* is sometimes called the 'intercept'.

Equation (3.5) is, for all its simplicity, one of the most important and most widely-used in the algebra of modern management. Any straight line you care to draw can be specified by choosing suitable values of *m* and *c*, and many business relationships obey a straight-line law.

Try taking a piece of squared paper, drawing an *x* axis and a *y* axis on it as in Figures 3.2 and 3.3, and graphing the equations you get by putting various values of *m* and *c* into equation (3.5). Use zero and negative values as well as positive ones,

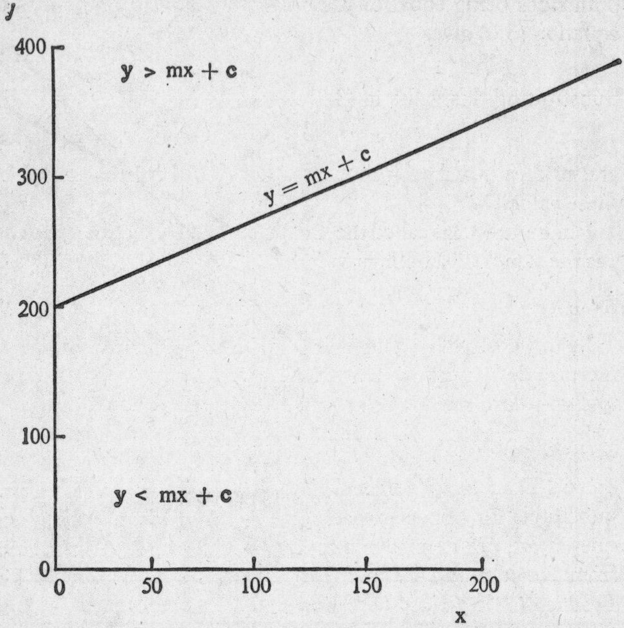

Fig. 3.4 Graphical representation of inequalities

and try to think up physical meanings for the variables x and y as well as the constants m and c which relate them.

Returning to Figure 3.3, it is easy to see that the two curves intersect at the 'break-even' point P where $x = 200$ miles and $y = 400$ shillings. For a weekly mileage below 200, casual hiring will cost less; above this figure hire purchase will be cheaper. This, then, is a geometrical or graphical solution; what is the corresponding algebraic procedure?

Point P is the only combination of x and y which is on both curves and therefore satisfies both equations simultaneously, so

$$y = 2x \qquad (3.3)$$

$$y = x + 200 \qquad (3.4)$$

It follows that

$$2x = x + 200 \qquad (3.6)$$

both sides being equal to y. Subtracting x from both sides of equation (3.6) gives

$$x = 200 \tag{3.7}$$

Substituting this value in (3.3) gives

$$y = 400 \tag{3.8}$$

and it is easy to check that equation (3.4) is also satisfied by these values.

P in Figure 3.3 is called the 'break-even point' because the cost y is the same, 400 shillings, whether the lorry is hired or owned.

Exercise 3.5

Rising costs have forced both the hirer and the owner to increase their mileage rates by 20%, but the fixed costs remain unchanged. Does the break-even figure change or not?

Exercise 3.6

The Purchasing Officer of Quaternion Ltd is obtaining quotations for a special spacing piece. Pascal's Pressings have quoted 3d. per item plus a toolmaking cost of £30; the price from Newton and Leibniz Ltd is simply 1/- per item. The Production Planning Department has not yet decided how many parts are required, so the Purchasing Officer calculates a 'break-even' figure. What is it? Find the answer algebraically and illustrate it with a graph.

For the example shown in Figure 3.3 and in the preceding exercise, we used both algebra and geometry to find the break-even point, but the final step of deciding which proposal was cheaper (i.e. which function gave the lower value of y for a given value of x) was by inspection rather than by a formal algebraic procedure. For such a procedure we need to consider inequalities as well as equations.

INEQUALITIES

Inequalities receive scant attention in school textbooks, which is not surprising since mathematicians in general have neglected them until quite recently.

T. Motzkin, in his doctoral thesis on linear inequalities in 1936, was able to cite after diligent search only some thirty references for the period 1900–1936, and about forty-two in all.[25]

The developments of the theory of linear inequalities described in the next two chapters have quickened the interest of mathematicians, and the number of references is now reckoned in thousands. This interest is reflected by the report of the Sub-Committee on Mathematics in the General School Course at the Southampton Mathematical Conference, 1961, which includes the following recommendation:

Inequalities should be considered at the same time as equalities. There is no inherent reason for not doing so. In fact positive advantages are to be gained.[26]

Inequalities may be expressed in several ways, but we shall only be concerned with four of them:

$$y > x \ (y \text{ is greater than } x) \qquad (3.9)$$

$$x < y \ (x \text{ is less than } y) \qquad (3.10)$$

$$y \geqq x \ (y \text{ is greater than or equal to } x \text{, i.e. } y \text{ is not less than } x) \qquad (3.11)$$

$$x \leqq y \ (x \text{ is less than or equal to } y, \text{ i.e. } x \text{ is not greater than } y) \qquad (3.12)$$

The difference between (3.9) and (3.11) is that the latter includes the case $y = x$ while the former does not. In practice, the difference between the two is usually trivial, but must be preserved if ambiguities are to be avoided. For instance, if we specify:

Choose y if $y > x$
Choose x if $y < x$

then the choice for the case $y = x$ is not clearly defined. We must write either

Choose y if $y \geqq x$
Choose x if $y < x$

or

Choose y if $y > x$
Choose x if $y \leqq x$

The inequality signs may be combined with all the more familiar mathematical operators, to give expressions such as

$$y \geqq mx + c \qquad (3.13)$$

Inequalities are difficult to manipulate mathematically; this may be overcome by transforming them into equations. In doing so, we make use of a property which many variables possess in industrial problems: they cannot have negative values. The number of items produced in a factory; the percentage of tin in an alloy; the value of last month's sales; the number of cases admitted to a hospital – these are all variables which may at times be zero, but otherwise must have positive values. They are called 'non-negative variables' and are themselves specified by inequalities such as $y \geqq 0$.

If $y \geqq x$ and both are non-negative, we can write

$$y = x + p, p \geqq 0 \tag{3.14}$$

p is itself a non-negative variable defined as the difference between y and x.

If y is annual income and x is annual expenditure, then equation (3.14) would summarize Mr Micawber's philosophy. 'Annual income twenty pounds, annual expenditure nineteen, nineteen, six, result happiness' with p as a measure of that happiness.

Exercise 3.7

A steel company has six blast furnaces with capacities a, b, c, d, e, and f. Write out the relationship between these capacities and the production x as an inequality, then turn it into an equation with the aid of a non-negative variable z. What is z a measure of?

In many practical situations, the gradient m and the intercept in equation (2.5) will both be non-negative. If m were negative, the hirer would be paying you to use his lorry.

A useful graphical analogue of an inequality is shown in Figure 3.4. The line $y = mx + c$ divides the total area between the x and y axes into two. The lower portion represents the inequality $y < mx + c$ or, if we consider the line itself to be included, $y \leqq mx + c$. In the same way, we can regard the x and y axes as the curves of the equations $x = 0$ and $y = 0$ respectively, dividing the plane in which the graph is drawn

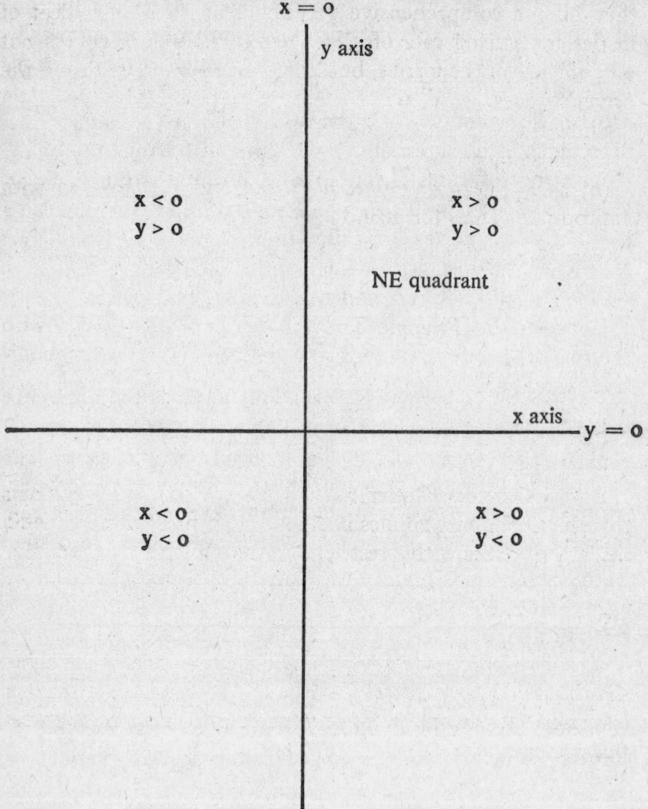

Fig. 3.5 Feasible and non-feasible quadrants

into four quadrants (Figure 3.5). Only the 'north-east' quadrant satisfies the requirement that x and y shall not have negative values.

Exercise 3.8

The Triangle Transport Corporation has now entered the field covered in Exercise 2.5, but with a different sort of bid;

they offer a comprehensive service using their own fleet of lorries for a fixed rate of £25 a week. This sum covers not only the use of the lorries, but also their running costs and the driver's wages.

Show this

(a) as a graph

(b) as a linear equation of the form $y = mx + c$ with appropriate values for m and c.

Exercise 3.9

Consider the Triangle Transport bid in competition with the two other offers shown in Figure 3.3. Under what conditions would you accept it?

Exercise 3.10

A supplementary letter from Triangle Transport explains that their offer only applies if the mileage does not exceed 400, i.e. $x \leqq 400$. Show this restriction graphically.

Exercise 3.11

The cost of insuring a 3-litre motor-car comprehensively in the Central London Area is £65 10s. 0d., if its value is £200 or less, plus 10/– for every £100 above this minimum. Express this graphically.

Exercise 3.12

Some investment managers use the variation in the price of a share as a measure of the risk associated with it, and compare it with the yield before deciding whether or not to buy.

The investment manager of Euclid Enterprises takes the highest and lowest values of a share in the previous year, and uses their ratio to measure its riskiness. He also has a maxim, 'Never buy unless the percentage yield is more than three times the price ratio'.

Draw a graph to illustrate this rule, with two areas labelled 'Buy' and 'Do not buy'. Plot the following shares on it:

Company	*Yield*	*High*	*Low*	*Ratio*
Principia Pty.	5·0%	8/3d	3/9d	2·2
Lagrange Multipliers Ltd	10·0%	2/8d	1/8d	1·6
Axioms Inc.	5·2%	12/9d	7/6d	1·7
Transcendental Corp.	8·3%	44/6d	22/3d	2·0
Vector Space Co.	7·5%	3/6d	1/6d	2·33
Quadratic Corp.	7·7%	27/-d	9/-d	3·0

PLANES AND PAYMENTS

The linear equations and inequalities considered up to now have contained a dependent variable y as a function of a single independent variable x. We now go on to consider a case in which y depends upon two independent variables x and z. Suppose that a chemical plant is producing 160 tons of product in a week, and that the manager decides to increase this figure by means of an incentive bonus scheme. The bonus is to be paid at the rate of one shilling for each ton of production in excess of 160. Then if y is the bonus and x is the production,

$$y = x - 160, \; x \geqq 160 \qquad (3.15)$$

The chemical engineers point out that increased production may affect the yield unless the plant is carefully controlled. The yield is the ratio of the amount of product obtained to the theoretical amount which would be produced under ideal conditions; at present it stands at 97%. The raw materials are expensive, and a lower yield would increase the cost of the product.

The manager therefore undertakes to apply a penalty of 10 shillings for a fall of 1 point in the yield, and a corresponding bonus for an increase. Such a scheme is called a 'multi-factor incentive', and its equation is

$$y = x - 160 + 10(z - 97),$$
$$y \geqq 0, \qquad x \geqq 160, \qquad z \leqq 100 \qquad (3.15)$$

in which

y is the bonus in shillings
x is the production in tons
z is the yield, as a percentage.

The restriction $y \geqq 0$ is necessary because a negative bonus would be a deduction from the basic rate of pay, which is a privilege permitted only to the Government or a trade union, not to an employer.

Equation (3.15) simplifies to

$$y = x + 10z - 1130 \tag{3.16}$$

This is still a 'linear function', that is, a straight-line relationship, because it does not contain terms like x^2 or z^3; however, its graph will need to show three variables and will therefore have to be drawn in three dimensions: in other words, it will be a solid, as shown in Figure 3.6.

The vertical axis is y, the bonus, and the two horizontal axes are seen in perspective, sloping upwards from the origin.

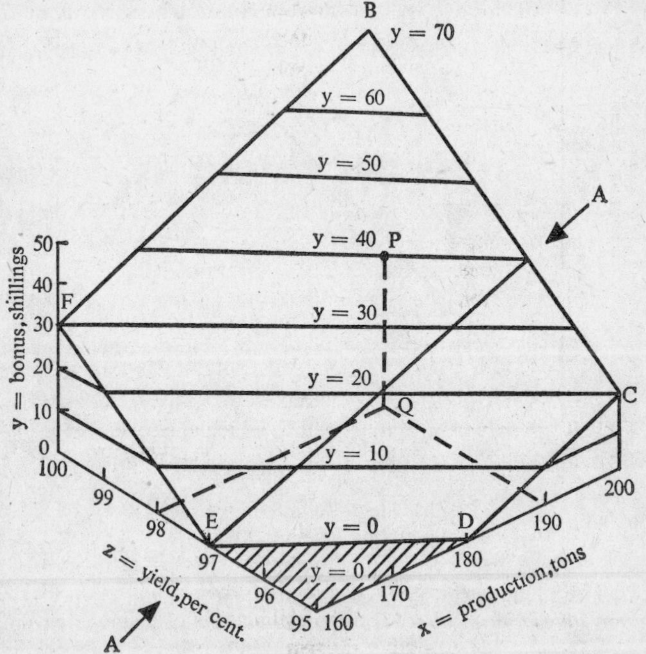

Fig. 3.6 Multi-factor bonus scheme

That on the left is the axis corresponding to z, the yield, and the triangle rising vertically is the graph of a relationship between y and z when the production, x, is 160 tons. Similarly, we can see on the right the dependence of the bonus on the production when the yield is 95%. To find the relationship between y and x which applies when the yield is 97% (as in the original single-factor scheme), we must take a cross-section at AA. This graph corresponds to equation (3.15) and is shown in Figure 3.7.

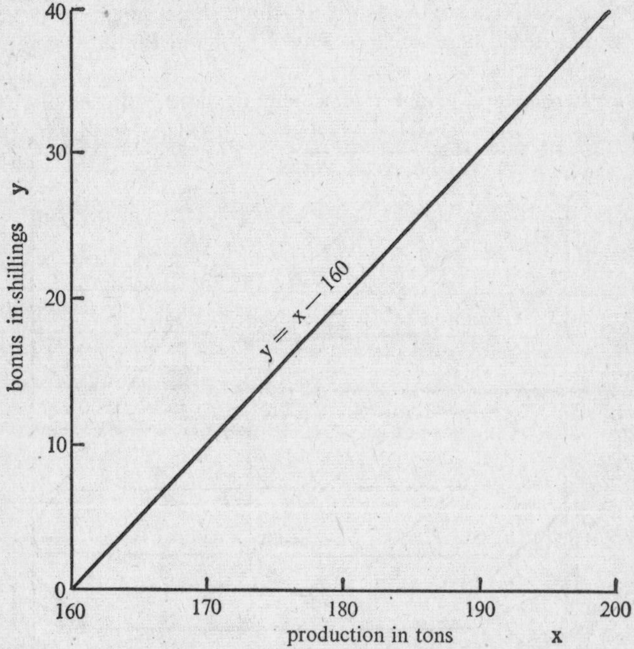

Fig. 3.7 Single-factor bonus scheme (cross-section AA from Figure 3.6)

The plane surface *BCDEF* is the graph of equation (3.16) and gives values of y for all combinations of x and z within the ranges shown. The contours drawn across it show its heights above the base, these heights being the appropriate values of y. For instance, the point Q on the base corresponds to the following combination:

$$x \text{ (production)} = 190 \text{ tons}$$
$$z \text{ (yield)} \quad = \ 98\%$$

If we draw a line vertically upwards from Q it will cut the y surface at P, on the '$y = 40$' contour and therefore 40 shillings above the base. Check this value by substituting for x and z in equation (3.16).

The shaded area represents combinations of x and z for which y would be negative, were it not for the restriction which does not allow it to fall below zero.

Figure 3.6 can be simplified by presenting it in plan view, as is done in Figure 3.8. The oblique lines again represent

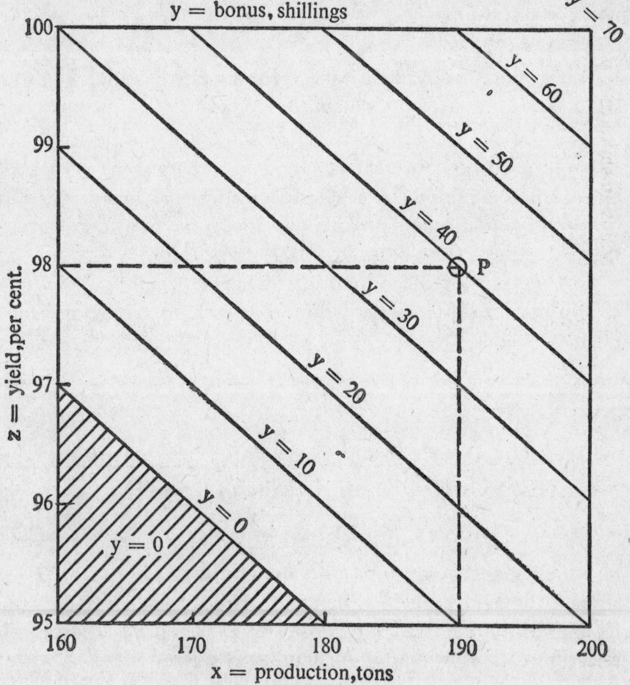

Fig. 3.8 Plan view of Figure 3.6

'bonus contours' and in this form the graph may be used as a ready-reckoner.

Exercise 3.13

The specified upper limit for the main impurity is 0·5%, and the manager wishes to introduce quality as the third factor in his incentive scheme. The rate is agreed with the union as 2 shillings for 0·4%, 4 shillings for 0·3% and so on, with corresponding intermediate values. Batches above the specification limit will be rejected and will not be counted towards the production figure, so no penalty need be applied to the quality factor.

Modify equation (3.16) so as to include this condition, and list the limits of all the variables.

Exercise 3.14

What bonus would be awarded for a week in which 174 tons were produced with a yield of 96·5% and 0·25% impurity?

An interesting contrast between the algebraic and geometric approaches can now be seen, for if the manager wished to bring in yet another factor, the algebraic treatment would merely require the addition of one more term.

The graph of this equation, however, would need to be drawn in four dimensions, which means that we cannot visualize it.

FAMILIES OF CURVES

Suppose we have a linear function of the form

$$2x + 3y = a \tag{3.17}$$

in which x and y are the variables and a is a constant. If we set a to have any selected constant value, then for each value of x there is one, and only one, value of y; y is therefore a function of x, and equation (3.17) may be rewritten as

$$y = -\tfrac{2}{3}x + \tfrac{1}{3}a \tag{3.18}$$

This is a linear function with a gradient of $-\frac{2}{3}$ and an intercept of $+\frac{1}{3}a$. The gradient is independent of the constant a, so all the curves corresponding to equation (3.18) will be parallel. Figure 3.9 shows a family of curves of this type.

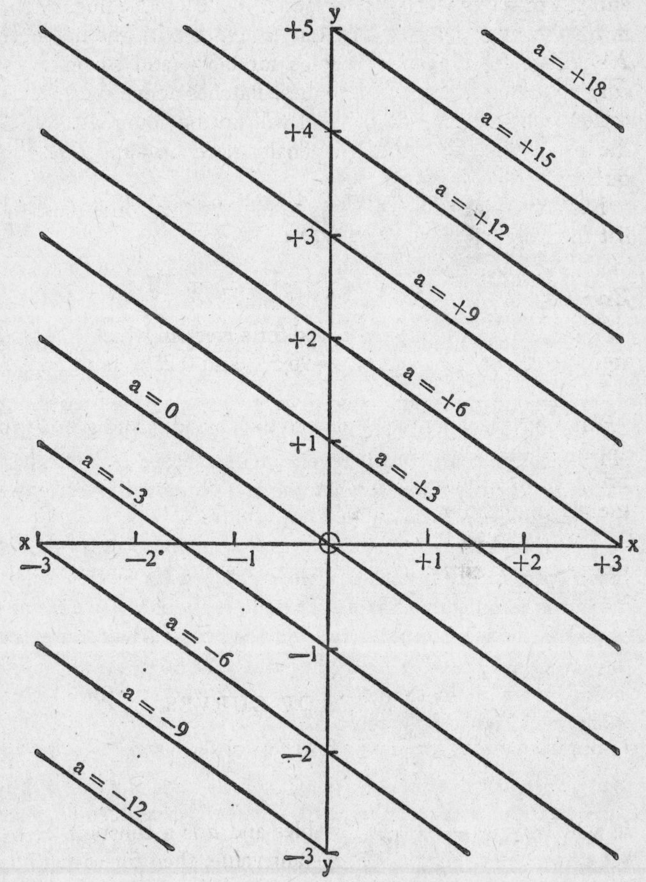

Fig. 3.9 Family of curves of the form $2x + 3y = a$
(The only difference between these straight lines is the value to which the constant a is set.)

The 'opportunity cost' concept of modern economics is derived from such graphs, as is the related idea of an 'indifference curve', although the latter is not usually a straight line. The underlying idea is of a choice between alternatives. For example, a dam may have to be built in an under-developed country, and a represents its total cost. The responsible manager can either plan to use heavy earth-moving machinery or cheap local labour. The latter will cost him 3 rupees per cubic yard of earth moved; bulldozers are more efficient but demand capital on which interest must be paid, which when added to the operating costs brings the total cost for mechanical earth-moving up to 2 rupees per cubic yard. Then the family of curves in Figure 3.8 gives the amounts of earth which may be moved by machinery (x) and labour (y) for any given total expenditure a.

In one actual case – the Maithon Dam of the Damodar Valley Project in West Bengal – a mixed effort of labour and machinery was used, with labour concentrated on the difficult corners and edges while machinery did the sheer 'bull-dozing' from which it takes its name. The problem in practice is not so simple as it has been made to appear here: the quick answer 'use machinery wherever possible because it is cheaper' is not necessarily the best when the non-employment of labour is unjustified on social or moral grounds.

A second point is that the use of machinery gives rise to fixed costs before it does any work at all, whereas the cost of labour is completely variable. The International Labour Office is currently sponsoring a study in the State of Bangalore, the object of which is to raise the efficiency of physical labour compared with mechanical handling so that the break-even point (see Figure 3.3) is raised.

Exercise 3.15

A man can move a cubic yard of earth over a given distance in one day, and his daily wage is 3 rupees. It costs 1,000 rupees to bring a bulldozer to the site, after which it can move a cubic yard of earth over the same distance for a cost of 1 rupee.

(a) how big a job (in terms of cubic yards) justifies the use of a bulldozer?

(b) how would this figure be affected if the man's daily output could be increased by 20% with no additional cost?

Exercise 3.16

The cost of hiring a London taxicab was calculated in the following way before the recent fare increases:

(a) For the first three fifths of a mile, or the first seven-and-a-half minutes, or a combination of parts of these: 1s. 9d.

(b) For every additional one fifth of a mile, or two and a half minutes: 3d.

(c) The charge for journeys greater than six miles or lasting for more than one hour is not bound by these rules, but is subject to negotiation.

Draw a graph of these rules as linear functions, using a to denote the total fare in pence, x the duration in minutes, and y the distance run, in miles.

Problems of great complexity can often be reduced to sets of linear equations and inequalities, thus making them easier to solve. Such problems are discussed in the next chapter.

3
Solutions to Exercises

Exercise 3.1

$x = 40, \qquad y = 10$

Exercise 3.2

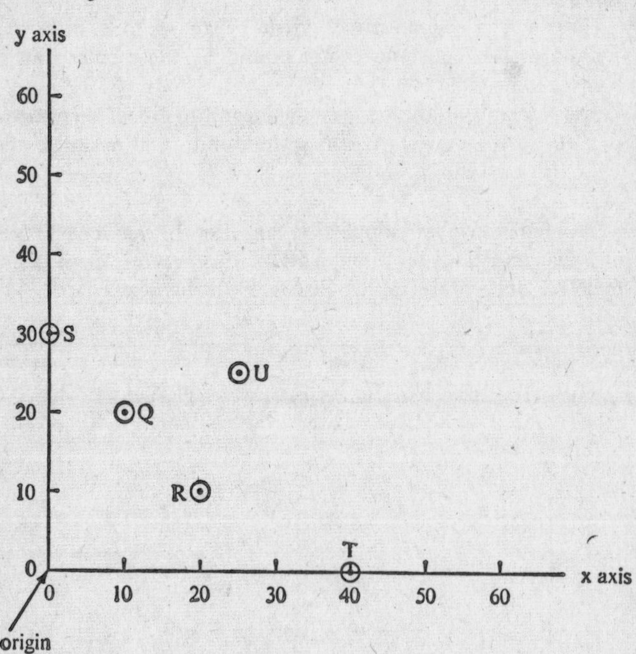

Exercise 3.3

(a) $y = 2x = 150$
(b) $x = \frac{1}{2}y = 100$
(c) $y = 2x = 0$
(d) At the origin

Exercise 3.4

All points $P(x, 0)$ lie along the x-axis.

Exercise 3.5

The new values for m in equations (3.3) and (3.4) are respectively 2.4 and 1.2. Then at the break-even point,

$$y = 2{\cdot}4x$$
$$y = 1{\cdot}2x + 200$$

Therefore

$$2{\cdot}4x = 1{\cdot}2x + 200$$
$$1{\cdot}2x = 200$$
$$x = 200/1{\cdot}2 = 167$$

The break-even point has changed. Now find the new value of y.

Exercise 3.6

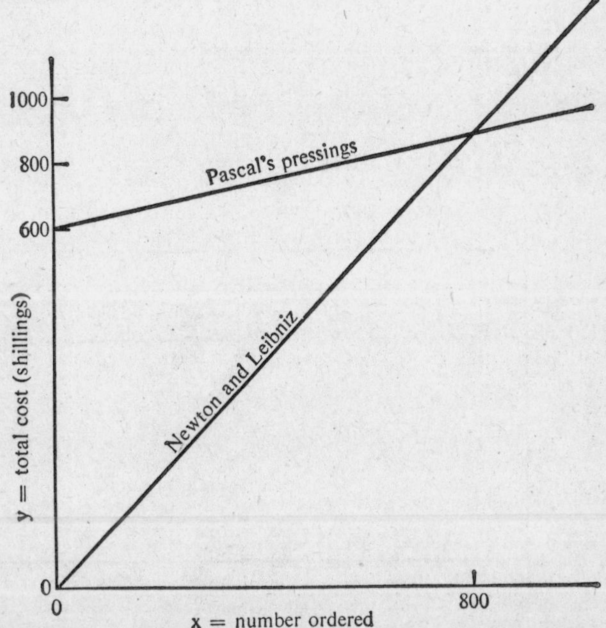

Pascal's Pressings $m = 0{\cdot}25$ shillings
$c = 600$ shillings
Newton & Leibniz $m = 1$ shilling
$c = 0$

$$x = \text{number ordered}$$
$$y = \text{total cost}$$

$$\left.\begin{aligned} y &= 0{\cdot}25x + 600 \\ y &= \phantom{0{\cdot}25}x \end{aligned}\right\} \text{Simultaneously true at the break-even point}$$

$$\text{from which } x = 800 = y$$

Pascal's Pressings are cheaper if the quantity to be ordered is 800 or more.

Exercise 3.7

$$y \leqq a + b + c + d + e + f$$
$$y + z = a + b + c + d + e + f$$

z is a measure of spare furnace capacity.

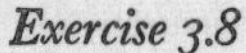

Exercise 3.8

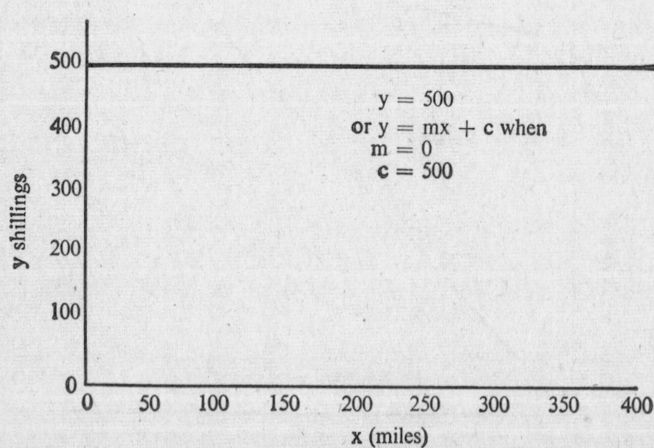

Exercise 3.9

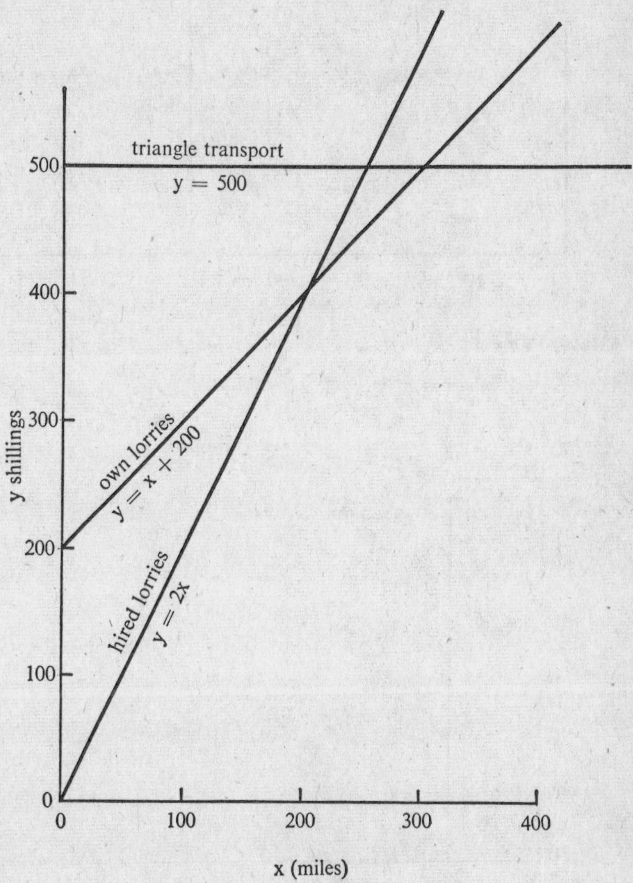

One would accept the Triangle Transport bid only when the weekly mileage was 300 or more.

Exercise 3.10

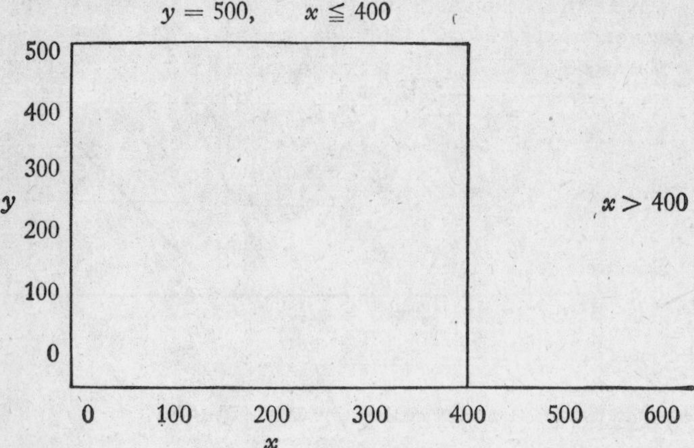

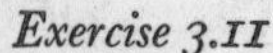

y = 500, x ≦ 400
500
400
300
y
200
100
0
x > 400
0
100
200
300
400
500
600
x

Exercise 3.11

£
80
70
60
50
40
30
20
10
0
premium = y
y = 65·5
y = 64·5 + 0·005x
x < 200
x > 200
0
200
400
600
800
1000
value of vehicle = x

$$y = 65{\cdot}5 + 0{\cdot}5\left(\frac{x - 200}{100}\right)$$
$$= 64{\cdot}5 + 0{\cdot}005x$$

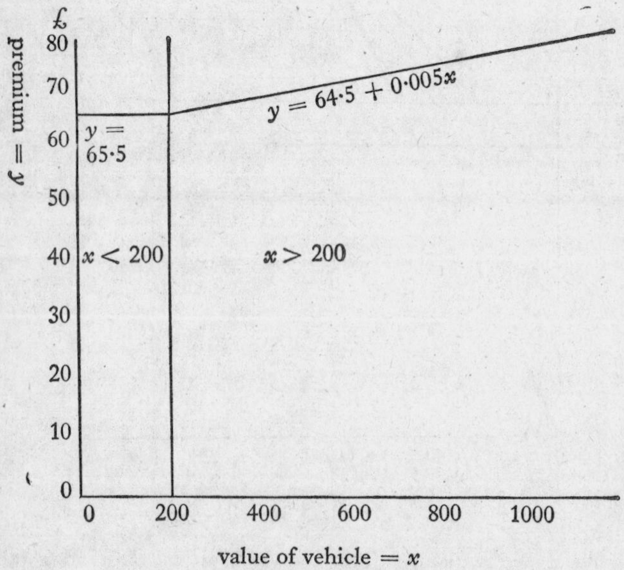

Note that, in practice, the premium would go up in steps at intervals of £50 or £100 along the x axis. This is also the case in most managerial problems, and the curves given here and elsewhere are, strictly speaking, approximations.

Exercise 3.12

$$\text{Let } y = \text{yield}$$
$$x = \text{risk}$$
$$\text{Then } y > 3x$$
$$\text{i.e. } y - 3x > 0$$

Sketch the curve $y - 3x = 0$.

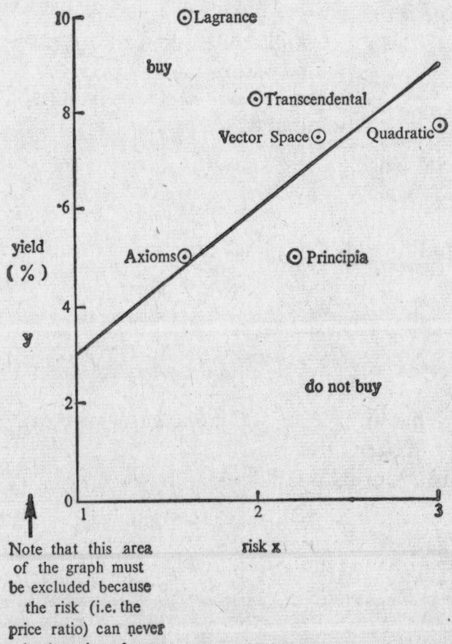

Exercise 3.13

Let w denote the percentage of the impurity.

$$\begin{aligned} \text{Then } y &= x + 10z - 1130 + 20\,(0{\cdot}5 - w) \\ &= x + 10z - 20w - 1120 \end{aligned}$$

$$y \geqq 0 \qquad x \geqq 160$$
$$z \leqq 100$$
$$w \geqq 0$$
$$w \leqq 0{\cdot}5$$

Note that w has a negative gradient, indicating that the bonus y increases as the percentage of impurity decreases.

Exercise 3.14

14/–. The higher quality and lower yield just cancel each other out.

Exercise 3.15

Let x = number of cubic yards moved,
y = total cost of moving x,
m = cost per cubic yard, in rupees,
c = initial fixed cost.

For manual work, $m = 3$, $c = 0$.

$$y = 3x$$

For the bulldozer

$$y = x + 1{,}000$$

At the break-even point,

$$3x = x + 1{,}000 \quad \text{so} \quad x = 500$$

It follows that any job of 500 cubic yards or more justifies the use of a bulldozer.
If the output per man is increased by 20%,

$$m \text{ becomes } 3 \div 1{\cdot}2 = 2{\cdot}5$$

At the new break-even point,

$$2{\cdot}5x = x + 1{,}000 \quad \text{so} \quad x = 667$$

The increase in output has raised the break-even point by 33%.

Exercise 3.16

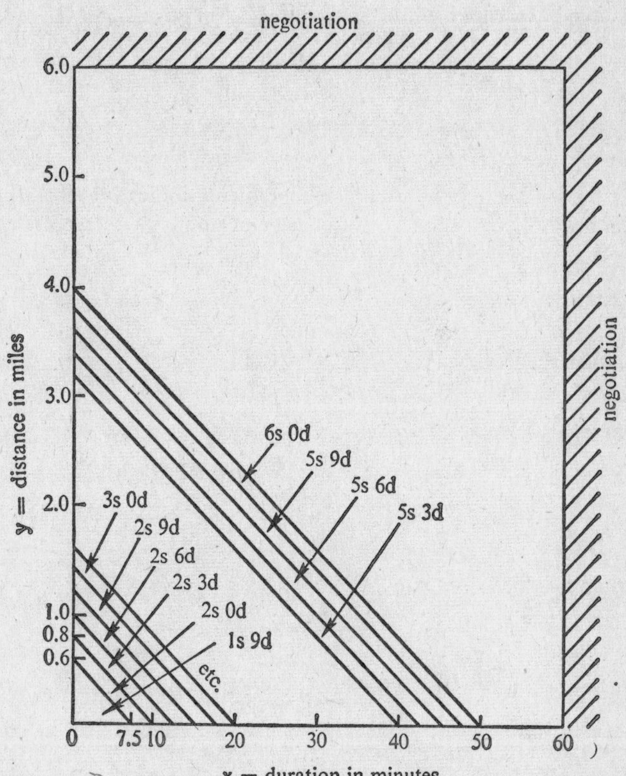

NOTES AND REFERENCES

25 Dantzig, G. B., *Linear Programming and Extensions* (Princeton University Press, 1963), p. 20.

26 Thwaites, B., and others, *On Teaching Mathematics* (*Southampton Mathematical Conference*) (1961), p. 31.

Opportunity cost and indifference curves are mentioned by (among others)

27 Lipsey, R. G., *An Introduction to Positive Economies* (Weidenfeld and Nicholson, 1963).

28 The use of break-even points is extensively discussed in Knoeppel, C. E., and Seybold, E. G., *Managing for Profit* (McGraw-Hill, 1937).

4
Allocation by Algebra

'The sum of all the parts of Such –
Of each laboratory scene –
Is Such?' While Science means this much
And means no more, why, let it mean!

ROBERT GRAVES, *Synthetic Such*

INTRODUCTION

Managers are as diverse in their interests as the companies they work in, but they all have one major problem in common: scarcity of resources. Labour, machinery, buildings, space, and labour are never available in unlimited quantities, and all management plans have to be made within the restrictions which they impose. The prudent allocation of resources is always a problem, but a powerful weapon for attacking it has been developed by mathematicians. It is known by the generic description of 'mathematical programming', but we shall consider here only the simplest and most widely-used member of the genus, linear programming. This is no mere academic curiosity, but a sound practical means of producing workable plans and increased profits. Transporting coal to power stations or gasworks, allocating cash to local branches, formulating foods and drawing up a maintenance schedule: these are all areas in which linear programming is at work today. Other examples are quoted later.

One could hardly expect the busy manager to slog through the calculations described in this chapter as part of his daily routine, but he ought to go through them for himself at least once. In doing so, he will learn a good deal about the limitations of the method as well as its potentialities, and be able to assess its appropriateness to his own circumstances. Furthermore, he will be able to set out his problem, possibly with some expert help, in a standardized form, and then delegate the routine calculations to either a human computer or an electronic one.

In the Glacier Metal case (described briefly at the end of Chapter 5), a girl with a desk calculating machine was able, after a week's training, to compute a re-melting plan in three hours. The plan had previously been drawn up by a research investigator, whose time was more costly, by rule of thumb. A comparison of the two methods showed that the girl got better answers.

Once the manager has acquired confidence in this remarkably versatile technique, he can afford to forget how he originally did the calculations and concentrate on the more interesting parts of the job – defining the problem and interpreting its solution in terms of practical decisions.

The descriptions which follow may at times make fairly heavy demands on the rusty non-mathematician; nevertheless, they consist entirely in juggling with simple equations as was done in the last chapter. Since one very common application of linear programming is to production control, the elementary case in this chapter is taken from that field of management.

A PRODUCTION PLANNING PROBLEM

The Fermat Furniture Company manufactures tables, chairs, desks, and bookcases. A table requires 5 feet of softwood and 2 feet of hardwood, and takes up 3 man-hours. These requirements and those for the other types are summarized in the table below:

Item	*Softwood (ft)*	*Hardwood (ft)*	*Man-hours*
Table	5	2	3
Chair	1	3	2
Desk	9	4	5
Bookcase	12	1	10

1,500 feet of softwood and 1,000 feet of hardwood are available. The factory employs 10 men, each of whom works 8 hours a day. (The man-hours given in the table above include suitable allowances for rest-periods, etc. Overtime is not permitted.) Production is planned over a 10-day period according to sales requirements.

The Sales Manager has asked for at least 40 tables, 130 chairs, and 30 desks, and says he can sell any production in excess of these figures. There is little demand for bookcases, so there is no minimum requirement and the Sales Manager does not think he could accept more than 10 for sale.

The question is how the production should be planned, and the first step in solving it is a simple one. We accept the Sales Manager's assessment of the market and assume that his minimum requirements will first be met in full. They will use some of the available resources as shown in the following table:

Item	*No.*	*Softwood (ft)*	*Hardwood (ft)*	*Man-hours*
Table	40	200	80	120
Chair	130	130	390	260
Desk	30	270	120	150
Bookcase	0	0	0	0
Sub-totals		600	590	530
Total Resources		1,500	1,000	800
Nett Resources Remaining		900	410	270

We are left with the problem of allocating the remaining productive resources – softwood, hardwood, and man-hours – to tables, chairs, desks, or bookcases, singly or in combination. Which of the many possible answers should we choose? In order to find an answer we must have some *criterion* of selection.

The simplest criterion of all is that of *feasibility* – that is to say, of finding a solution which lies within the limits of the resources available; in our example, we might decide to make 10 bookcases and 80 chairs above the minimum requirements.

Exercise 4.1

Confirm that 10 bookcases and 80 chairs constitute a feasible plan.

The criterion of feasibility is a crude one: why then is it so widely used? Simply because real-life problems are so much more complex than our over-simplified example that merely to achieve feasibility is a considerable feat of mental agility. As Doctor Johnson said of 'a dog's walking on his hinder legs. It is not done well; but you are surprised to find it done at all'.

A more refined criterion which is also used extensively is minimum idle time. Since the plant presumably makes a profit when it is running and merely incurs costs when it is idle, the plan which most utilizes the productive resources will, one assumes, be the best. In the Fermat Furniture Company, the only measure of 'plant capacity' is the number of man-hours worked: the feasible solution we have already proposed leaves 10 idle hours which we might allocate to, say, 2 desks. Although minimum idle time can give an improvement on mere feasibility, its employment as a criterion can sometimes give fallacious results, as will be shown later.

The most modern method is to use a financial criterion, usually minimum cost or maximum profit, the latter being preferable. To this end we need to know costs and prices which for Fermat Furniture are:

Softwood costs 2/– per foot.
Hardwood costs 5/– per foot.

The labour cost, including machine costs and all direct costs (e.g. electricity, lubricants) but excluding overheads, is 10/– per hour.

The prices at which the products are offered to the trade are:

Table	£3	2	0
Chair	£2	2	0
Desk	£5	3	0
Bookcase	£6	19	0

Calculating the profit on each item is a straightforward procedure:

								Shillings	
	Soft-wood 2/–		*Hard-wood 5/–*		*Man-hours 10/–*		*Total*	*Sell-ing*	*Gross*
Item	*ft*	*Cost*	*ft*	*Cost*	*Hours*	*Cost*	*Cost*	*Price*	*Profit*
Table	5	10	2	10	3	30	50	62	12
Chair	1	2	3	15	2	20	37	42	5
Desk	9	18	4	20	5	50	88	103	15
Book-case	12	24	1	5	10	100	129	139	10

The gross profit on our feasible solution would be

10 bookcases:	100 shillings
80 chairs:	400 shillings
2 desks:	30 shillings
Total:	530 shillings

(plus, of course, a profit of 1,580 shillings made by manufacturing and selling the minimum requirements, which from now on will be taken for granted).

It is not difficult to select better plans now that we know about costs, as the two exercises which follow will show.

Exercise 4.2

(a) Which item shows the greatest profit per unit manufactured?
(b) How many can we make?
(c) What would be the profit?
(d) What stops us from making any more?

Exercise 4.3

(a) Which item shows the greatest profit per man-hour?
(b) How many can we make?
(c) What would be the profit?
(d) What stops us from making any more?

In this small example, it is not difficult to work out that the most profitable plan is to make 90 tables, but the fact that taking profit-per-man-hour leads us to the best solution in this example should not be taken to mean that this is always so.

ALGEBRAIC STATEMENT OF THE PROBLEM

Let us now set out in formal algebraic terms the second part of the problem – that is, of employing the resources remaining after the minimum requirements have been satisfied.

Let t = number of tables made,
c = number of chairs made,
d = number of desks made,
b = number of bookcases made.

The amount of softwood used in making t, c, d and b, will be expressed by the linear function:

$$5t + c + 9d + 12b$$

Since the amount used cannot exceed what is available, i.e. 900 ft, we have the inequality:

$$5t + c + 9d + 12b \leq 900 \tag{4.1}$$

which can be transformed into an equation by adding a non-negative variable p, (see equation 1.17):

$$5t + c + 9d + 12b + p = 900 \tag{4.2}$$

p represents the amount of softwood available for use but not taken up, and we must remember that t, c, d and b are also non-negative variables.

Exercise 4.4

Write down the equation corresponding to (4.2) but which relates to man-hours instead of softwood.

What does the additional variable represent?

Exercise 4.5

Write down an equation which expresses algebraically the limit on the number of bookcases which can be sold.

Exercise 4.6

Write down an equation for the profit P which is a linear function of t, c, d and b.

Proceeding in this way, we arrive at a set of simultaneous linear equations defining the restrictions within which we must work. They are:

Softwood:	$5t + c + 9d + 12b + p$	$= 900$	(4.2)
Hardwood:	$2t + 3c + 4d + b + q$	$= 410$	(4.3)
Man-hours:	$3t + 2c + 5d + 10b + r$	$= 270$	(4.4)
Market:	$b + s$	$= 10$	(4.5)

By covering up the labels on the left-hand side, we can see that the 'man-hours' equation does not differ in form from the two 'wood' equations, implying that there is no reason for treating man-hours as having any special quality. Why should we not use, say 'minimum idle softwood' as a guide to the best solution?

Before answering this question, we must consider the mathematical problem of equations (4.2) to (4.5). There are only four of them, but they contain eight unknown variables. We cannot therefore 'solve' them in the conventional sense of obtaining a single value for each of the variables: apparently we have reached a dead end.

The way out is indicated by the profit equation

$$P = 12t + 5c + 15d + 10b \qquad (4.6)$$

because P is a quantity we want to make as large as possible. We need to find a set of values for the eight variables which will simultaneously satisfy the restrictions imposed by equations (4.2) to (4.5) and maximize the profit P: this will give us the unique solution we are seeking.

METHOD OF SOLUTION

It is convenient to transpose the equations so that the problem is stated in the following form:

$$p = 900 - 5t - c - 9d - 12b \qquad (4.7)$$
$$q = 410 - 2t - 3c - 4d - b \qquad (4.8)$$
$$r = 270 - 3t - 2c - 5d - 10b \qquad (4.9)$$
$$s = 10 - b \qquad (4.10)$$

Maximize $\quad P = 12t + 5c + 15d + 10b \qquad (4.6)$

The procedure for finding maximum profit starts from any feasible solution: we could take one of those already described, but the calculation in this case is easier if we take the simplest possible solution, which is to do nothing. Then t, c, d and b are all zero; $p = 900$ because all the softwood is available but not used; similarly $q = 410$, $r = 270$, $s = 10$ and of course there is no profit, so $P = 0$.

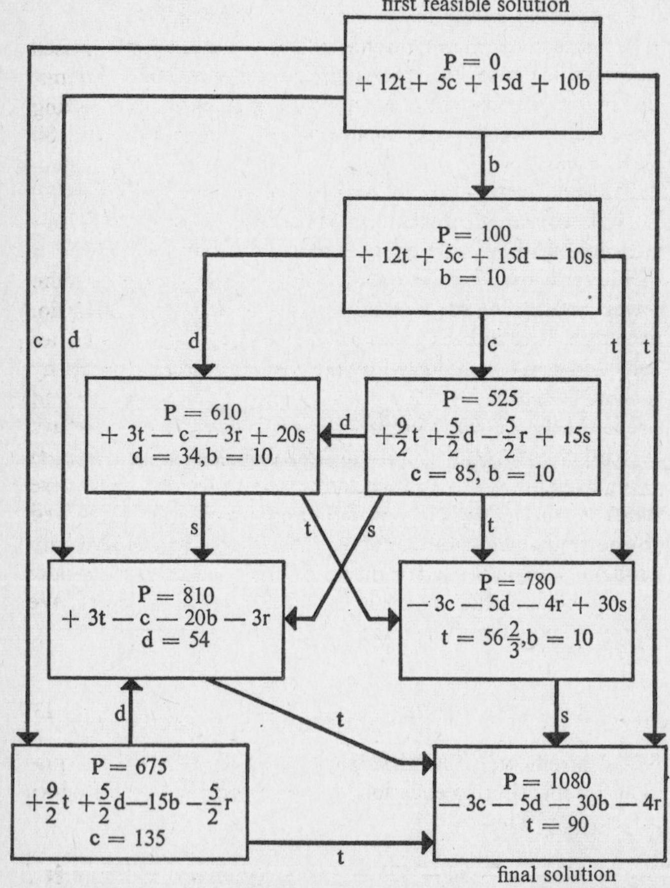

Fig. 4.1 Summary of all possible ways of arriving at the solution of equations (3.6) to (3.10)

We go on to consider the various possibilities for increasing P. All the terms on the right-hand side of equation (4.6) have positive signs in front of them, so to increase any of t, c, d or b will automatically increase P. None of them may be increased indefinitely, however, as may be seen by considering the first variable, t. From equation (4.7), if c, d and b are held at zero, we have

$$p = 900 - 5t.$$

p becomes zero when t reaches 180, so t cannot be increased beyond this figure if p is to remain non-negative. In real terms, if our 900 feet of softwood are used exclusively for making tables, then at 5 feet per table we have enough to make 180 tables with none left over ($p = 0$). The hardwood equation (3.8) restricts t to $\frac{410}{2} = 205$; man-hours restrict it to $\frac{270}{3} = 90$, but no restriction is imposed by the market for bookcases, equation (4.10).

The operative restriction will be the one which gives the lowest value, $t = 90$; it is equation (4.9). What we may do, therefore, is to increase t up to the point at which r becomes zero – in real terms, to use up all the available man-hours by making 90 tables. We have now taken a step towards improved profit. At this stage (and also in any subsequent steps) we have increased one variable, t, *from* zero and reduced another, r, *to* zero. The particular method of solution we are using here demands that all variables which become zero must be moved to the right-hand side of the equations and all the non-zero ones must be on the left; r therefore has to be moved across to the right-hand side, where it joins the other zero values. We transpose equation (4.9) into:

$$3t = 270 - 2c - 5d - 10b - r$$
$$\therefore \quad t = 90 - \tfrac{2}{3}c - \tfrac{5}{3}d - \tfrac{10}{3}b - \tfrac{1}{3}r \qquad (4.13)$$

We also remove t from the right-hand side of the other equations by substituting equation (4.13). In doing so, we introduce a term in r. Thus:

$$p = 900 - c - 9d - 12b - 450 + \tfrac{10}{3}c + \tfrac{25}{3}d + \tfrac{50}{3}b + \tfrac{5}{3}r$$
$$= 450 + \tfrac{7}{3}c - \tfrac{2}{3}d + \tfrac{14}{3}b + \tfrac{5}{3}r \qquad (4.11)$$

Exercise 4.7

Find the new expression for the profit, P, by substituting equation (4.13) into equation (4.6).

The final result is the following group of equations:

$$p = 450 + \tfrac{7}{3}c - \tfrac{2}{3}d + \tfrac{14}{3}b + \tfrac{5}{3}r \qquad (4.11)$$
$$q = 230 - \tfrac{5}{3}c - \tfrac{2}{3}d + \tfrac{17}{3}b + \tfrac{2}{3}r \qquad (4.12)$$
$$t = 90 - \tfrac{2}{3}c - \tfrac{5}{3}d - \tfrac{10}{3}b - \tfrac{1}{3}r \qquad (4.13)$$
$$s = 10 - b \qquad (4.14)$$
$$P = 1080 - 3c - 5d - 30b - 4r \qquad (4.15)$$

Look first of all at the new expression for P: whereas all the terms on the right-hand side of equation (4.6) had positive signs, all those in equation (4.15) have negative signs; that is to say, any increase in c, d, b or r will *decrease* P, and since negative values are not permitted, no further increase in P is possible. The value of 1080, obtained by putting c, d, b and r equal to zero, is therefore the maximum value of P. The set of equations (4.11) to (4.15) is called the optimum solution; 'optimum' is a general expression signifying a maximum or minimum, whichever is appropriate. Here it means maximum, but for a minimum-cost criterion it would denote the final minimum value.

Since one of the computational rules was that *all* the variables on the right-hand side of any equation must be zero, it follows that c, d, b and r are all zero. Substituting these zero values in equations (4.11) to (4.15) gives the values of p, q, t, s and P as being equal to 450, 230, 90, 10 and 1080 respectively. Every one of these values has some practical significance as follows:

$\left.\begin{array}{l} c = 0 \\ d = 0 \\ b = 0 \end{array}\right\}$ No chairs, desks or bookcases are to be made.

$r = 0$ No man-hours will remain unused.

$\left.\begin{array}{l} p = 450 \\ q = 230 \end{array}\right\}$ These are the amounts of softwood and hardwood respectively which are not used.

$t = 90$ Gives the number of tables to be made.

$s = 10$ None of the market for bookcases will be taken up.

SELECTING A DIFFERENT ROUTE

Supposing we had not picked on t as the variable to be increased – what then? An alternative candidate is d, because it has the largest coefficient in equation (4.6). The restrictions on increasing d are:

From equation	(4.7)	$\frac{900}{9} = 100$
	(4.8)	$\frac{410}{4} = 102{\cdot}5$
	(4.9)	$\frac{270}{5} = 54$
	(4.10)	None

Man-hours are, as before, the operative restriction, so we again transpose equation (4.9), but this time bringing d over to the left-hand side:

$$d = 54 - \tfrac{3}{5}t - \tfrac{2}{5}c - 2b - \tfrac{1}{5}r \qquad (4.18)$$

Substituting (4.18) in the remaining equations gives:

$$\begin{aligned} p &= 414 + \tfrac{2}{5}t + \tfrac{13}{5}c + 6b + \tfrac{9}{5}r && (4.16)\\ q &= 194 + \tfrac{2}{5}t - \tfrac{7}{5}c + 7b + \tfrac{4}{5}r && (4.17)\\ d &= 54 - \tfrac{3}{5}t - \tfrac{2}{5}c - 2b - \tfrac{1}{5}r && (4.18)\\ s &= 10 - b && (4.19)\\ P &= 810 + 3t - c - 20b - 3r && (4.20) \end{aligned}$$

The profit has again increased, but to a lower figure than before, and equation (4.20) still has a term with a positive sign, namely, $+3t$. We know from this that P can be made even greater by increasing t, and the only equation restricting the increase is (4.18) which gives $t = 54 \div \frac{3}{5} = 90$ as the point beyond which d would become negative. Equation (4.18) is therefore the one we must transpose in order to bring the variable d, with its new value of zero, to the right-hand side:

$$t = 90 - \tfrac{2}{3}c - \tfrac{5}{3}d - \tfrac{10}{3}b - \tfrac{1}{3}r$$

which is identical with equation (4.13) and substitution into (4.16), (4.17), (4.19) and (4.20) gives the optimum solution shown in (4.11) to (4.15).

Had we started with c instead of d, we should first have arrived at a plan to make 135 chairs and a profit equation as follows:

$$P = 675 + \tfrac{9}{2}t + \tfrac{5}{2}d - 15b - \tfrac{5}{2}r \qquad (4.21)$$

Here there are two positive terms in the equation: increasing t would take us straight to the optimum solution, whereas increasing d would take us there by the indirect route through equations (4.16) to (4.20).

No matter which variable we choose in equation (4.6), the routine just described will lead us to the optimum solution, as is shown in Figure 4.1. As long as variables with positive signs are chosen, the choice of variable at each stage does not affect the solution, but only the number of 'iterations' needed to arrive at it. (An iteration is a complete set of transpositions.)

Exercise 4.8

If the variables transposed are b, c, d, s and t in that order, what is the form of the profit function at the end of the third iteration?

TWO OPERATIVE RESTRICTIONS

The Fermat Furniture Company have decided to make 90 tables when they are told that the timber merchant no longer has the full amount of softwood available: he can only deliver up to 980 feet. Since 600 feet are used for satisfying the minimum requirements, only 380 feet are available. The problem is now expressed by the following equations:

$$p = 380 - 5t - c - 9d - 12b \qquad (4.22)$$
$$q = 410 - 2t - 3c - 4d - b \qquad (4.8)$$
$$r = 270 - 3t - 2c - 5d - 10b \qquad (4.9)$$
$$s = 10 - b \qquad (4.10)$$
$$P = 12t + 5c + 15d + 10b \qquad (4.6)$$

The extent to which t may be increased is now limited by the softwood equation (4.22) instead of the man-hours equation. Transposing t and p in (4.22) and substituting the result in the other equations gives:

$$t = 76 - \tfrac{1}{5}c - \tfrac{9}{5}d - \tfrac{12}{5}b - \tfrac{1}{5}p \qquad (4.23)$$
$$q = 258 - \tfrac{13}{5}c - \tfrac{2}{5}d + \tfrac{19}{5}b + \tfrac{2}{5}p \qquad (4.24)$$
$$r = 42 - \tfrac{7}{5}c + \tfrac{2}{5}d - \tfrac{14}{5}b + \tfrac{3}{5}p \qquad (4.25)$$
$$s = 10 - b \qquad (4.26)$$
$$P = 912 + \tfrac{13}{5}c - \tfrac{33}{5}d - \tfrac{94}{5}b - \tfrac{12}{5}p \qquad (4.27)$$

and a further iteration on c gives the final solution:

$$t = 70 - \tfrac{13}{7}d - 2b - \tfrac{2}{7}p + \tfrac{1}{7}r \qquad (4.28)$$
$$q = 180 - \tfrac{8}{7}d + 9b - \tfrac{5}{7}p + \tfrac{13}{7}r \qquad (4.29)$$
$$c = 30 + \tfrac{2}{7}d - 2b + \tfrac{3}{7}p - \tfrac{5}{7}r \qquad (4.30)$$
$$s = 10 - b \qquad (4.31)$$
$$P = 990 - \tfrac{41}{7}d - 24b - \tfrac{9}{7}p - \tfrac{18}{7}r \qquad (4.32)$$

Exercise 4.9

Remembering that all variables on the right-hand side are put equal to zero, write out the interpretation of equations (4.28) to (4.32) as was done on page 98.

It is noteworthy that *two* factors – softwood and man-hours – are now restricting the profit in the final solution, and the plan calls for *two* products to be manufactured. Finding the solution by linear programming required no more effort than when one restriction was operative, whereas obtaining a two-product solution by trial and error would have been a long and tedious process.

THE VALUE OF OVERTIME

Knowing that man-hours are one of the operative restrictions on profit, the management of the Fermat Furniture Company decides to re-examine its policy on overtime. What would be the effect of allowing a single extra hour of overtime to be worked? First, the original equation for man-hours, (4.4), would become:

$$3t + 2c + 5d + 10b + r = 271. \qquad (4.33)$$

This equation could be transposed and the whole calculation worked through again: there is, however, a quicker way.

Suppose we define a new variable u, such that

$$u = r - 1.$$

Then:

$$3t + 2c + 5d + 10b + u = 270. \qquad (4.34)$$

which has exactly the same form as the original equation (4.4). In other words, increasing the number of available man-hours by 1 is the same as letting r, previously a non-negative variable, decrease as far as -1 instead of to 0.

In the solution equations (4.28) to (4.32), if r becomes -1, P increases to $990 - (\frac{13}{7} \times -1) = 991\frac{6}{7}$. It follows that working overtime will increase the profit provided that the premium paid for overtime does not exceed $\frac{13}{7}$ shillings – about 1s. 10d. – per hour: this is therefore a break-even figure, above which overtime is not profitable.

Exercise 4.10

If more softwood could be obtained from another supplier at a higher price, up to how much extra should we be prepared to pay for it?

Exercise 4.11

What is the corresponding figure for hardwood?

The coefficients of the variables on the right-hand side of equation (4.32) are called 'incremental values', and it is interesting to examine the others. The coefficient of d, for instance, is $-\frac{41}{7}$: what can we deduce from it?

PROFIT ON DESKS

Allowing d to become zero means that no desks other than the minimum requirements are to be made. For d to become negative, the Sales Manager's original estimate must be questioned. Making one desk less ($d = -1$) would cause the profit to increase by $\frac{41}{7}$ shillings (5s. 10d.) This result appears paradoxical, until we look at the results of putting $d = -1$ in the other equations. Because of integral restrictions – we cannot make fractions of items of furniture – it is more sensible to put $d = -7$, giving

$$\begin{aligned} t &= 70 + 13 = 83 \\ q &= 180 + 8 = 188 \\ c &= 30 - 2 = 28 \\ s &= 10 \\ P &= 990 + 41 = 1031 \end{aligned}$$

The extra profit is earned by making 7 desks less, simultaneously reducing the number of chairs made by 2 and using the softwood and man-hours so released for the manufacture of 13 additional tables.

Exercise 4.12

Verify that the softwood and man-hours released are enough to make the extra tables.

THE PRICE OF BOOKCASES

If one bookcase less were made, the profit would increase by 24 shillings, but we cannot do this because there are no minimum requirements to be dipped into, as there were for desks. There is, however, a clear implication that the price of bookcases is too low in relation to the other items: if it were increased by 25 shillings, equation (4.32) would become

$$P = 990 - \tfrac{41}{7}d + b - \tfrac{9}{7}p - \tfrac{13}{7}r \qquad (4.38)$$

and a further iteration would be needed to get the final solution:

$$\begin{aligned}
t &= 50 - \tfrac{13}{7}d - \tfrac{2}{7}p + \tfrac{1}{7}r + 2s & (4.34)\\
q &= 270 - \tfrac{8}{7}d - \tfrac{5}{7}p + \tfrac{13}{7}r - 9s & (4.35)\\
c &= 10 + \tfrac{2}{7}d + \tfrac{3}{7}p - \tfrac{5}{7}r + 2s & (4.36)\\
b &= 10 - s & (4.37)\\
P &= 1000 - \tfrac{41}{7}d - \tfrac{9}{7}p - \tfrac{13}{7}r - s & (4.38)
\end{aligned}$$

20 tables and 20 chairs have been sacrificed to make 10 bookcases for an extra profit of 10 shillings. Incidentally, the term in s in equation (4.38) shows that it would now pay us to spend up to 1 shilling, per bookcase sold, on expanding the market for bookcases.

It is not difficult to show that this result is consistent with the other incremental values. The scarcity of softwood justified a premium of $\frac{9}{7}$, bringing the price up to $2 + \frac{9}{7} = 3\frac{2}{7}$ shillings per foot. Hardwood had no scarcity value, but the break-even cost of man-hours was $10 + \frac{13}{7} = 11\frac{6}{7}$ shillings per hour. Then every bookcase contains

12 feet of softwood at $3\frac{2}{7}$ shillings	=	$39\frac{3}{7}$ shillings
1 foot of hardwood at 5 shillings	=	5 shillings
10 man-hours at $11\frac{6}{7}$ shillings	=	$118\frac{4}{7}$ shillings
Total price	=	163 shillings
Actual price	=	139 shillings
Difference	=	24 shillings

The difference is the increase in price needed to make bookcases compete on equal terms with the other two products for the productive resources available. At any higher price increase, such as the 25 shillings extra we chose, bookcases will have the advantage.

Exercise 4.13

An investigation into the unprofitability of bookcases has led to a new design, which would use 14 feet of softwood, 2 feet of hardwood and use 7 man-hours. What should its price be?

RANGES OF VALIDITY

We have already seen that the coefficient of r in equation (4.38) indicates an incremental value of $\frac{13}{7}$, but this is only valid over a limited range of values of r. These values may be both positive and negative, for we shall lose profit by increasing r just as we gain it by letting r become negative. The other equations define the range of validity: in (4.34), if r takes on a negative value of -350, t will become zero and an equation will have to be transposed. The corresponding values from (4.35) and (4.36) are $-145\frac{5}{13}$ and $+14$, while (4.37) has no restrictive effect. The latter two values give the range of validity, and may be interpreted as follows.

If we make more man-hours available, then 'profit per foot of softwood' becomes more important than 'profit per man-hour', and consequently we find tables being replaced by chairs in the production plan. This would go on until all the tables had been replaced by chairs, thus consuming 350 extra man-hours, were it not for the fact that with $145\frac{5}{13}$ extra man-hours, we run out of hardwood. If, instead of making more man-hours available, we reduce the original figure of 270, chairs will be driven out of the solution in favour of tables, until all the chairs have gone.

Exercise 4.14

'It will pay us to expand the market for bookcases at a cost of not more than one shilling for each extra bookcase sold.'

At what point will this statement cease to be valid, in the solution equations (4.34) to (4.38)?

WORK FOR WORK'S SAKE?

It was pointed out in an earlier section that using 'minimum idle time' as a criterion may lead to fallacious results; so may such superficially laudable policies as 'keep all the customers satisfied'. The following example by Coaker[29] illustrates this.

John Smith runs a one-man woodworking business; he works an eight-hour day producing alpenstocks, bookshelves and chairs which sell at £3, £2 and £2 each respectively. He has the choice of working any one of three processes:

Process *P* costs £5 an hour to run, in which time it produces one alpenstock and two bookshelves.
Process *Q* costs £6 an hour, producing two alpenstocks and three chairs.
Process *R* costs £7 an hour, producing one alpenstock, one bookshelf and two chairs.

The local retailers have told Smith that they can sell anything up to nine alpenstocks, eleven bookshelves and nine chairs a day. How should he plan his work and how much profit will he make?

If we assume that our market must be fully satisfied and

If p, q and r are the number of hours worked on the three processes, then

Number of alpenstocks made will be:

$$p + 2q + r = 9 \qquad (4.39)$$

Number of bookshelves made will be:

$$2p + r = 11 \tag{4.40}$$

Number of chairs made will be:

$$3q + 2r = 9 \tag{4.41}$$

and solving these simultaneous equations will give us the answer $p = 4$ hours, $q = 1$ hour and $r = 3$ hours. The cost and revenue calculations show that Smith's profit will be £20 a day:

	£
Process *P*, 4 hours at £5	20
Process *Q*, 1 hour at £6	6
Process *R*, 3 hours at £7	21
	£47

Sale of alpenstocks, 9 at £3	27
Sale of bookshelves, 11 at £2	22
Sale of chairs, 9 at £2	18
	£67

giving £20 profit for 8 hours work.

If, however, we replace these equations by inequalities and select the solution which maximizes profit (easily calculated as £2 an hour on processes *P* and *R* and £6 an hour on *Q*), the problem becomes:

$$p + q + r \leqq 8 \tag{4.42}$$
$$p + 2q + r \leqq 9 \tag{4.43}$$
$$2p + r \leqq 11 \tag{4.44}$$
$$3q + 2r \leqq 9 \tag{4.45}$$

Maximize:

$$P = 2p + 6q + 2r \tag{4.46}$$

for which the solution is:

$$s = 2 - \tfrac{2}{3}r + t - \tfrac{1}{3}v \tag{4.47}$$
$$p = 3 + \tfrac{1}{3}r - t + \tfrac{2}{3}v \tag{4.48}$$
$$u = 5 - \tfrac{5}{3}r + 2t - \tfrac{4}{3}v \tag{4.49}$$
$$q = 3 - \tfrac{2}{3}r - \tfrac{1}{3}v \tag{4.50}$$
$$P = 24 - \tfrac{4}{3}r - 2t - \tfrac{2}{3}v \tag{4.51}$$

In this solution, s, t, u and v are the variables added to the left-hand sides of (4.42) to (4.45) respectively so that they become equations instead of inequalities.

	£
Process P, 3 hours at £5	15
Process Q, 3 hours at £6	18
Total cost	£33

Sale of alpenstocks, 9 at £3	27
Sale of bookshelves, 6 at £2	12
Sale of chairs, 9 at £2	18
Total revenue	£57

By working two hours less, Smith has increased his profit by £4.

Although this is a theoretical example, there is abundant evidence that some of the products with which manufacturers occupy their plant are unprofitable. The real-life problem is complicated by such considerations as setting-up times, the spreading of overheads, and the future pay-off from a currently unprofitable development; these may render the linear programming formulation more difficult, but do not necessarily invalidate it.

TACTICAL AND STRATEGIC APPLICATION

The first purpose to which we applied linear programming was finding the most efficient allocation of an existing set of limited resources. This we may call the tactical problem, and such problems are the essence of day-to-day management. However, the study of incremental costs led us to consider changing the availability of resources, as in making more man-hours available by authorizing overtime: these are strategic measures, generally associated with a higher level of management and the policy-making function. The contribution which linear programming makes in this second field may well prove to exceed in importance its already established usefulness in the tactical area.[30]

In the next chapter we shall go on to re-examine both these aspects of linear programming, but from a geometrical rather than an algebraic point of view.

4
Solutions to Exercises

Exercise 4.1

	Resources consumed		
	Softwood, ft	*Hardwood, ft*	*Man-hours*
10 bookcases	120	10	100
80 chairs	80	240	160
	200	250	260
Resources available	900	410	270

In each case, the resources consumed are less than the resources available, and therefore the plan is a feasible one.

Exercise 4.2

(a) Desks (15 shillings per unit)
(b) 54.
(c) £40 10s. 0d. (810 shillings).
(d) All the available man-hours have been used up.

Exercise 4.3

(a) Tables (4 shillings per man-hour).
(b) 90.
(c) £54 0s. 0d. (1,080 shillings).
(d) All the available man-hours have been used up.

Exercise 4.4

$$3t + 2c + 5d + 10b + r = 270.$$

r is a non-negative variable representing the number of man-hours available but not used.

Exercise 4.5

$$b \leqq 10$$

i.e.

$$b + s = 10$$

in which s is the market capacity not taken up.

Exercise 4.6

$$P = 12t + 5c + 15d + 10b$$

Exercise 4.7

$$\begin{aligned} P &= 5c + 15d + 10b + 1080 - 8c - 20d - 40b - 4r \\ &= 1080 - 3c - 5d - 30b - 4r. \end{aligned}$$

Exercise 4.8

$$P = 610 + 3t - c - 3r + 20s \quad \text{(from Figure 4.1)}$$

Exercise 4.9

$t = 70$	Make 70 tables.
$c = 30$	Make 30 chairs.
$d = 0$, $b = 0$	Make no desks nor bookcases.
$p = 0$	No softwood is left over.
$q = 180$	Gives amount of hardwood left over.
$r = 0$	No man-hours are left over.
$s = 10$	The market capacity for bookcases is not taken up.
$P = 990$	Gives the profit in shillings.

Exercise 4.10

The extra variable representing the amount of softwood not used is p; its coefficient in (4.32) is $-\frac{9}{7}$; allowing p to take on a value of -1 would increase P by $\frac{9}{7}$ shillings, i.e. 1s. 3½d., and we should be prepared to pay anything up to this figure.

Exercise 4.11

Nothing. Hardwood is not an operative restriction.

Exercise 4.12

	Softwood, ft	*Man-hours*
From 7 desks:	63	35
From 2 chairs:	2	4
Total	65	39
For 13 tables:	65	39

Exercise 4.13

£6 19s. 0d. i.e. 139 shillings as at present, given by:

	Incremental Value		Actual Cost
14 feet of softwood	46		28
2 feet of hardwood	10		10
7 man-hours	83		70
Total	139		108
Profit		31	

Exercise 4.14

Expanding the market for bookcases means allowing s to take on negative values. The equations which restrict negative values of s are (4.34) and (4.36), the former giving $t = 0$ when $s = -25$, and the latter giving $c = 0$ when $s = -5$. The value put on market expansion is therefore valid only for an extra 5 bookcases.

NOTES AND REFERENCES

29 Battersby, A., *The Accountant*, 1 July 1961, p. 5 and 19 August 1961, p. 226.

30 Jewell, W., *Operations Research* (1960), Vol. 8, No. 4, p. 565.

The following books are recommended to the reader who wishes to pursue the subject of linear programming in greater detail:

31 Vajda, S., *Theory of Games and Linear Programming* (2nd edn, Methuen, 1962).

32 Vajda, S., *Readings in Mathematical Programming* (2nd edn, Pitman, 1962) (contains a good bibliography).

33 Gass, S. M., *Linear Programming* (2nd edn, McGraw-Hill, 1964).

The original statement of the problem discussed in this chapter was given by Gass as Exercise 2 of his Chapter 1. He does not, however, give any solution to it.

5
Blending and Boundaries

The Kingdom of Number is all boundaries
Which may be beautiful and must be true;

W. H. AUDEN, *Numbers and Faces*

GEOMETRICAL REPRESENTATION

The Fermat Furniture example has been dealt with throughout by algebraic methods, but, as Chapter 3 suggested, problems of this type may also be represented geometrically. This will be shown by a new example from a different field of application of linear programming: blending. One of the earliest successful applications of the technique was to the production of commercial fuels by blending the outputs of an oil refinery, and it has also been used to find the cheapest way of making food mixtures, and to investigate the cost of diets.

A PROBLEM IN BLENDING

The Weasel Oil Company is a small business which specializes in blending oil for Weasel engines, to the following specification:

Specific Gravity	at least 0·88
Viscosity	not more than 32 units
Sulphur	not more than 0·35%

The sulphur and viscosity figures in this and the other specifications have been corrected for specific gravity so that any blending calculations can be done directly by volume. We can also assume that all the specification figures blend according to linear rules. For example, one gallon of oil with viscosity 40 units blended into one gallon with viscosity 44 units will yield a blend with viscosity 42 units.

The company holds a stock of 100,000 gallons of oil with the following characteristics:—

Specific Gravity	0·89
Viscosity	20 units
Sulphur	0·30%

and the manager wants to increase his stock by blending without going outside the specification. To do so, he can blend in Boozle Oil or Fizzle Oil, which he can buy at the same price per gallon. Boozle Oil is available in unlimited quantities, but the manager can only buy up to 90,000 gallons of Fizzle Oil.

What is the greatest amount of Weasel Oil that he can make by blending, if the oils available for blending have the following specifications?

	Boozle Oil	*Fizzle Oil*
Specific Gravity	0·92	0·86
Viscosity	40	40
Sulphur	0·45	0·25

USING SUBSCRIPTS

To solve this problem algebraically, we must first express it as a set of linear equations and a function to be maximized or minimized. It can then be dealt with by manipulating the equations as shown in the previous chapter, so that the 'profit', or in this case the total amount of blended oil, is brought step by step to its maximum value.

This is an opportune point at which to learn a bit of mathematical notation which is not generally dealt with in schools, that is, the use of subscripts. We could call the amounts of Boozle Oil and Fizzle Oil b and f respectively, just as we denoted tables and chairs by their initials in the last chapter. However, since they both represent the same *sort* of variable – quantities of oil – professional mathematicians prefer to use the symbols x_1 and x_2, where 1 and 2 are called subscripts. The symbol x_1 is pronounced 'x-one' or sometimes 'x-sub-one'.

Exercise 5.1

Rewrite the inequality (4.1) in the previous chapter, using x_1 for tables, x_2 for chairs, x_3 for desks and x_4 for bookcases.

Exercise 5.2

Rewrite equation (4.2), allocating the subscript 5 to the variable previously represented by p.

Exercise 5.3

In the equations (4.3), (4.4) and (4.5), what new symbols would you suggest substituting for q, r and s respectively?

The mathematician uses subscripts for convenience and not, as you may have suspected, to make his work more difficult to understand. Remember that he will be dealing with much bigger equations than the ones used here, and ask yourself what you would do if the Fermat Furniture Co. made a hundred different items instead of four. With subscripts, one has only to call them x_1, x_2, x_3 and so on up to x_{100} (and there are other benefits such as the ability to reduce long equations to simple shorthand forms with the aid of signs like Σ, 'the sum of').

If x_1 and x_2 represent the amounts of Boozle Oil and Fizzle Oil respectively, in units of 1,000 gallons, then since we have to maximize the total amount P of blend produced:

$$P = 100 + x_1 + x_2 \qquad (5.1)$$

The specific gravity of the mixed oils will be:

$$\frac{0{\cdot}89 \times 100 + 0{\cdot}92x_1 + 0{\cdot}86x_2}{100 + x_1 + x_2} \geqq 0{\cdot}88$$

Multiplying both sides by the denominator gives:

$$89 + 0{\cdot}92x_1 + 0{\cdot}86x_2 \geqq 88 + 0{\cdot}88x_1 + 0{\cdot}88x_2$$

which reduces to

$$1 + 0{\cdot}04x_1 - 0{\cdot}02x_2 \geqq 0$$

Multiplying throughout by 50 gives:

$$50 + 2x_1 - x_2 \geqq 0$$

which is transposed to

$$-2x_1 + x_2 \leqq 50 \tag{5.2}$$

Note that in manipulating these inequalities we used some of the rules applicable to equations, such as that the expression is still valid if equal quantities are added or subtracted on both sides of the inequality sign, or if all the terms in the expression are multiplied or divided by the same factor.

Exercise 5.4

Draw a graph of the inequality (5.2) for non-negative values of x_1 and x_2. (See Figure 3.4.) Label the appropriate areas 'S.G. outside specification' and 'S.G. within specification'.

The corresponding equations for viscosity and sulphur are respectively

$$\frac{20 \times 100 + 44x_1 + 40x_2}{100 + x_1 + x_2} \leqq 32$$

and

$$\frac{0{\cdot}30 \times 100 + 0{\cdot}45x_1 + 0{\cdot}25x_2}{100 + x_1 + x_2} \leqq 0{\cdot}35$$

which reduce to

$$3x_1 + 2x_2 \leqq 300 \tag{5.3}$$

and

$$x_1 - x_2 \leqq 50 \tag{5.4}$$

We can now assemble these expressions, including the restriction on Fizzle Oil, into the complete algebraic statement of the problem. (The variable x_3 is reserved for use later.)

$$-2x_1 + x_2 + x_4 = 50 \tag{5.5}$$
$$3x_1 + 2x_2 + x_5 = 300 \tag{5.6}$$
$$x_1 + x_2 + x_6 = 50 \tag{5.7}$$
$$x_2 + x_7 = 90 \tag{5.8}$$

Maximize $$P = 100 + x_1 + x_2 \tag{5.1}$$

The four restrictions (5.5) to (5.8) can be drawn as graphs, and this has been done in Figure 5.1. In the top right-hand corner is shown the quadrant within which all the values of x_1 and x_2 must lie, and the shading indicates the areas within which they must not lie if they are to be non-negative. The next graph down, (b), shows the restriction imposed by equation (5.8): the shaded area above the horizontal line corresponds to blends containing more than 90,000 gallons of Fizzle Oil, which are not feasible. In the third graph, (c), the oblique line corresponds to equation (5.6) when x_5 is held equal to zero; it is therefore the graph of $3x_1 + 2x_2 = 300$.

Exercise 5.5

Using the equation $3x_1 + 2x_2 = 300$, find

(i) x_1 when $x_2 = 0$
(ii) x_2 when $x_1 = 0$
(iii) x_1 and x_2 when they are equal.

Check that they all lie on the straight line in Figure 5.1(c)

Exercise 5.6

In equation (5.6), what is the value of x_4 when

(i) $x_1 = 50$, $x_2 = 75$
(ii) $x_1 = 50$, $x_2 = 50$
(iii) $x_1 = 100$, $x_2 = 100$?

Check that negative values of x_4 correspond to points outside the feasible area, and positive values to points within it.

It is worth spending a little time on section (d) of Figure 5.1, so as to make yourself familiar with the idea of feasible and non-feasible areas, which are finally combined to give the total solution area. It is the irregular hexagonal space in the middle and it contains all the feasible blends, from which the best is to be chosen – that is, the blend which maximizes P in the control equation (5.1). The equation for this control function represents a family of parallel straight lines, each member of which has a gradient of -1. The value of P increases as the line moves away from the origin. Figure 5.2 shows a set of these lines drawn for various values of P, and we can see that the best blend is that for which $P = 230$, when $x_1 = 40$ and $x_2 = 90$.

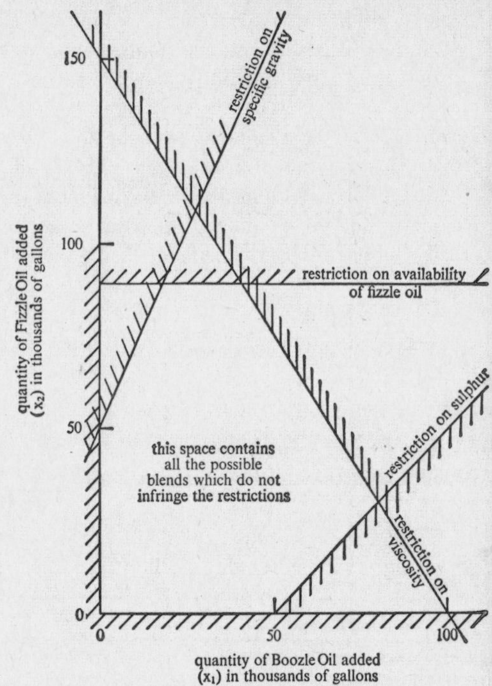

Fig. 5.1 A problem in blending: graphical solution (1) restrictions

The corresponding algebraic solution is:

$$x_4 = 40 - \tfrac{2}{3}x_5 + \tfrac{7}{3}x_7 \qquad (5.9)$$
$$x_2 = 90 - x_7 \qquad (5.10)$$
$$x_1 = 40 - \tfrac{1}{3}x_5 + \tfrac{2}{3}x_7 \qquad (5.11)$$
$$x_6 = 100 + \tfrac{1}{3}x_5 - \tfrac{5}{3}x_7 \qquad (5.12)$$
$$P = 230 - \tfrac{1}{3}x_5 - \tfrac{1}{3}x_7 \qquad (5.13)$$

The additional variables are x_4 to x_7. Every item in the algebraic solution has its counterpart in the graphical one. The two operative restrictions are seen to be on viscosity and on the quantity of Fizzle Oil; Figure 5.3 shows the incremental value of the latter to be

$$\frac{233\tfrac{1}{3} - 230}{100 - 90} = \tfrac{1}{3}$$

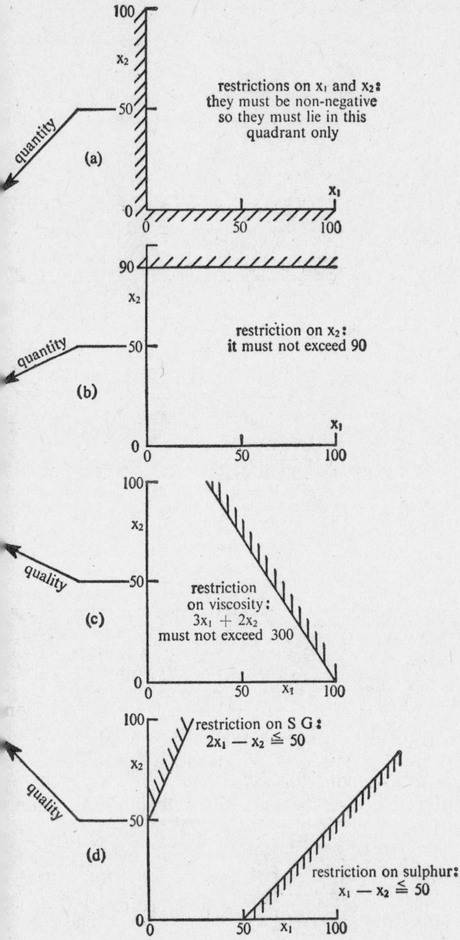

which may also be obtained from the coefficient of x_7 in equation (5.13). Point Z, at which specific gravity becomes an operative restriction, is one limit of the range of validity for this incremental value.

Suppose that, instead of an upper limit on Fizzle Oil, we impose a lower limit of not less than 150,000 gallons to be

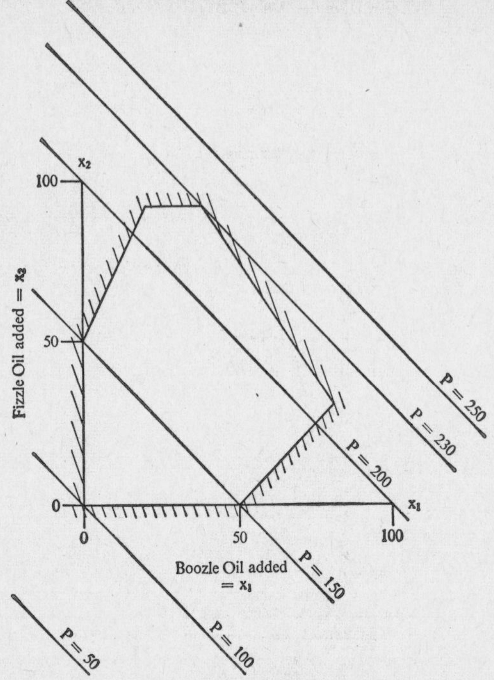

Fig. 5.2 A problem in blending: graphical solution
(2) function to be maximized; (3) possible routes to final solution

added. Then it is immediately apparent from Figure 5.4 that there is no feasible solution to the problem, because all the blends above the lower limit infringe the quality specifications.

Exercise 5.7

Use Figure 5.2 to find the optimum solution to the blending problem with the restrictions on sulphur and quantity of Fizzle Oil removed.

Exercise 5.8

If the profit on every 1,000 gallons of Boozle Oil added is £3, and is £2 on every 1,000 gallons of either Fizzle Oil or the existing stock,

(a) write down the new profit function
(b) find an optimum solution graphically.

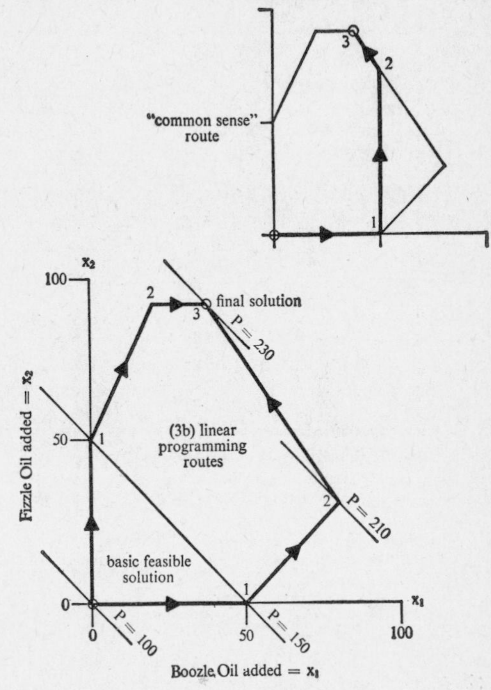

ROUTE TO THE SOLUTION

Figure 5.5 shows the part of Figure 5.2 in the region near the origin, but the drawing has been rotated through 45° so that the control function P appears as a horizontal line. Increasing x_1 from zero is equivalent to moving along the line OA, and the vertex A is the point at which equation (5.4) restricts any further improvement in P. Similarly, increasing x_2 takes us along OB to B, the specific gravity restriction. The rates of increase of P with x_1 and x_2 are the same, which may be seen algebraically because x_1 and x_2 have the same coefficient in the control function, and geometrically because they have the same gradient in Figure 5.5. The usual practice in solving linear programming problems is to begin by increasing the

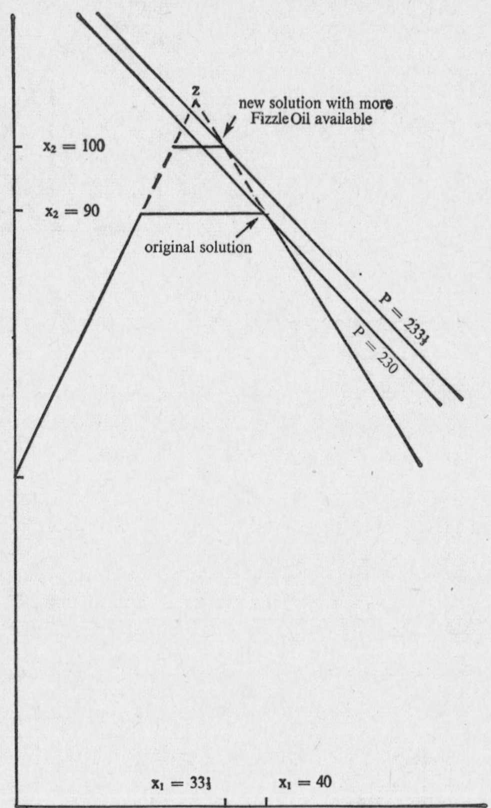

Fig. 5.3 Effect of changing restriction on x_2

term with the greatest coefficient, i.e. the steepest gradient. The gradients being the same in this case, we shall arbitrarily select x_2 and move to the vertex B. The route to the solution consists of a number of such moves along edges to vertices, choosing only such edges as have an upward gradient (or sometimes a horizontal one) – that is, choosing only terms with positive coefficients in the control function. The solution is found at the summit, from which all routes lead downwards (or, in rare cases, horizontally as in Exercise 5.8).

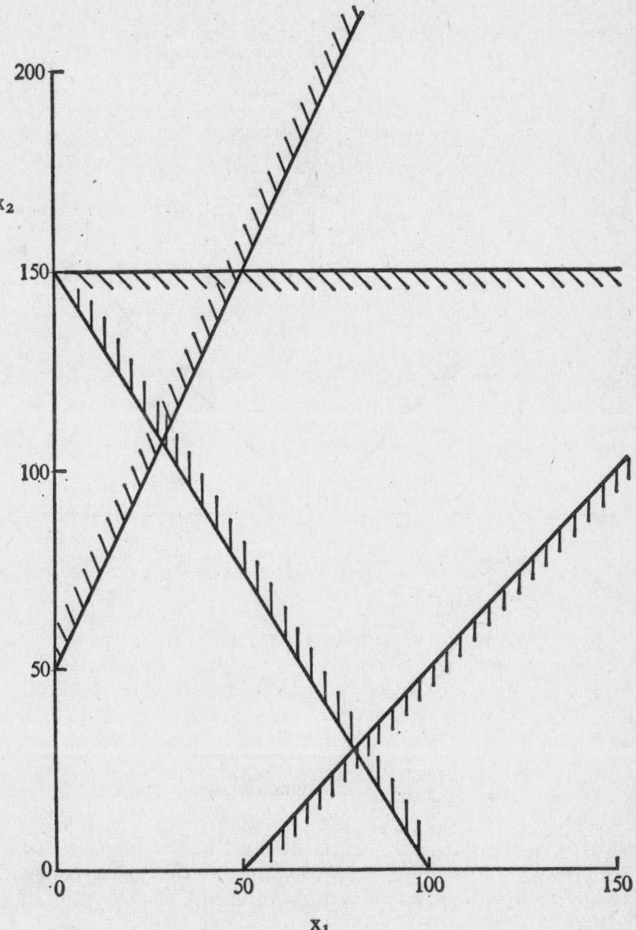

Fig. 5.4 Blending problem with lower limit on Fizzle Oil and no feasible solutions

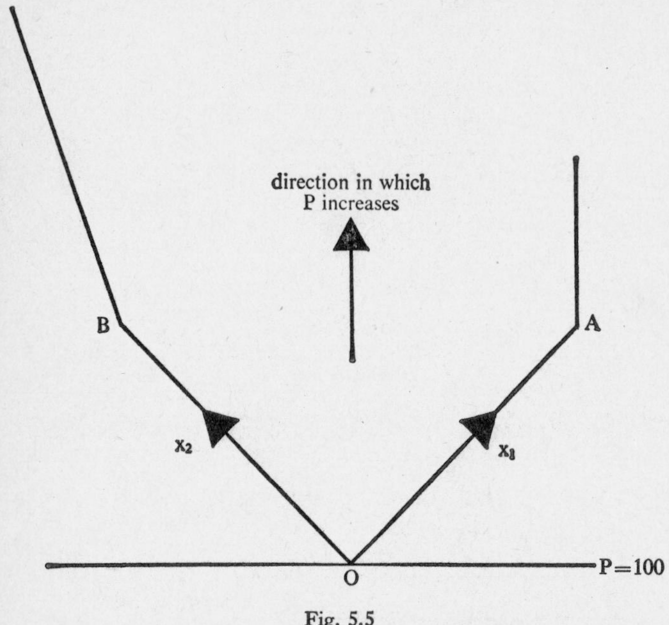

Fig. 5.5

BLENDING THREE OR MORE ADDITIVES

Suppose that a third component, Muzzle Oil, becomes available to the extent of 60,000 gallons if required. Its specification is:

Specific Gravity	0·87
Viscosity	36 units
Sulphur	0·40%

A graphical solution will now extend into three dimensions, one for each of the quantities x_1, x_2 and x_3.

Instead of the restrictions being lines bounding an area of feasibility, they are now planes enclosing a solution space, which will be a convex polyhedron. Two views of the polyhedron are given in Figure 5.7 and 5.8. All blends which satisfy the specification are contained within this irregular octahedron, and in each figure it is cut by a plane corresponding

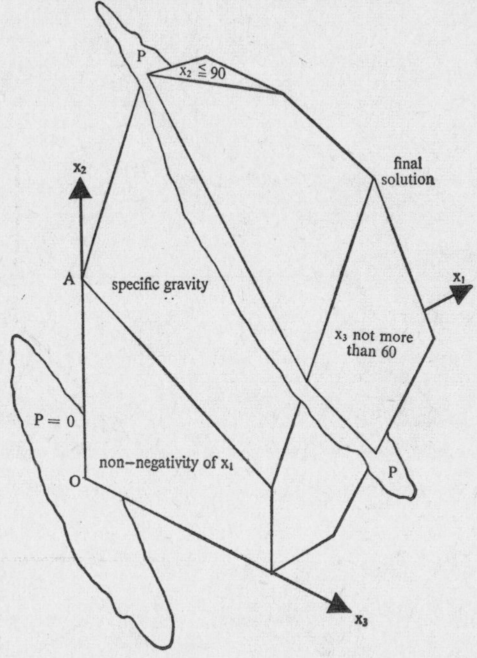

Fig. 5.7

to the profit P, which is shown at an intermediate value. As this plane moves outwards from the origin, it eventually reaches a single vertex to which the final solution corresponds. In this instance the solution is:

Boozle Oil:	$x_1 = 28\frac{4}{7}$	i.e. 28,571 gallons
Fizzle Oil:	$x_2 = 77\frac{1}{7}$	i.e. 77,143 gallons
Muzzle Oil:	$x_3 = 60$	i.e. 60,000 gallons
Total Blend	$P = 265\frac{5}{7}$	i.e. 265,714 gallons

The solution is again reached by starting from the origin and moving along the edges to successive vertices, always in a direction which improves P, to the final solution. (Figure 4.1 was a symbolic representation of different routes around a polyhedron, with the boxes representing conditions at its

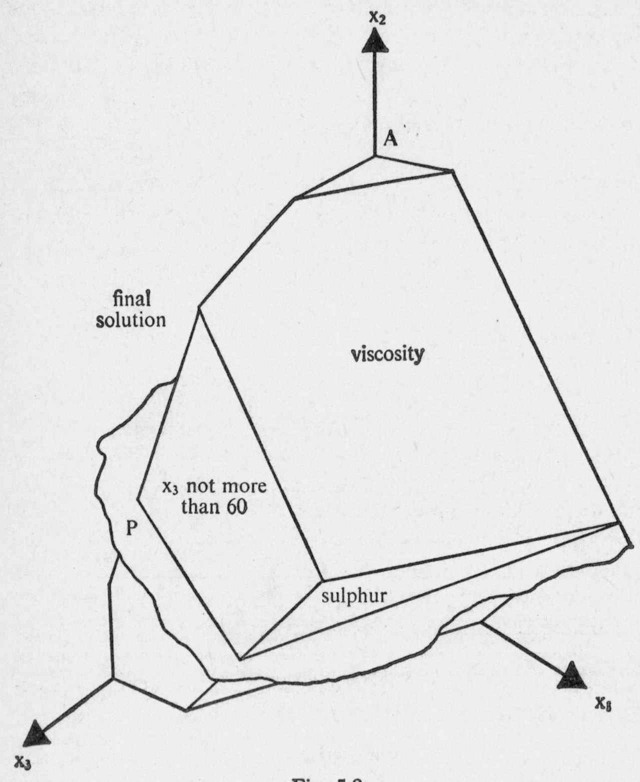

Fig. 5.8

vertices.) Although the problem with two additives could have been found easily by trial and error, it is unlikely that any approach other than linear programming would solve the three-dimensional problem.

When the number of variables exceeds three, a complete graph of the solution cannot be drawn, although for four variables we could represent the process of solution by a series of three-dimensional solid bodies showing successive cross-sections of the solution space when cut by the 'hyper-plane' of P.

The reader who finds such excursions into many dimensions interesting would be well advised to read Abbott's light-hearted essay 'Flatland', originally published in 1890 but recently re-issued.[34] It is strange to reflect on the relevance of this fantasy to the daily operation of an oil refinery.

Exercise 5.9

Draw a rough sketch of the control function in the problem of the Fermat Furniture Company ignoring bookcases, i.e.

$$B = 12t + 5c + 15d$$

for the value $B = 60$.

TABLEAUX

If we were to ask an Organization and Methods expert to study the Linear Programming calculations, he might well point out that there is a good deal of time wasted in carrying out the calculations as previously described. He would probably say 'Do you have to write all those x's down every time? Why not just make a column of the coefficients and write the appropriate x at the top of it?' By following this advice we arrive at a presentation known as a 'Tableau'. A simple tableau corresponding to equations (5.1) to (5.5) is given below:

Quantity	x_1	x_2		
50	−2	+1	x_4	(5.2)
300	+3	+2	x_5	(5.3)
50	+1*	−1	x_6	(5.4)
90	0	+1	x_7	(5.5)
100	−1	−1	P	(5.1)

The equations have again been transposed, but if we read the double vertical line as an 'equals' sign, we can see that they correspond to those whose numbers appear in brackets alongside.

We arrive at the final solution, as before, in a series of steps. At each step, the tableau is transformed into a new one by a set of systematic rules. These rules correspond exactly to the rearrangement of the equations as already described in Chapter 4. The first rule is to look in the bottom row to the right of the double line and pick out the greatest number which is preceded by a negative sign. In this case, we can choose either x_1 or x_2, and have arbitrarily begun with x_1. We next look for positive coefficients in the column above, and for each of these we divide the figure in the 'Quantity' column by the coefficient: the ratios obtained in this way are 100 and 50, as before. The coefficient corresponding to the smaller result is selected, and is called the 'pivot': it is marked with an asterisk in the tableau above. Once the pivot has been identified, the variable above it (in this case x_1) is interchanged with the variable alongside it (x_6). We can then transform the tableau, and need only four rules to do this (assuming that certain fairly rare complications do not occur):

For the row which contains the pivot

(1) Replace the pivot itself by its own reciprocal.

(2) For all the other coefficients in this row, divide the original value by the pivot to obtain the new value.

For all the other rows (including the 'P' row)

(3) For the coefficient in the same column as the pivot, divide the original value by the pivot and reverse the sign.

(4) For each of the other coefficients, draw an imaginary rectangle with the coefficient at one corner and the pivot diagonally opposite (as they appear in the old tableau).

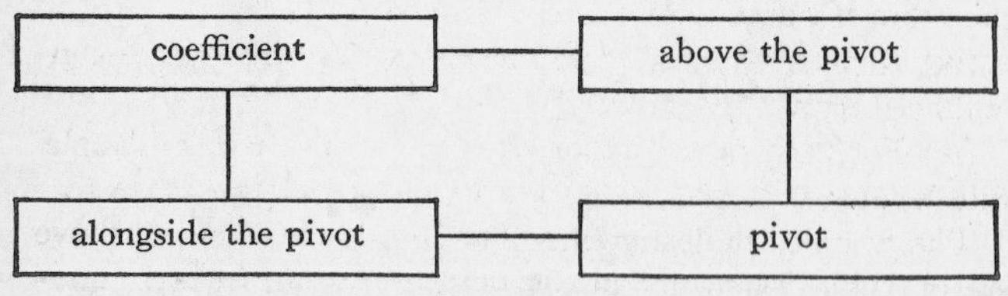

Fig. 5.12

(a) Multiply 'above the pivot' by 'alongside the pivot'.

(b) Divide the product so obtained by the pivot.

(c) Subtract the quotient from the coefficient to obtain the new value of the coefficient.

These rules apply to the coefficients in the Quantity column and those in the 'P' row as well as the others. The second tableau, derived by these rules, is given below.

Quantity	x_6	x_2	
150	+2	−1	x_4
150	−3	+5	x_5
50	+1	−1	x_1
90	0	+1	x_7
150	+1	−2	P

Exercise 5.10

Write out in full the set of equations corresponding to the tableau immediately above.

The tableaux have been presented like this in order to show as closely as possible their relationship to the sets of simultaneous equations discussed earlier. In this form, they are rather a hodge-podge because some of the variables appear along the top and some down the right-hand side. A more usual form of presentation is the Simplex tableau in which all the variables have columns allocated to them. The rules for manipulating these tableaux differ slightly from those already given, because each column now corresponds to one and only one variable throughout the whole set of calculations. The rules are:

(i) Select the pivot as before.

(ii) Divide the numbers in the row containing the pivot by the value of the pivot itself.

(iii) Replace all the remaining numbers in the column containing the pivot by zero.

(iv) For each of the other coefficients, use the 'rectangle' rule (4) above.

The Simplex tableaux corresponding to those given above are in Table 5.1, which also gives the two subsequent iterations leading to the final solutions.

TABLE 5.1

Simplex Tableaux of the Two-Dimensional Problem

First Tableau

Quantity	x_1	x_2	x_4	x_5	x_6	x_7
50	−2	+1	+1	0	0	0
300	+3	+2	0	+1	0	0
50	+1*	−1	0	0	+1	0
90	0	+1	0	0	0	+1
100	−1	−1	0	0	0	0

Second Tableau

Quantity	x_1	x_2	x_4	x_5	x_6	x_7
150	0	−1	+1	0	+2	0
150	0	+5*	0	+1	−3	0
50	+1	−1	0	0	+1	0
90	0	+1	0	0	0	+1
150	0	−2	0	0	+1	0

Third Tableau

Quantity	x_1	x_2	x_4	x_5	x_6	x_7
180	0	0	+1	$+\frac{1}{5}$	$+\frac{7}{5}$	0
30	0	+1	0	$+\frac{1}{5}$	$+\frac{3}{5}$	0
80	+1	0	0	$+\frac{1}{5}$	$+\frac{2}{5}$	0
60	0	0	0	$-\frac{1}{5}$	$+\frac{3}{5}$*	+1
210	0	0	0	$+\frac{2}{5}$	$-\frac{1}{5}$	0

Fourth Tableau (optimum solution)

Quantity	x_1	x_2	x_4	x_5	x_6	x_7
40	0	0	+1	$+\frac{2}{3}$	0	$-\frac{7}{3}$
90	0	+1	0	0	0	+1
40	+1	0	0	$+\frac{1}{3}$	0	$-\frac{2}{3}$
100	0	0	0	$-\frac{1}{3}$	+1	$+\frac{5}{3}$
230	0	0	0	$+\frac{1}{3}$	0	$+\frac{1}{3}$

Exercise 5.11

Set up a Simplex tableau for the Fermat Furniture problem, using equations (4.6) to (4.10) inclusive as a starting point.

Exercise 5.12

Set up and solve the Simplex tableau for the blending problem with three additives. (Start from Table 5.1, inserting an extra column for x_3. Use variable x_1 as the first pivot.)

SOME PRACTICAL APPLICATIONS OF LINEAR PROGRAMMING

Wyatt[35] has given an interesting factual account of a blending problem in the Glacier Metal Company Ltd which makes white metal bearings. The problem was to blend the maximum value of recovered melt with virgin tin, antimony, copper and lead in making up alloys to required specifications, that is, to maximize a function F such that

$$F = m_1x_1 + m_2x_2 + m_3x_3 + m_4x_4$$

(Note that in this equation the use of subscripts has been extended to the coefficients m by which the variables x are to be multiplied.)

The m's are the values per pound of the recovered melts and the x's are the weights used. There were two types of restriction: those on weight of the general form $x_1 \leqq W_1$, W_1 being the weight of melt available, and those of the form

$$t_1x_1 + t_2x_2 + t_3x_3 + t_4x_4 \leqq T,$$

with T as the total weight of tin required, and the t's representing the tin contents of the recovered melts.

The tableaux contained about a dozen variables, and, as already mentioned, was solved by a girl with an electric desk-calculating machine. About 5 per cent more recovered metal was utilized with the aid of linear programming, giving a worthwhile saving. Moreover, a 'bonus' was obtained in the form of a quicker turnover of the recovered metal, with consequently lower stocks.

Dr Morton of the London School of Economics has described[36] how linear programming was introduced into an Indian textile mill as a means of planning production for maximum profit. Much of his work was devoted to reducing a potentially huge tableau to manageable size: for instance, he found it possible to reduce the total production flow to a small range of possible 'bottlenecks'; 40 principal products were selected from the full list of 400; 100 different kinds of loom were sorted into 12 groups. The final set of equations contained about 160 columns and 20 rows, the latter corresponding to the restrictions; they were solved without the aid of an electronic computer.

Morton deals with some of the *J*-factors introduced:

> If some kind of equipment is not restrictive under a given solution, if, e.g. an extra spindle hour could not increase total profits because spindles were not fully used, the apparent contribution of the spinning department to profits appears to be nil. It raises the question how to counteract the psychological effect of partly understood numerical details, or perhaps how to keep certain items of information from middle grade management. This is also related to the difficulty of persuading management that it may be better to keep certain items of equipment idle.

and again

> The only risk is the well-known, psychological one of assuming accurate knowledge merely because a number has been put on paper.

Koenigsberg[37] has compared the costs of different computers in solving a problem in the plywood industry. The function to be maximized was the total return from the products manufactured under restrictions on raw material, market and plant capacity: the resulting tableau contained about 50 equations and 100 variables, and the computer times and costs are given in Table 5.2.

He quotes two other problems in the same paper, one concerning the distribution of grain and the other a fermentation process in which a production schedule is drawn up over several successive periods. Amongst his pertinent comments are the following:

... in all three instances, the linear programming study was carried out for companies that were relatively small. The solutions yielded very worthwhile results in real terms, showing that the technique does not necessarily have to be applied to very large-scale operations to be effective.

Experience has shown that merely the process of writing down the pertinent relations in an operation leads to a better understanding of the industry itself as well as of the problem.

TABLE 5.2

Machine	*Time*	*Cost/hour*	*Total cost*	*Remarks*
IBM 650	16 hr	\$50	\$800–1,280	No tape
Burroughs 205	$2\frac{3}{4}$ hr	\$100–150	\$275–415	Tape
Burroughs 220	5 min.	\$300–400	\$30–40	Min. charge is for 1/10 hr
Philco 2000	1 min.	\$375	\$37·50	Min. charge is for 1/10 hr
IBM 704	6 min.	\$300–500	\$30–50	Min. charge is for 1/10 hr
Ferranti Mercury	5 min.	£75	£7	

Further, the process of solution always provides more information than just giving the solution itself. The formulations may therefore change with the passage of time as the operational research worker and the manager learn to understand one another and both learn more about the complex relationships between the variables of the industrial pattern.

Published work dealing with oil refineries is fairly extensive, and papers by Catchpole[38] and Newby and Deam[39] are noteworthy. The latter deals in detail with the conditions under which a production schedule is compiled for a single oil refinery, and the former shows how integrated operations render the problem even more complex and introduces some difficulties brought about by the sheer size of the matrix.

The installation of a planning system in a food factory is the subject of a paper by Jones and Rope of Fisons' Limited.[40] The factory manufactures ten different food products by nine different processes from two basic raw materials which are highly perishable and have a highly seasonal pattern of availability. Two models are used for planning, one covering six successive periods of one month each, the other adding two further periods of three months each.

The restrictions considered include those on production, maximum and minimum stock levels, availability of raw material and certain contractual obligations. The control function was essentially an expression for maximizing profit, but it needed to be modified in various ways. Products for which a sales forecast has been made will have a constant expected revenue from sales, and, since the cost of raw material is the principal variable element in their manufacture, a function which minimizes this cost is adequate. Other products are essentially users of residual raw materials, and their contributions have to be taken as expected gross profit margins. Stockholding costs are included, including the hiring of outside warehousing space if necessary.

Much careful thought has to be put into a practical formulation. One can easily over-complicate a model, and the manager and mathematician must collaborate closely to decide not only what is relevant, but what is significant.[41–5] For instance, Jones and Rope say that they first tried to incorporate restrictions specifically based on types of labour available, but abandoned them: limitation of the allowable range of production rates on groups of related plants was found to be a far more effective way of controlling labour requirements. Their model is being extended to embrace several factories linked by a network of transportation facilities. The latter may be dealt with by a particular form of the linear programming model which is the subject of the next chapter.

5
Solutions to Exercises

Exercise 5.1

$$5x_1 + x_2 + 9x_3 + 12x_4 \leqq 900$$

Exercise 5.2

$$5x_1 + x_2 + 9x_3 + 12x_4 + x_5 = 900$$

Exercise 5.3

$$q = x_6 \qquad r = x_7 \qquad s = x_8$$

Exercise 5.4

See Figure S.12.

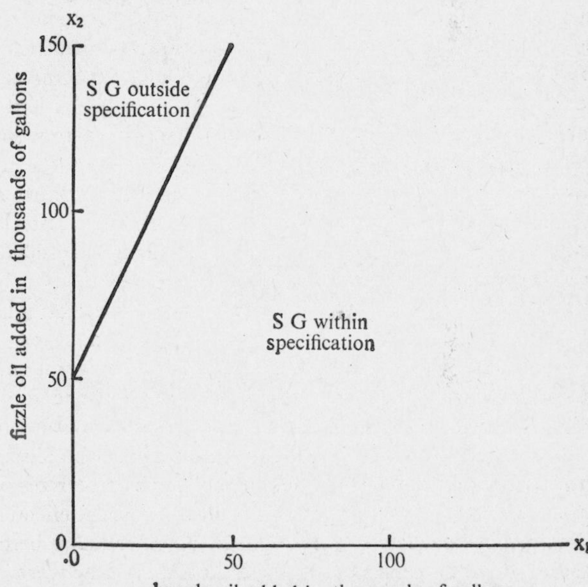

Fig. 5.12

Exercise 5.5

(i) $x_1 = 100, \quad x_2 = 0$
(ii) $x_1 = 0, \quad x_2 = 150$
(iii) $x_1 = 60, \quad x_2 = 60$

Exercise 5.6

(i) $x_4 = 0$
(ii) $x_4 = +50$
(iii) $x_4 = -200$

Exercise 5.7

P can be made as large as we choose; there are no operative restrictions and therefore there is no single solution. In geometric terms, we can put the P-line at an infinite distance from the origin.

Exercise 5.8

(a) $P = 200 + 3x_1 + 2x_2$
(b) See Figure S.13. The profit function has the same

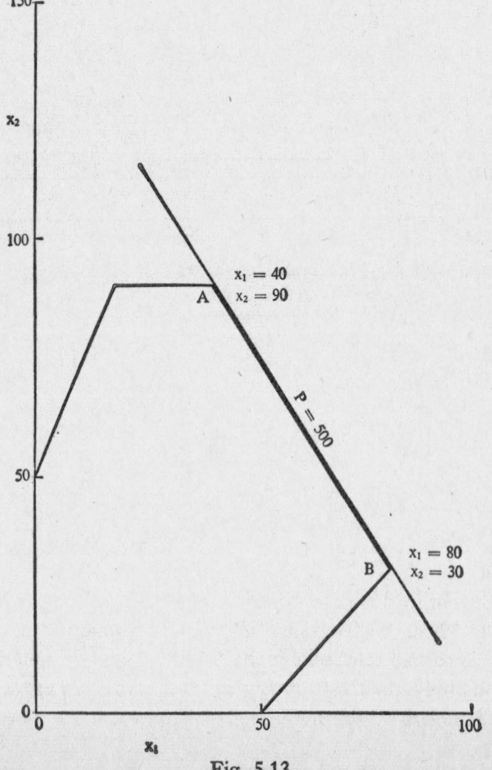

Fig. 5.13

gradient as the sulphur restriction, and coincides with it when P is maximized. Any pair of values between A and B constitute an optimum value; for example $x_1 = 60$, $x_2 = 60$ gives $P = 500$.

Exercise 5.9

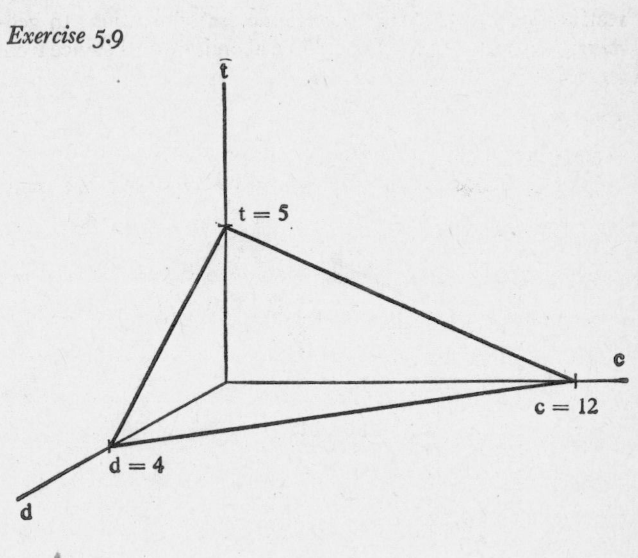

Exercise 5.10

$$\begin{aligned} x_4 &= 150 + x_2 - 2x_6 \\ x_5 &= 150 - 5x_2 + 3x_6 \\ x_1 &= 50 + x_2 - x_6 \\ x_7 &= 90 - x_2 \\ P &= 150 + 2x_2 - x_6 \end{aligned}$$

Note that in this case the area of feasible solutions is defined by only three restrictions. Those who wish to delve more deeply into the relationship between geometric and algebraic methods may like to study Figure S.15 and ponder its implications. It is the graph of this set of equations.

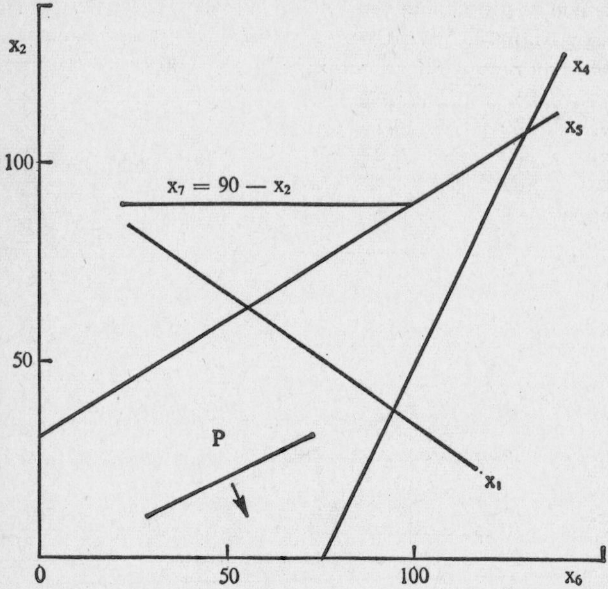

Fig. 5.15

Exercise 5.11

Let $x_1 = t,\quad x_2 = c,\quad x_3 = d,\quad x_4 = b$

$x_5 = p,\quad x_6 = q,\quad x_7 = r,\quad x_8 = s$

Q	x_1	x_2	x_3	x_4	x_5	x_6	x_7	x_8
900	+5	+1	+9	+12	+1	0	0	0
410	+2	+3	+4	+1	0	+1	0	0
270	+3	+2	+5	+10	0	0	+1	0
10	0	0	0	+1	0	0	0	+1
0	−12	−5	−15	−10	0	0	0	0

Exercise 5.12

First Tableau

		x_1	x_2	x_3	x_4	x_5	x_6	x_7	x_8
x_4	100	−4	+2	+1	+1	0	0	0	0
x_5	300	+3	+2	+1	0	+1	0	0	0
x_6	100	+2*	−2	+1	0	0	+1	0	0
x_7	90	0	+1	0	0	0	0	+1	0
x_8	60	0	0	+1	0	0	0	0	+1
	100	−1	−1	−1	0	0	0	0	0

Second Tableau

		x_1	x_2	x_3	x_4	x_5	x_6	x_7	x_8
x_4	300	0	−2	+3	+1	0	+2	0	0
x_5	150	0	+5*	$-\frac{1}{2}$	0	+1	$-\frac{3}{2}$	0	0
x_1	50	+1	−1	$+\frac{1}{2}$	0	0	$+\frac{1}{2}$	0	0
x_7	90	0	+1	0	0	0	0	+1	0
x_8	60	0	0	+1	0	0	0	0	+1
	150	0	−2	$-\frac{1}{2}$	0	0	$+\frac{1}{2}$	0	0

Third Tableau

		x_1	x_2	x_3	x_4	x_5	x_6	x_7	x_8
x_4	360	0	0	$+\frac{14}{5}$	+1	$+\frac{2}{5}$	$+\frac{7}{5}$	0	0
x_2	30	0	+1	$-\frac{1}{10}$	0	$+\frac{1}{5}$	$-\frac{3}{10}$	0	0
x_1	80	+1	0	$+\frac{2}{5}$	0	$+\frac{1}{5}$	$+\frac{1}{5}$	0	0
x_7	60	0	0	$+\frac{1}{10}$	0	$-\frac{1}{5}$	$+\frac{3}{10}$	+1	0
x_8	60	0	0	+1*	0	0	0	0	+1
	210	0	0	$-\frac{7}{10}$	0	$+\frac{2}{5}$	$-\frac{1}{10}$	0	0

Fourth Tableau

		x_1	x_2	x_3	x_4	x_5	x_6	x_7	x_8
x_4	192	0	0	0	+1	$+\frac{2}{5}$	$+\frac{7}{5}$*	0	$-\frac{14}{5}$
x_2	36	0	+1	0	0	$+\frac{1}{5}$	$-\frac{3}{10}$	0	$+\frac{1}{10}$
x_1	56	+1	0	0	0	$+\frac{1}{5}$	$+\frac{1}{5}$	0	$-\frac{2}{5}$
x_7	54	0	0	0	0	$-\frac{1}{5}$	$+\frac{3}{10}$	+1	$-\frac{1}{10}$
x_3	60	0	0	+1	0	0	0	0	+1
	252	0	0	0	0	$+\frac{2}{5}$	$-\frac{1}{10}$	0	$+\frac{7}{10}$

Fifth Tableau

		x_1	x_2	x_3	x_4	x_5	x_6	x_7	x_8
x_6	$137\frac{1}{7}$	0	0	0	$+\frac{5}{7}$	$+\frac{2}{7}$	+1	0	−2
x_2	$77\frac{1}{7}$	0	+1	0	$+\frac{3}{14}$	$+\frac{2}{7}$	0	0	$-\frac{1}{2}$
x_1	$28\frac{4}{7}$	+1	0	0	$-\frac{1}{7}$	$+\frac{1}{7}$	0	0	0
x_7	$12\frac{6}{7}$	0	0	0	$-\frac{3}{14}$	$-\frac{2}{7}$	0	+1	$+\frac{1}{2}$
x_3	60	0	0	+1	0	0	0	0	+1
	$265\frac{5}{7}$	0	0	0	$+\frac{1}{14}$	$+\frac{1}{35}$	0	0	$+\frac{1}{2}$

This is the final solution.

NOTES AND REFERENCES

34 Abbott, E. A., *Flatland: a Romance of Many Dimensions* (Blackwell, 1950).

35 Wyatt, J. K., *Operational Research Quarterly* (1958), vol. 9, No. 2, p. 154.

36 Morton, G., *Operational Research Quarterly* (1958), vol. 9, No. 3, p. 198.

37 Koenigsberg, E., *Operational Research Quarterly* (1961), vol. 12, No. 2, p. 105.

38 Catchpole, A. R., *Operational Research Quarterly* (1962), vol. 13, No. 2, p. 163.

39 Newby, W. J., and Deam, R. J., *Planning for Productivity in the Oil Industry* (The Institute of Petroleum), p. 68.

40 Jones, W. G., and Rope, C. M., *Operational Research Quarterly* (1964), vol. 15, p. 293.

Other useful references include:

41 Charnes, A., Cooper, W. W., and Mellon, B., *Ecometrica* (1952), Vol. 20, No. 2.

42 Brigham, G., *Operations Research* (1959), vol. 7, 524–33.

43 Jewell, W. S., *Operations Research* (1960), vol. 8, 565–70.

44 Dantzig, G. B., *Linear Programming and Extensions* (Princeton University Press, 1963), chap. 27.

45 Brown, J. A. C., *Symposium on Linear Programming* (1954), Ferranti Ltd., London.

6
Transportation by Tabulation

Lines, circles, scenes, letters and characters;
Ay, these are those that Faustus most desires.
Oh, what a world of profit and delight,
Of power, of honour, of omnipotence
Is promis'd to the studious artisan!

MARLOWE, *Dr Faustus*

CERTAIN complex problems in distributing goods may be reduced to a simple routine; it will be described arithmetically in this chapter, but we shall not bother with the theoretical justification, contenting ourselves with the comment that it is a special case of the linear programming method already described. The Heinz Company in the U.S.A. was a pioneer in the industrial application of this method, which was originally devised for planning convoys across the Atlantic in the Second World War. One large oil company is also using it to decide which distribution areas in Western Europe should be allocated to each of the refineries it controls.

The Pythagoras Processed Plankton Co. is an imaginary enterprise operating in the future when much of our protein intake may be harvested from the sea. This company owns factories at the four ports where its edible plankton is landed and processed; they are –

Amsterdam	Capacity	50,000	tons per year
Barcelona	,,	72,000	,,
Copenhagen	,,	57,000	,,
Dieppe	,,	21,000	,,
Total		200,000	

It also has five main centres for distribution to the European market, which are listed below together with their estimated annual demand:

Milan	36,000	tons per year
Paris	69,000	,,
Rome	35,000	,,
Strasbourg	20,000	,,
Turin	40,000	,,
Total	200,000	

A map of the factories and market centres is given in Figure 6.1.

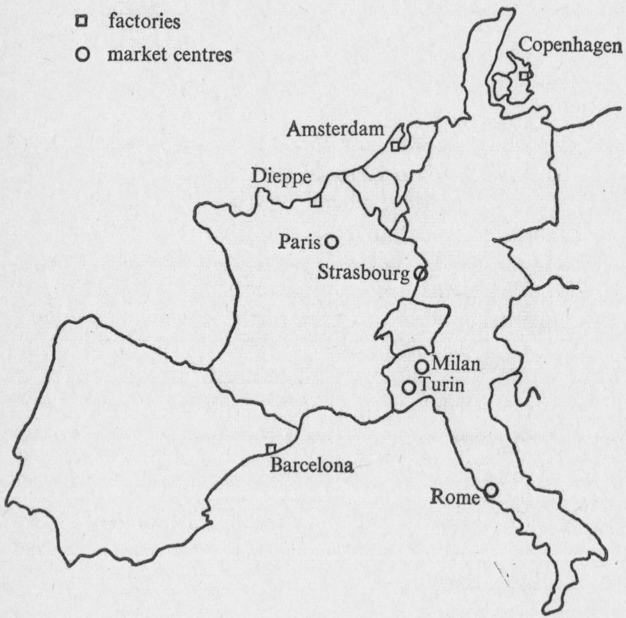

Fig. 6.1 Centres of manufacture and distribution for Pythagoras' Processed Plankton

The company runs its own fleet of delivery vehicles, which have a uniform cost of one shilling per mile. The Transport Manager has the problem of deciding how the factories and distribution centres are to be linked to each other so that the cost of distribution is as low as possible. His first job is to compile a table of distances, Table 6.1.

TABLE 6.1

Distances between Plankton Factories and Centres
(in miles, single journey only)

Factory	Market Centre				
	Milan	*Paris*	*Rome*	*Strasbourg*	*Turin*
Amsterdam	678	307	1,059	363	683
Barcelona	648	685	887	684	564
Copenhagen	937	731	1,248	631	982
Dieppe	639	103	1,016	367	602

(The figures in this table were taken from the Automobile Association's Foreign Touring Guide, 1963.)

His present method is to begin with the centre of highest demand, Paris, and allocate as much as possible from the nearest factory, Dieppe. Its capacity is not enough, so he completes the Paris allocation from the next nearest factory, which is Amsterdam. When he has satisfied Paris, he selects the next biggest market, Turin, and proceeds in the same way. Eventually he arrives at the 'common-sense' allocation shown in Table 6.2.

TABLE 6.2

Plankton Allocation. First 'Common-Sense' Solution
(in thousands of tons)

Factory	Market Centre					
	Milan	*Paris*	*Rome*	*Strasbourg*	*Turin*	*Total*
Amsterdam	2	48				50
Barcelona	32				40	72
Copenhagen	2		35	20		57
Dieppe		21				21
Total	36	69	35	20	40	200

The total ton-mileage (not counting return journeys) is 119,725 which at two shillings per mile (out-and-return) would cost £11,972,500. Can this total be reduced?

This is an allocation problem, and may be solved by linear

programming. We can set up linear equations (or inequalities) to ensure that no factory is called on to distribute more than it can produce and that no market receives more than it can sell; we then have to minimize a total cost function, made up of individual terms like the following:

Amount supplied to Milan from Amsterdam ×
Cost of supplying a unit amount to Milan from Amsterdam.

For the common-sense solution in Table 6.2, this term would be

$$(2000 \times 2) \times 678 \text{ shillings}$$

where the multiplier 2000 is needed because of the double journey and the use of thousands of tons as a unit in Table 6.2.

Exercise 6.1

In Table 6.2, what terms would express the costs of supplying

(i) Milan from Barcelona?
(ii) Rome from Amsterdam?

Exercise 6.2

If we minimize the ton-mileage, shall we automatically minimize the cost in this example?

Exercise 6.3

Use the values in Tables 6.1 and 6.2 to check that the total mileage of 119,725,000 in the 'common-sense' solution is correct.

The problem could be solved by the algebraic methods already described, but it has a special property which makes an even simpler routine possible: all the variables in the equations turn out to have unit coefficients, giving what is known as a 'transportation matrix'. (A matrix is a rectangular array of numbers.) One of these simple routines is called the method of 'fictitious costs'. It starts from any feasible solution – we shall use Table 5.2 as a starting-point – and improve it in successive iterations until a demonstrable optimum is found.

It must be emphasized here that the 'fictitious costs' are a technical term for an aid to calculation and have no real meaning in the accountants' sense.

For convenience, we shall from now on refer to individual entries as being in the 'cells' of the matrix; each cell will be described by the initials of the factory and the market corresponding to it. For instance, the entry in cell *CR* of Table 6.1 is 1,248.

First we can simplify the matrix of mileages (i.e. costs) in Table 6.1 so as to ease the subsequent burden of arithmetic. The first row gives all the distances from Amsterdam, the shortest being 307 miles to Paris. This means that the 50 units (50,000 tons) processed at Amsterdam will all have to be shipped *at least* 307 miles each, a total of $50 \times 307 = 15{,}350$ (in units of a thousand ton-miles), and the subsequent allocation will determine the extent to which this minimum will be exceeded. If we add 15,350 to the cost function, we may reduce all the cost elements in the first row of the matrix by 307.

Exercise 6.4

Simplify the second row (Barcelona) in Table 6.2 by the method just described.

How much must then be added to the cost function?

Reducing all the rows in this way gives Table 6.3.

TABLE 6.3

Plankton Allocation: First Stage in Matrix Reduction

Factory	*Market* *M*	*P*	*R*	*S*	*T*	*Mileage Sub-tracted*	*Amount Deliv-ered*	*Product in ton-miles, to be added to cost function*
A	371	0	752	56	376	307	50	15,350
B	84	121	323	120	0	564	72	40,608
C	306	100	617	0	351	631	57	35,967
D	536	0	913	264	499	103	21	2,163
						Sub-total		94,088

The reduction ensures that the lowest cost in each of the rows is zero, and may now be carried a stage further by doing the same for the columns. Each of these contains a zero except M and R; the lowest entry in the former is 84. If we reduce all the entries in column M by this amount, we must increase the cost function by $84 \times 36 = 3024$; similarly, by subtracting 323 from all the entries in column 5 we add 11,305 to the cost function and arrive at the completely reduced matrix in Table 6.4 which has at least one zero in each row and column.

TABLE 6.4

Plankton Allocation: Final Stage in Matrix Reduction

	Market						
Factory	*M*	*P*	*R*	*S*	*T*		
A	287	0	429	56	376	Sub-total from previous	
B	0	121	0	120	0	reduction	94,088
C	222	100	294	0	351	Sub-total from this reduction	14,329
D	452	0	590	264	499	Grand total	108,417
Mileage Subtracted	84	0	323	0	0		
Amount Delivered	36	69	35	20	40		
Product to be added to cost function	3,024	0	11,305	0	0	Sub-total 14,329	

The figure 108,417 belongs to a useful class of estimates called 'lower bounds'. We know that, whatever the final allocation may be, it cannot possibly give a lower 'cost' than this – a valuable, though incomplete, piece of information in many problems.

We now combine Tables 6.2 and 6.4 into Table 6.5, where the reduced costs appear in the small rectangles within each cell, and the common-sense allocations are also entered, zero values being omitted. The row and column totals are included for checking.

TABLE 6.5
Plankton Allocation: Feasible Solution

	Market	*M*	*P*	*R*	*S*	*T*
	Totals	36	69	35	20	40
		287	0	429	56	376
A	50	2	48			
		0	121	0	120	0
B	72	32				40
		222	100	294	0	351
C	57	2		35	20	
		452	0	590	264	499
D	21		21			

Table 6.6 shows how the 'fictitious costs' are calculated from cost elements in rows and columns. Column *M* has been arbitrarily chosen as the starting-point, and a cost element of zero entered at its foot. Taking the occupied cells in this column – those containing unencircled figures – we enter cost elements in the corresponding rows in such a way that the cost entry in any occupied cell is the sum of its corresponding row and column elements. Thus we have 287 as the cost element in the first row, and this in turn generates —287 at the bottom of the second column in order to agree with the zero in cell *AP*.

The fictitious costs are then found by adding together the row and column cost elements for the unoccupied squares: they are the encircled figures in Table 6.6. If none of the fictitious costs exceeds the true cost, the allocation as a whole has minimum cost.

There are two cells in Table 6.6 where this is not so; the

TABLE 6.6

Plankton Allocation: Calculation of Fictitious Costs

Factory	*Market* Totals	*M* 36	*P* 69	*R* 35	*S* 20	*T* 40	Fictitious Cost Element
A	50	[287] 2	[0] 48	[429] (359)	[56] (65)	[376] (287)	287
B	72	[0] 32	[121] (−287)	[0] (72)	[120] (−222)	[0] 40	0
C	57	[222] 2	[100] (−65)	[294] 35	[0] 20	[351] (222)	222
D	21	[452] (287)	[0] 21	[590] (359)	[264] (65)	[499] (287)	287
Fictitious Cost Element		0	−287	72	−222	0	

first is *AS* where the fictitious cost, 65, exceeds the true cost by 9. In cell *BR*, the fictitious cost exceeds the true cost by 72, an even greater difference. We therefore choose the latter, and cheapen the solution by allocating to it as great an amount as possible: it is marked with a plus sign in the left-hand part of Table 6.7. We now look along the row for an entry in a column which also contains at least one other occupied cell and mark it with a minus sign – in this case, cell *BM* with an entry of 32. Next we look down the same column for an entry in a row which also contains another occupied cell, and mark it with a plus sign. This goes on with alternate plus and minus signs until we eventually arrive back at cell *BR*: the route is shown in the left hand part of Table 6.7.

TABLE 6.7

Plankton Allocation: First Iteration

	M	*P*	*R*	*S*	*T*
A					
B	32−		+		
C	2+		35−		
D					

	M	*P*	*R*	*S*	*T*
A					
B			32		
C	34		3		
D					

TABLE 6.8

Plankton Allocation: Result of First Iteration

	Market	*M*	*P*	*R*	*S*	*T*	
Factory	Totals	36	69	35	20	40	Fictitious Cost Element
A	50	[287] 2 −	[0] 48	[429] (359)	[56] + (65)	[376] (359)	287
B	72	[0] (−72)	[121] (−359)	[0] 32	[120] (−294)	[0] 40	−72
C	57	[222] 34 +	[100] (−65)	[294] 3	[0] 20 −	[351] (294)	222
D	21	[452] (287)	[0] 21	[590] (359)	[264] (65)	[499] (359)	287
Fictitious Cost Element		0	−287	72	−222	72	

Having found the route, we move as large a number as possible into cell *BR*, adding and subtracting to preserve the factory and market totals. Negative allocations are meaningless, so the largest number in this case must be 32; it leads to a zero in cell *BM* as shown in the right-hand side of Table 6.7. The reduction in cost so obtained is 72 × 32 = 2,304 (which may readily be checked by comparing the total costs for Tables 6.6 and 6.8).

Table 6.8 shows the situation at the end of the first iteration, with the new fictitious costs. Cell *AS* still has an excess of fictitious over true cost of 9 units; the plus and minus signs show the route for adjustment, and Table 6.9 gives the result of

TABLE 6.9

Plankton Allocation: Optimum Solution

	Market	*M*	*P*	*R*	*S*	*T*	
Factory	Totals	36	69	35	20	40	Fictitious Cost Element
A	50	[287] (278)	[0] 48	[429] (350)	[56] 2	[376] (350)	278
B	72	[0] (−72)	[121] (−350)	[0] 32	[120] (−294)	[0] 40	−72
C	57	[222] 36	[100] (−56)	[294] 3	[0] 18	[351] (294)	222
D	21	[452] (278)	[0] 21	[590] (350)	[264] (56)	[499] (350)	278
Fictitious Cost Element		0	−278	72	−222	72	

the second iteration, which is the optimum solution. Its overall cost is 8,986 units, which when added to the original minimum total obtained by reducing the matrix (108,417) gives a grand total of 117,403.

Exercise 6.5

What reduction in cost would you expect between Tables 6.8 and 6.9? Check your answer against the costs of these two allocations.

Exercise 6.6

What is the total cost of transportation given by the optimum solution? What is the saving over the original 'common-sense' solution of Table 6.2?

Exercise 6.7

The Assistant Transport Manager was also asked to produce a common-sense solution. He used almost the same method, except that he began with the biggest *factory* and allocated its output to the nearest markets. His result is tabulated below. Find the cost of this solution and use the method of fictitious costs to derive the optimum.

Factory			*Centre*			
	Milan	*Paris*	*Rome*	*Strasbourg*	*Turin*	*Total*
Amsterdam	4	32	14			50
Barcelona	32				40	72
Copenhagen		37		20		57
Dieppe			21			21
Total	36	69	35	20	40	200

It is possible, as in the Simplex method, to calculate ranges of validity for the solution. For instance, in cell *AM* of Table 6.9, the fictitious cost is 9 units greater than the true cost: it follows that a reduction in the true cost of up to 9 units will not affect the solution, but a change greater than this will. If a new Dutch motorway were to reduce the distance from Amsterdam to the Italian cities by 25 miles, the true costs in the cells for Amsterdam to Milan, Rome and Turin (Table 6.9) would fall to 262, 404 and 351 respectively. The fictitious cost for Amsterdam to Milan, cell *AM*, would then be less than the true cost and Amsterdam would supply Milan rather than Strasbourg, with corresponding adjustments in the shipments from Copenhagen to those two centres.

The Plankton problem was such that the total productive and market capacities were exactly equal, but the transportation method may also be used for inequalities. An example can easily be constructed by supposing that the Turin centre and its market no longer exist, so that the total productive capacity exceeds the total demand by 20 units.

The problem can still be expressed in the same general form, with only a few changes. The column which previously represented the Turin outlet now becomes a disposal column. Each cell in it is given an artificially high cost, much greater than any other cost, which we shall call Z – this device ensures that all these cells will have the lowest priority. By altering Table 6.9 in this way, and using it as a first feasible solution, we arrive at the statement of the problem given in Table 6.10.

The occupied cell in column T is CT which contains 40 units; its cost in the original table was 0 and is now Z, so the cost of the solution as a whole becomes $8{,}968 + 40Z$. The corresponding fictitious costs are also shown in Table 6.10, and we can see that all the cells in column T now have fictitious costs greater than the actual ones, the greatest difference being in cell AT. By transferring the greatest possible number – two – into this cell, we arrive at Table 6.11, and a further iteration gives Table 6.12, the optimum solution.

The first iteration decreased the cost by $2 \times 350 = 700$, and the second by 1×294, making a total decrease of 994. It is easy to confirm that the cost of the allocation in Table 6.12 is 7,992 units, which is 994 less than that for Table 6.9. The additional 'cost', $40Z$, is not counted because it was introduced as an artificial device for dealing with an inequality.

A similar device is used when the total manufacturing capacity is less than the total market: an extra row would be added,

TABLE 6.10

Plankton Allocation with Turin Excluded: First Feasible Solution

	Market	*M*	*P*	*R*	*S*	*T*	
Factory	Totals	36	69	35	20	40	Fictitious Cost Element
A	50	[287] (278)	[0] 48	[429] (350)	[56] 2 −	[Z] + (Z+350)	278
B	72	[0] (−72)	[121] (−350)	[0] 32 +	[120] (−294)	[Z] 40 −	−72
C	57	[222] 36	[100] (−56)	[294] 3 −	[0] 18 +	[Z] (Z+294)	222
D	21	[452] (278)	[0] 21	[590] (350)	[264] (56)	[Z] (Z+350)	278
Fictitious Cost Element		0	−278	72	−222	Z+72	

representing an imaginary additional factory with an output exactly equal to the deficiency in manufacturing capacity. All the cells in this row would have a 'penalty' cost of *Z*, and the resulting distribution plan would show which parts of the total market should be satisfied.

Using an artificial penalty cost to exclude certain sets of solutions is a convenient method which is widely used in cost-minimization problems; similarly, we may use zero or negative costs to impose priorities. Thus, if local politics made it

TABLE 6.11

Plankton Allocation with Turin Excluded: Result of First Iteration

Factory	Market Totals	*M* 36	*P* 69	*R* 35	*S* 20	*T* 40	Fictitious Cost Element
A	50	[287] (−72)	[0] 48	[429] (0)	[56] (−294)	[Z] 2	−72
B	72	[0] (−72)	[121] (0)	[0] 34 +	[120] (−294)	[Z] 38 −	−72
C	57	[222] 36	[100] (294)	[294] 1 −	[0] 20	[Z] + (Z+294)	222
D	21	[452] (−72)	[0] 21	[590] (0)	[264] (−294)	[Z]	−72
Fictitious Cost Element		0	+72	72	−222	Z+72	

necessary for Strasbourg to be supplied from a French source, a negative cost for cell *DS* would ensure that the full capacity of the Dieppe factory was allocated to Strasbourg.

Exercise 6.8

Pythagoras Plankton have decided that plankton processed in Amsterdam shall not be sold in the Italian market. How would you represent this decision in the allocation problem, and what would be its effect on the company's distribution costs?

TABLE 6.12

Plankton Allocation with Turin Excluded: Optimum Solution

	Market	*M*	*P*	*R*	*S*	*T*	
Factory	Totals	36	69	35	20	40	Fictitious Cost Element
A	50	[287] (222)	[0] 48	[429] (0)	[56] (0)	[Z] 2	222
B	72	[0] (222)	[121] (0)	[0] 35	[120] (0)	[Z] 37	222
C	57	[222] 36	[100] (0)	[294] (0)	[0] 20	[Z] 1	222
D	21	[452] (222)	[0] 21	[590] (0)	[264] (0)	[Z] (Z)	222
Fictitious Cost Element		0	−222	−222	−222	Z−222	

WIDER USES OF THE TRANSPORTATION METHOD

The idea of transportation can be extended to cover not only physical movement but other changes of state with which costs are associated. One common group of applications considers various periods of time as the 'destinations' – as was done in the planning problem of Jones and Rope described in the previous chapter – and may even use them as 'sources' as well.[47] The next exercise shows how quite complex situations can be described in terms of transportation.

Exercise 6.9

Clark and Maxwell Ltd make a chemical compound, 3-blindmycin. The demand for this product is seasonal, and the productive capacity allocated to it follows roughly the seasonal trend. The sales forecast for 1970 is:

1st Quarter	60,000 mg.
2nd Quarter	97,000 mg.
3rd Quarter	118,000 mg.
4th Quarter	95,000 mg.
Total	370,000 mg.

The productive capacity allocated is:

1st Quarter	51,000 mg.
2nd Quarter	80,000 mg.
3rd Quarter	119,000 mg.
4th Quarter	100,000 mg.
Total	350,000 mg.

There is therefore a deficiency of 20,000 mg. in total productive capacity, and the company's usual practice is to make this up by buying from an outside supplier at a price of £70 per 1,000 mg. The price is falling, however, and the Chief Buyer estimates that it will fall at a uniform rate from £70 in the first quarter to £67 in the last.

The internal production cost is £50 per 1,000 mg. and this holds good as long as the chemical is sold in the same quarter as it is produced. If it is sold in the following quarter, it incurs a storage cost of £1 per 1,000 mg. If it is sold two quarters afterwards, the storage cost goes up to £2, but there is an additional cost of £10 for filtering and re-testing the material. If it is sold three quarters afterwards, it must also be re-distilled at a total extra cost (including sortage charges) of £30 per 1,000 mg. For any further delay, the product must be scrapped.

If orders are held over for one-quarter, the loss (in customer

Productive Capacity \ Sales Forecast		1st Quarter 60	2nd Quarter 97	3rd Quarter 118	4th Quarter 95
1st Quarter	51	50	51	62	80
2nd Quarter	80	55	50	51	62
3rd Quarter	119	59	55	50	51
4th Quarter	100	63	59	55	50
Buy Outside	20	70	69	68	67

Sales and Productive Capacity are in units of 1,000 mg.

Costs are given in £ per 1,000 mg.

goodwill and extra administration) is estimated at £5; for two quarters, £9 and for three quarters' delay, £13. Check that the following matrix is an adequate description of the problem, and find the optimum solution.

NON-INTUITIVE SOLUTIONS

The solution to Exercise 6.9 is an interesting example of a result which goes against our intuition. The Purchasing Department in procuring 3-blindmycin from outside sources, would almost certainly recommend intuitively that it be bought in the last quarter when it is cheapest, but the linear programming solution suggests otherwise.

Non-intuitive solutions of this sort will usually occur when either

(a) the problem has not been properly defined in the first instance, or

(b) the linear programming formulation expresses a broad view of the problem which cuts across departmental responsibilities.

An example of the first type is afforded by dietary problems. If we know the prices and nutritional factors for a range of foods and the minimum nutritional requirements for a family, we may set up a linear programming matrix which produces a mimimum-cost diet. This may well contain a ridiculously large proportion of potatoes because they are a cheap source of Vitamin C, and because the problem did not specify any maximum restrictions on individual foodstuffs. One exercise closely resembling the Fermat Furniture example was carried out in a chemical factory with similar results.[46] The solution indicated the manufacture of a product in quantities far above the most optimistic estimate of the total market. A maximum as well as a minimum sales figure had to be specified, and the whole pricing policy was called into question as a result.

Examples of the second type tend to occur in fairly large matrices, when the data are obtained from a variety of origins. The individual managers within the several departments tend to organize work so that the department itself is at maximum efficiency (technically called 'sub-optimization') whereas maximum *overall* efficiency may conflict with this. Suppose a shop in a motor-car factory is making pistons and has some spare capacity. Increasing the output of pistons will lower their unit cost, but will produce a useless excess if it is not accompanied by a corresponding increase in the number of cylinder blocks.

The linear programming solution may also suggest methods of working. Newby and Deam found in scheduling an oil refinery that

The optimum blends as determined by the computer were in some cases considerably different from current practice. These blends were physically checked in the laboratory and found to agree with the properties as formulated by the solution and to meet appropriate specification requirements.[39]

Thus linear programming may not only solve our current problems but may contribute to our insight of the whole business of being managers. One industrial statistician has summed up in these words: 'Unless my solution generates at least four new problems, I consider that I have failed'.

6

Solutions to Exercises

Exercise 6.1

(a) 2,000 × 32 × 648 shillings = 41,472,000 shillings
= £2,073,600

(b) Nil, because no allocation has been made under this heading

Exercise 6.2

Yes, because the cost of transportation per mile is the same throughout.

Exercise 6.3

Working in units of one thousand tons, we have:

2 × 678 =	1,356
48 × 307 =	14,736
32 × 648 =	20,736
40 × 564 =	22,560
2 × 937 =	1,874
35 × 1,248 =	43,680
20 × 631 =	12,620
21 × 103 =	2,163
Total	119,725

Exercise 6.4

Lowest mileage 564 (Barcelona to Turin)

New row:	*M*	*P*	*R*	*S*	*T*
	84	121	323	120	0

Total amount from Barcelona = 72 thousand tons (Table 6.2)
Amount to be added to cost function = 564 × 72 = 40,608

Exercise 6.5

The difference between fictitious and true costs in cell *AS* was 9, and 2 units were moved into it. The saving would be $9 \times 2 = 18$ units. Each unit represents 1,000 tons making an out-and-return journey of 2 miles at one shilling per mile, giving a cost per unit of £100 – the monetary saving is therefore £1,800.

Check. Total from Table 6.8 = 9,004 units
,, ,, ,, 6.9 = 8,986 ,,
Difference 18 units

Exercise 6.6

'Lower bound' cost = 108,417 units
Optimum additional cost = 8,986 ,,
Total cost = 117,403 units
= £11,740,300

Cost of 'common-sense' solution = £11,972,500

Saving = £232,200

Saving as percentage of original total = 1·94%

Exercise 6.7

The cost of this solution is £13,166,100.
The optimum solution is as shown in Table 6.9.

Exercise 6.8

Enter a penalty cost *Z* in cells *AM*, *AR* and *AT*. Since these cells are unoccupied in Table 6.9, the original solution would not be changed and so the distribution costs would not be affected.

Exercise 6.9

	Sales Forecast / *Productive Capacity*	*1st Quarter* 60	*2nd Quarter* 97	*3rd Quarter* 118	*4th Quarter* 95
1st Quarter	51	[50] 51	[51]	[62]	[80]
2nd Quarter	80	[55]	[50] 80	[51]	[62]
3rd Quarter	119	[59]	[55] 1	[50] 118	[51]
4th Quarter	100	[63]	[59] 5	[55]	[50] 95
Buy Outside	20	[70] 9	[69] 11	[68]	[67]

NOTES AND REFERENCES

46 Battersby, A., *Linear Programming in a Small Batch Chemical Plant* (1962). Paper delivered to the Manchester Branch of the Institution of Chemical Engineers, December.

47 Magee, J. F., *Production Planning and Inventory Control* (McGraw-Hill, 1958), p. 146.

More information about 3-blindmycin will be found in:
Comfort, A., *Come Out to Play* (Eyre & Spottiswoode, 1961).

7
Simulation by Symbols

The little actor cons another part.
Filling from time to time his 'humorous stage'
With all the Persons, down to palsied Age,
That life brings with her in her equipage;
    As if his whole vocation
    Were endless imitation.

WORDSWORTH, *Ode on Intimations of Immortality*

THE study of computers will show us how close is the connexion between the 'new' mathematics of the business world and the systematic studies of logical relationships which originated with Aristotle. This association is evident in the study of business systems by the method known as 'simulation'. As its name implies, simulation enables a manager to study the system which he controls by imitating or 'simulating' its behaviour. As examples of simulation in its widest sense, we have:

1. A model in a wind-tunnel test, for deducing the aerodynamic behaviour of a new type of aircraft.

2. The 'flight simulator' used for training airline pilots; this is a full-scale representation of a flight-deck, which responds to the pilot's handling of the controls in the same way as a real air liner.

3. The mechanical 'tortoises', Elmer and Elsie, built by Dr W. Gray Walter. They illustrate the nervous system of an animal, building up astonishingly lifelike behaviour from the interactions of simple electrical circuits.

These are all physical models with the common characteristic of reproducing the *behaviour* of the real object which they represent. In theory, the behaviour of any system can be deduced in all circumstances provided that its structure is completely known: given the exact shape, surface characteristics and speed of a supersonic aircraft, we ought to be able to compute the nature of the shock wave, but the calculation would be so laborious and liable to error that the 'simulation' in a wind-tunnel is cheaper and more convenient.

A simulation model need not be mechanical; the diagram in Figure 7.1 is a rather frivolous example of an *abstract* model. It represents the game of Snakes and Ladders. There is, for example, a snake with its head on square 16 and its tail on square 4; there is a ladder from square 2 to square 62.

Throwing the die is represented by 'Select a number at random from 1 to 6 inclusive'. See how precisely the rules have been designed: if you throw a six, and have a second throw, do you go down a snake if the six alone lands you on its head? These rules show clearly that you do not. Notice also that the rules for finishing the game have been carefully defined.

Exercise 7.1

Is any skill involved in the game of Snakes and Ladders?

PROBLEMS OF ORGANIZATIONS

How does all this affect the executive who is concerned with the more serious problems of controlling some sort of *organization*? There is a fundamental resemblance between his problem and that of the aircraft designer: the manager, like the designer, knows the *structure* of what he is dealing with, but its complexity prevents him from deducing its behaviour. Consequently, he is obliged to make decisions of which the effect can be only imperfectly predicted.

CONTROL LOOPS

Imperfect decisions of this sort mean that the manager is experimenting with the business itself – making changes, observing the results and modifying his instructions accordingly. He has set up a 'feedback control loop' between himself and

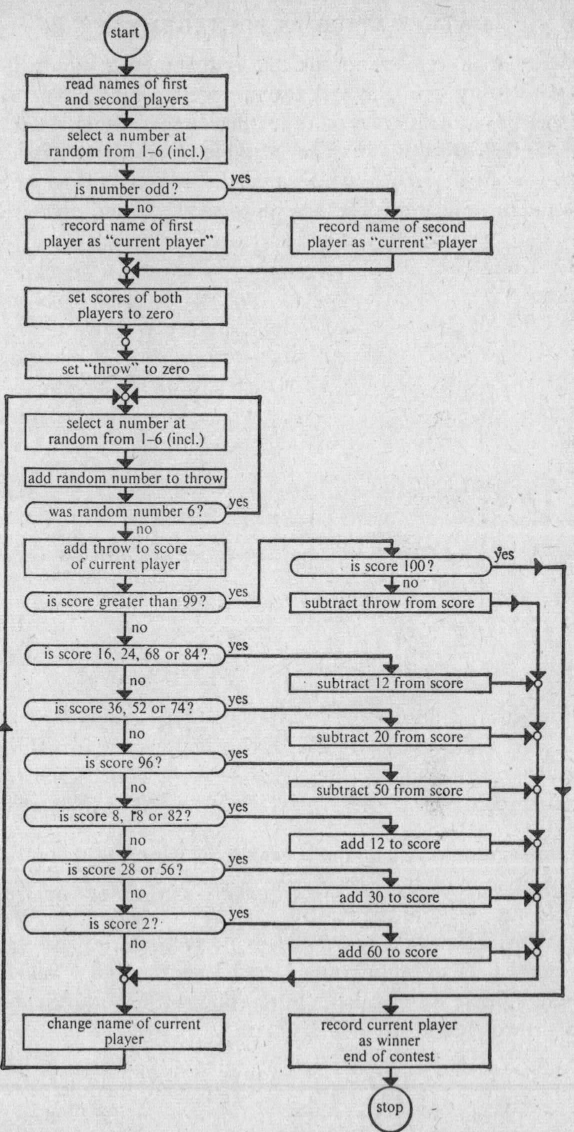

Fig. 7.1 Simulation of a contest: logical flow diagram

the system, which is the left-hand loop shown in Figure 7.2. Experimenting with the real system in this way is expensive and can be risky; it is no more justifiable than using a real air liner for training a pilot to meet emergencies. The pilot has his flight simulator: what can we offer the executive who needs a 'business simulator'? The answer is shown in the right-hand

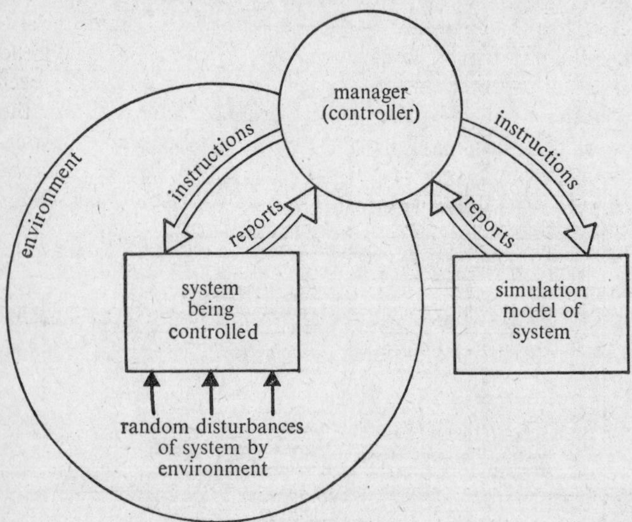

Fig. 7.2 Relationship of system, environment, controller and mode

loop of Figure 7.2. By giving him a model which will reproduce the behaviour of the real system, we enable the manager to try out the effect of his control actions before applying them to the business itself. No model is perfect, so the answer he obtains will be an approximate one; nevertheless, a skilfully-designed model can be made to reproduce the workings of the original to a remarkably close extent.

APPLICATIONS OF SIMULATION

The steel industry has been one of the most successful industrial exploiters of simulation models; one of the earliest papers is a very readable description of a problem in a melting shop,[48] and the B.I.S.R.A. Annual Report for 1961 mentions a similar problem (p. 84). Planning the work of soaking pits at the Abbey Works of the Steel Company of Wales has been improved with the help of a simulation model[49]; the unloading of iron ore at Ijmuiden has also been studied.[50] A recent paper dealing with steel fabrication showed that an extra crane costing £15,000 would not be needed in a new materials-handling system.[51] A rather unusual study investigated the effect of weather on production scheduling for sugar-beet factories in the U.S.A.[52] Pit-haulage in France [53] and the method of warning miners in a colliery[54] have also been simulated, as well as a wide variety of traffic and transport problems.[55,56] Much of the simulation work in the military field is kept secret, but occasionally some information dribbles out; a paper from the United States Air Force[57] describes a case in which direct experimentation on the system would be undesirable, to say the least – simulating 'a large-scale two-sided global war'. Could simulation do more?

DEFINING THE SYSTEM

In order to build a model we must break down the system into its component parts, but before doing this we need to say more precisely what we mean by a 'system'. This word has been used so far to mean 'that which is being controlled', and we cannot hope to define it more exactly until we have examined the range of control actions which is to be studied.

To make this rather abstract point clearer, consider a transport company whose operations we wish to study by building a model. It consists of a fleet of lorries operating from a central warehouse; do these physical components, then, make up the whole system? If all we wish to observe is the effect of different speeds or scheduling procedures, then the answer is probably yes. If, however, we are concerned with the desirability of opening a new warehouse or adding more lorries to the fleet, we must include those *potential* components in the system; if we wish to observe the effects of our actions on the service to customers, then the customers themselves must be represented in some way.

BOUNDARIES

In short, the system is defined by a *boundary* which we draw around it. Everything inside the boundary is 'the system'; everything that lies outside constitutes 'the environment' in which the system operates. Drawing this boundary correctly is difficult: some day, perhaps, operational researchers may discover 'cleavage planes' between a system and its environment, and use them to separate the system as a lapidary cuts his gems. In the meantime, the best definition of a boundary remains a matter for individual judgement – a part of the *art* of simulation, as distinct from the more methodical procedures to be mentioned later.

ANALYSING THE SYSTEM

Suppose we have decided that our system is to contain so many warehouses, lorries and customers' unloading bays; then the next question to be answered is, 'How much detail must we include?' Obviously, a highly detailed model will reproduce the real system more faithfully, but it will also tend to be cumbersome and clumsy. On the other hand, a very rough model will cover a narrower range of activities and give answers with a wider margin of error. Should we, for example, consider each driver to be an integral part of his vehicle or not? Here again we are faced with deciding just what sorts of questions we want the model to deal with. If the driver and the vehicle are to all intents inseparable in real life, then it is pointless to separate them in the model. If, on the other hand, we want to know what will happen if we run our vehicles on two shifts from a pool of drivers, the drivers will have to be represented as separate entities.

In this way we shall arrive at a list of all the physical

components which help to make up the system. Our imaginary transport company might well yield the following list:

Central Warehouse
with two existing bays for loading and up to three possible extra ones.

Five Lorries
and up to three possible extra ones.

Ten Destinations
each with one unloading bay.

STATES OF THE COMPONENTS

Writing down a description of a real process is never an easy job; one is faced with what at first appears to be a chaotic jumble of men and machines. In order to unravel the separate threads of activity, the investigator needs a methodical procedure. Work study, for instance, has given us the flow process chart, the multiple activity chart and so on. These can be helpful, although they are not sufficient in themselves; a more specialized procedure is needed for a simulation. One widely-used method is to list the 'states' of each component and then to discover the rules which govern changes from one state to another.

To take a simple example, our loading bays can be 'Vacant' or 'Occupied', which we call State 1 and State 0 respectively. The lorries, however, can exist in any one of five states.

State 1 = At warehouse, waiting to load.
State 2 = At loading bay, taking on load.
State 3 = Full, moving from loading bay to destination.
State 4 = At destination, unloading.
State 5 = Empty, moving from destination to warehouse.

The possible transitions between these five states are very restricted. They are shown in Figure 7.3.

We shall use this diagram to build up a simulation routine, but it should be pointed out that in practice we should almost

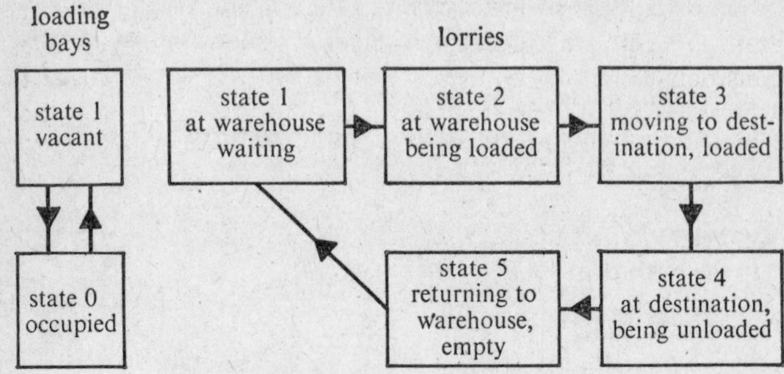

Fig. 7.3 States of the components of a system

certainly need a wider range of states and transitions, as exemplified by Figure 7.4. The 'non-existent' state which this shows (State 0) is a useful device when we are dealing with an

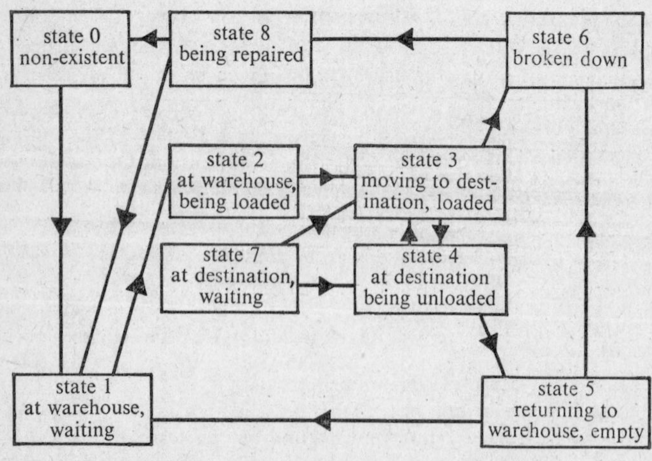

Fig. 7.4 A more complicated set of lorry states

expanding business and want to bring in new vehicles during a simulated period of operation. Another big difference from Figure 7.3 is that *alternative* transitions are possible: a vehicle may go from State 3 to any of States 4, 6 or 7.

Some builders of simulation models would prefer to put Figure 7.4 into a different form – a table or 'matrix' of possible transitions; Figure 7.5 shows the diagram from Figure 7.4 expressed in this alternative way. The entry '1' means that the

first state \ second state	0	1	2	3	4	5	6	7	8
0	1	1	0	0	0	0	0	0	0
1	0	1	1	0	0	0	0	0	0
2	0	0	1	1	0	0	0	0	0
3	0	0	0	1	1	0	1	1	0
4	0	0	0	1	1	1	0	0	0
5	0	1	0	0	0	1	1	0	0
6	0	0	0	0	0	0	1	0	1
7	0	0	0	0	1	0	0	1	0
8	1	1	1	0	0	0	0	0	1

Fig. 7.5 Matrix corresponding to Figure 7.4

transition is possible, whereas '0' shows it to be impossible. A brief study will show that Figures 7.4 and 7.5 do in fact represent the same set of connexions between states.

Finally, returning to Figure 7.3, we can see that this abstract diagram is a general one and could be used to represent not only a lorry, but also a goods train, a ship, an aircraft or even a man with a wheelbarrow.

Exercise 7.2

Draw up a list of states which would adequately describe some repetitive process with which you are familiar. Possible examples are:

(a) Wallpapering a room.
(b) Answering a mixed pile of correspondence.
(c) Mowing a lawn.
(d) The work of a barber's shop.

CLOCKS

The components of the system have been selected, their states defined and their possible transitions listed; what is the next step? Obviously we must now find out the *rules* which govern the transitions. One simple and common rule is that a transition from one state to another occurs purely because time has elapsed. The simulation therefore needs a *clock*, which is no more than a simple counter, to govern its changes.

There is no reason why the time kept by the clock should be the same as time in the real world – indeed, there is good reason why it should not. One of the objects of a simulation is to accumulate experience at a much faster rate than is possible in real life, so our 'simulated time' will usually pass more quickly than natural time.

The clock in our model will go on counting up seconds, minutes, hours or days until it reaches some pre-set figure at which it stops the simulation run, itself included, like the time switch on an electric cooker.

How long should each 'tick' be? We have met a similar question before, in considering the physical components of the system: essentially it can be reduced to 'How much detail do we want the model to include?' Here again we must strike a balance between precision and practicability: simulating the flow of neutrons in a nuclear reactor may call for a 'tick' of a millionth of a second, but in an industrial model such as our transport company we are more likely to need a unit of several minutes or even an hour. The decision rests with the simulator – he is free to choose a time unit as long or as short as he pleases, knowing that the longer the unit, the faster but cruder his simulation will be.

TRANSITIONS OF STATE

Let us look at a specific transition in Figure 7.3 – from State 4 to State 5. Suppose that in real life a lorry is always unloaded in one hour, and that we have chosen an hour as our 'tick', or unit of time. The transition rule is a simple one: 'A lorry in State 4 automatically passes to State 5 in the next time period'. In terms of the flow diagram in Figure 7.1, the same rule can be expressed as follows:

Advance clock by one unit.
Was lorry in State 4?
If the answer is yes, change the state of the lorry to 5.

When the lorry reaches State 5, we must know the circumstance in which it will pass to State 1. This obviously depends on the duration of the return journey – say, 3 hours. One convenient way of effecting the transition is to put a counter in the lorry which can be set to three hours and which will count down as the clock ticks away. The rule for the next transition is then, 'If the lorry is in State 5 and its counter registers zero, then change its State to 1'. This rule may be condensed into a mathematical notation such as

$$L\,5 \rightarrow 1, \qquad C = 0 \tag{7.1}$$

(reading L as 'Lorry State' → as 'becomes' and the comma as 'if').

RANDOM EFFECTS

Sometimes we cannot say definitely whether a lorry will take 2, 3 or 4 hours for the return journey, because the time varies randomly between these three values. Then before we can set the counter on our lorry we must know the relative frequencies of these periods in real life; suppose they were:

2 hours: 25% of the journeys
3 hours: 50% ,, ,, ,,
4 hours: 25% ,, ,, ,,

This simple frequency distribution is easy to simulate. Whenever we wish to set the counter for a return journey we may toss two coins and use the rule –

For 2 heads, take 2 hours:
For a head and a tail, take 3 hours:
For 2 tails, take 4 hours,

– because a head and a tail together will occur twice as frequently as either two heads or two tails.

In this way, we make a random selection from a frequency distribution. Simulations are especially useful when many random factors have to be considered, and a good deal of the research into the subject is devoted to the methods of generating random numbers and reproducing frequency distributions. The methods which are used may be grouped into two main classes: first, truly random numbers may be taken from a table; secondly, a device like 'Ernie' (Electronic Random Number Indicating Equipment) may be used. Both are rather clumsy; for convenience, genuinely random numbers are replaced by 'pseudo-random' numbers; these are generated by fairly simple calculations which are known to produce strings of numbers indistinguishable in the short run from truly random ones.

Typical of these calculations is the 'mid-square' method, in which a large number is squared and its middle digits taken as a random sequence. They in turn are squared and produce the next sequence: Tocher[65] quotes the following example:

$$76^2 = 5776$$
$$77^2 = 5929$$
$$92^2 = 8464$$
$$46^2 = 2116$$
$$11^2 = 0121$$
$$12^2 = 0144 \quad \text{etc.}$$

This method, due to Von Neumann, is by no means infallible, as the following sequence shows:

$$84^2 = 7056$$
$$05^2 = 0025$$
$$02^2 = 0004$$
$$00^2 = 0000$$
$$00^2 = 0000$$

There seems little point in striving too earnestly after perfection in this matter, since eminent mathematicians themselves have been known to disagree on the question of what 'truly random' means.

The frequency distribution quoted above is much simpler than any we should meet in reality. One is more likely to find the journey times distributed in a less tidy way – for example,

Journey Time	*Frequency*	*Random Numbers Allocated*
1 hour	nil	
2 hours	23%	01–23
3 hours	36%	24–59
4 hours	29%	60–88
5 hours	11%	89–99
6 hours	1%	100
Total	100%	

Then to obtain the time for any single journey we pick a random number from the range 1 to 100 inclusive and look up the corresponding journey time in the table.

If the frequency distribution can be fitted to one of the known statistical patterns, (e.g. Gaussian or Poisson), the time for a single journey can be calculated mathematically from a random number without the need for a tabulated list of values. For simulations on an electronic computer, sub-routines which will generate pseudo-random numbers and derive statistics from standard frequency distributions are usually preferred to those which use tables, because they make less demands on the limited storage capacity of the machine.

A roulette wheel is a simple mechanical method of producing a string of random numbers, and consequently this part of the simulation process is often referred to as 'the Monte Carlo method'. The same phrase is sometimes used for describing an entire simulation in which random effects are introduced, and is therefore ambiguous.

CONDITIONAL TRANSITIONS

The transition from State 1 to State 2 differs from those already discussed, in that it depends upon the states of the loading bays. If all of these are occupied, then, obviously, no more lorries can pass from State 1 to State 2 until a bay becomes free.

Conditions such as this one link the various components

together, and to enumerate them completely calls for careful logical analysis. If a computer is to be used, then even such elementary rules as 'No two bodies can occupy the same space at the same time' must be explicitly stated, otherwise the misnamed 'electronic brain' will overlook them. In fact, the time spent on conventional mathematics in the average industrial simulation is likely to be small in comparison with that devoted to logic.

Exercise 7.3

If 'State 0' means 'Occupied' when applied to a loading bay, can you think of a simple test which would tell whether *any* bay was free? (Try addition.)

TRANSITION PROBABILITIES

How often does a lorry break down? In our imaginary transport company, only rarely – once in every thousand deliveries, let us say. If we wish to include breakdowns in our simulation, as in Figure 7.4, then we must arrange for the transition from State 3 to State 6 to have a probability of 0·001. Each time a vehicle is in State 3, a random number from 1 to 1,000 is selected: if it happens to be 1,000, the next transition will be to State 6 instead of State 7 or State 4.

TIME-CONTROLLED TRANSITIONS

When listing the physical components of the system, we took into account certain vehicles which might be added to the system during a simulated period of operation; similarly, they could be removed from the system. Changes of this sort would take place at times which were specified beforehand; an 'unborn' lorry would carry a 'date of birth' as part of its specification, and the transition from State 0 to State 1 would take place when the clock reached this date.

CRITERION OF PERFORMANCE

There can be no point at all in simulating a system unless we measure its performance in some way. In other words, the right hand control loop in Figure 7.2 must be closed with a 'feed-back' to the controller.

The criterion of performance will usually be some measure of cost or profit: indeed, Figure 7.2 suggests that it will correspond to the returns which the executive receives from the real-life system.

For the sake of simplicity, we may choose to use a measure such as 'idle machine-hours', on the grounds that a reduction in idleness will automatically bring down operating costs. These are only valid for the simplest models; when several diverse activities take place in the simulation, measurement in terms of money is the only way of reducing them to a common unit.

A SIMPLE EXAMPLE

In order to show how all these parts are assembled into a complete model let us consider the imaginary case of the Fetter Lane Transport Company. It has a central warehouse with two loading bays, and five lorries which run continuously to various destinations. The average time for an outward journey is 2 hours 50 minutes; for a return journey it is 2 hours 40 minutes. These times are not constant: they vary in a random manner as follows:

Time of Journey	*Percentage of Occasions* *Outward*	*Inward*
	(State 3)	(State 5)
2 hours	33⅓%	50%
3 hours	50%	33⅓%
4 hours	16⅔%	16⅔%

Loading at the warehouse takes 2 hours and unloading at the destination takes 1 hour. After returning to the warehouse, each lorry must wait at least 1 hour for service and paper work, and may have to wait longer if there is no loading bay vacant.

The complete cycle of operations can therefore be represented by Figure 7.3; the expected time for a return trip is 9½ hours, made up of:

Waiting	(State 1)	1 hour
Loading	(State 2)	2 hours
Delivering	(State 3)	2 hours 50 minutes
Unloading	(State 4)	1 hour
Returning	(State 5)	2 hours 40 minutes
	Total	9 hours 30 minutes

Each lorry spends less than a quarter of its total journey time at a loading bay, so one bay should be adequate to deal with four lorries if they arrive in a steady stream. However, variations in the journey times sometimes cause lorries to 'bunch' together so that they have to wait for a loading bay to fall vacant.

These delays are not serious at present, but the company proposes to buy three more lorries to deal with increasing business. The congestion at the bays will obviously get worse: how serious will it be? Would it be bad enough to justify a third loading bay?

The flowsheet for the simulation model is shown in Figure 7.6. The criterion of performance is the pattern of delays suffered by the lorries, and we have arranged to count the number of delays of 1 hour each, the number lasting 2 hours and so on. These numbers are to be stored in a set of 'delay registers' which are set to zero at first (Box 1) and increased (Box 18) whenever a lorry which has been delayed moves to the loading bay.

The 'tick' of the master clock is one hour. Each simulated lorry is given its own private clock, called the 'counter', which is arranged to count down to zero. When the counter reaches zero, the lorry moves to the next state unless it happens to be in State 1 and no loading bay is available: it must then wait, and the delay is registered as a negative number on the counter.

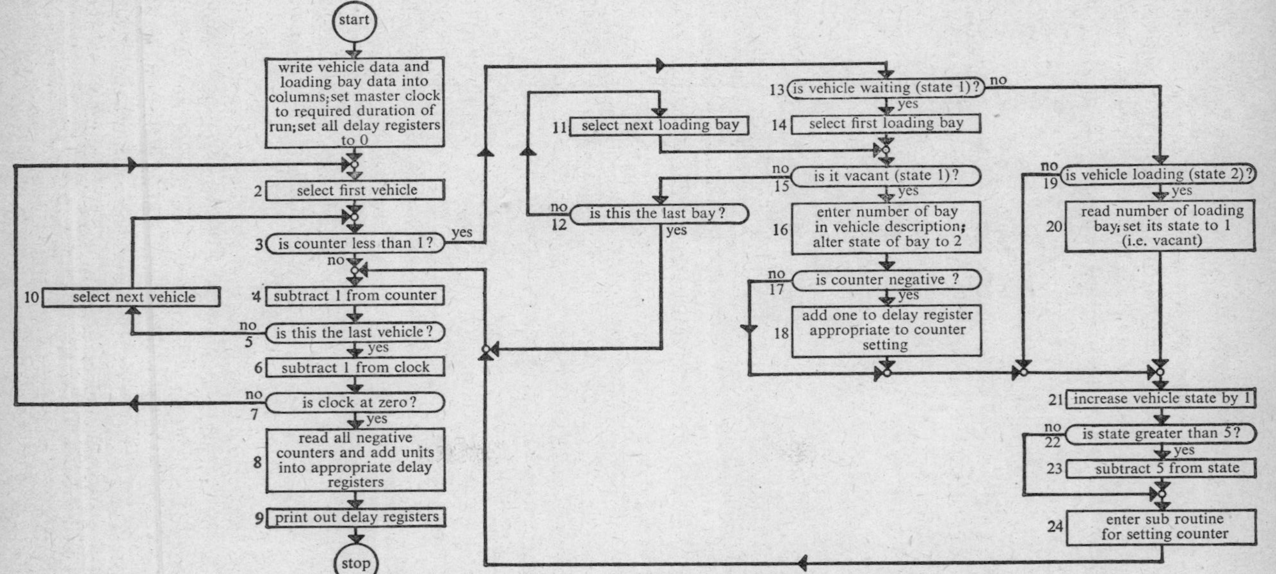

Fig. 7.6 Simulation flowsheet for the Fetter Lane Transport Company

The rest of the flowsheet is not difficult to follow; the sub-routine in Box 24 uses the throw of a die to select the journey times for States 3 and 5; Figure 7.7 gives it in detail.

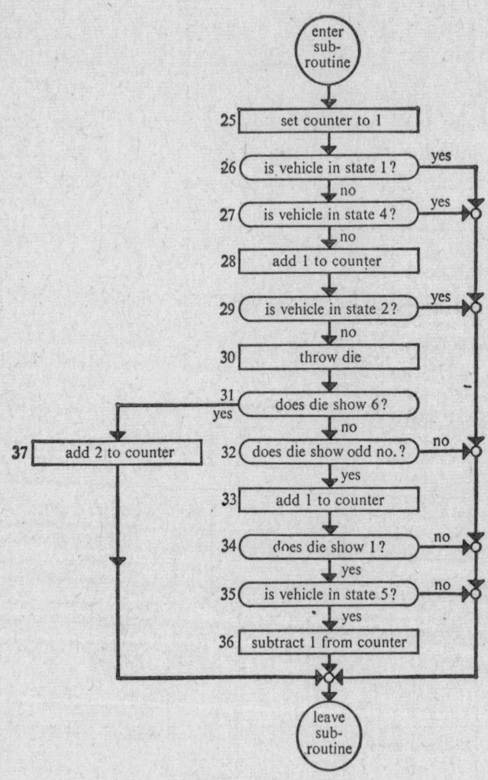

Fig. 7.7 Sub-routine for setting counters

The routine shown in Figures 7.6 and 7.7 is interesting in two ways. First, it can deal with any number of lorries and any number of bays without modification. Secondly, it leaves nothing to imagination or common-sense, and can therefore be used as the basis for a computer programme, as is explained in the next chapter. It can also be used to 'programme' or teach a human being: you will find that if you work your way through the routine it will not be long before you start skipping odd steps here and there. It only needs about a hundred simulated time periods to impress the whole routine on your memory.

INPUT DATA

In order to start the model working, we must describe the current states of the components, as shown in the first column of Figure 7.8. Here we are simulating the existing fleet of five

		clock settings											
lorry no.	100 input	99	98	97	96	95	94	93	92	91	2	1	0
1 state	5	1	2		3			4	5		5		
counter	0	1	2	0	3	1	0	1	2	0	1	0	
counter		0	1		2			0	1				
bay			1										
2 state	2		3		4	5		1	2		4	5	
counter	1	0	2	0	1	2	0	1	2	0	1	3	
counter			1		0	1		0	1		0	2	
bay	2								2				
3 state	3		4	5			1	2		3	2		
counter	1	0	1	3	1	0	1	2	0	3	2	0	
counter			0	2			0	1		2	1		
bay								1			2		
4 state	3				4	5		1		2	5		
counter	3	2	1	0	1	2	0	1	–1	2	2	0	
counter					0	1		0		1	1		
bay										1			
5 state	2	3				4	5			1	3		
counter	0	4	2	1	0	1	3	1	0	1	2	0	
counter		3				0	2			0	1		
bay	1												
loading bay no.													
1 state	2	1	2		1			2		1	1		
state										2			
2 state	2		1						2		2		
state													
delay registers													
–1	0									1			6
–2	0												2
–3	0												0
–4	0												0
–5	0												0

Fig. 7.8 Results of simulation

lorries; No. 1 will complete its return journey in the next hour; No. 2 is loading at the second bay and No. 5 is about to finish loading at the first; Nos. 3 and 4 are on the outward journey.

Both loading bays are occupied, and the master clock is set so that the model will stop after it has simulated 100 hours' working.

The first delay occurs in the eighth hour (column 92) and affects lorry No. 4. By the time the run has ended, six delays of one hour and two of two hours have been registered. If the simulated delays agree with those observed in the real system, we are justified in assuming that the model is good enough for our needs, and using it as a basis for experimentation.

EXPERIMENTING WITH THE MODEL

Putting another three lorries into the model is very simple: we simply add their descriptions to the input data and repeat the simulation run.

With eight lorries, for instance, we get the following comparison:

Number of delays of	*5 lorries*		*8 lorries*	
	2 bays	*3 bays*	*2 bays*	*3 bays*
1 hour	6	0	25	0
2 hours	2	0	5	0
More than 2 hours	0	0	0	0

These results, being derived from random numbers, are themselves liable to random variations, and the prudent experimenter will carry out several runs for each combination of bays and lorries, and apply statistical tests of significance to his results. If the runs are to yield the greatest possible amount of information, they should be arranged according to modern principles of experimental design.[58]

The model described above has been purposely kept simple, but in fact a very similar routine has been used by a large distributor of petroleum products as an aid to designing the loading points in a depot.

EXTENSIONS OF THE MODEL

Sometimes the first definition of a model turns out to be inadequate, because one cannot always assess the problems perfectly in the first place: this follows the scientific tradition, in which one experiment may point the way to the next.

If we study the working of which Figure 7.8 is a summary, we find that as many as three lorries may be in State 4 (unloading at destination) simultaneously. An observation like this may well lead us to ask, 'Have we been too vague about the destinations? Should we identify them as separate components and take account of possible delays there as well?' Such questions may lead us to extend the model into a more detailed form.

OTHER METHODS

The method used for building the model of the Fetter Lane Transport Company is only one of several which are available. It was appropriate to this example because at least one 'event' or change of state occurs in each time period. When the 'tick' of the master clock is short compared with the journey times, it may be more appropriate to jump forward by the amount shown on the lowest counter – that is to say, to the next event. We may go further and include the next event but one, and so on, so that we find ourselves *sorting* the lorries into the order of their counters.

This and other problems of model-building are discussed in a survey by Conway and others,[59] Harling,[60] Youle and others[61] and Tocher.[62] A bibliography of papers has also been compiled by Malcolm[63]; it is significant that of the 94 papers on industrial simulation listed in it, only 4 were published before 1954.

HUMAN DECISIONS IN SIMULATION

Sometimes a system we want to simulate contains human beings who inject decisions based on judgement. How can we incorporate them into our model?

An investigation may show that the allegedly 'inspired' decisions can be reduced to a set of logical rules or replaced by an optimizing technique such as linear programming. It is not uncommon for the scientific analysis of the system to show up its present inadequacies, and suggest means of overcoming them before the model is even built. (A similar phenomenon has been observed in computer feasibility studies.)

Alternatively, we may acknowledge the impossibility of rationalizing the decisions and stop the simulation run each time one is required. Then the model will supply the data on which the decision is based; after it has been made, the results are fed in as a fresh set of input data and the run is resumed. A typical example is in preparing a machine-loading programme or a delivery schedule for vehicles.

MANAGEMENT GAMES

We have already seen that a model can provide a means of experimenting with decisions and learning by mistakes. This forms the basis of management games, in which human beings are made to play major parts in a simulated business organization. Management games have become a subject in their own right, and can only be given a passing mention here.

THE ROLE OF COMPUTERS IN SIMULATION

A computer is not a prerequisite for a simulation model: much of the work quoted in the literature has been done with no more equipment than pencil and paper. Nevertheless, this type of work lends itself very readily to electronic computation, because it comprises a number of repetitive 'loops' of instructions, controlled by simple 'yes-no' decisions.

The high speed of an electronic computer allows us to accumulate 'experience' with the model much more quickly than in real life. For example, the British Petroleum Company have used their 'Mercury' computer to investigate the distribution of petrol and fuel oil in Belgium. One year's operations can be simulated in great detail in rather less than an hour, and the results are printed out as estimates of monthly operating costs. The effects of seasonal variations in demand have been analysed; so have the economics of changing the constitution of the barge fleet and providing additional storage at selected points. In effect, the simulation sorts out the possibilities of new capital investment according to their profitability; it also predicts the cost savings which will accrue from alterations in the day-to-day running of the business.

Some teams of investigators, including those at B.I.S.R.A. and the United Steel Company, have developed general simulation programmes for computers; these are essentially ways of describing the system in a methodical layout, which the computer itself can interpret into its own 'language' of instructions. The question of applying computers will be dealt with at greater length in the next chapter.

SIMULATION AND ANALYSIS

The problem of the Fetter Lane Transport Company, as laid out in Figure 7.3, could have been solved analytically by using a branch of mathematical statistics called the 'theory of queues'. One of the criticisms directed at people who build simulation models is that they are lazy men looking for some way of avoiding the mathematical analysis which would give them a more elegant, more general and ultimately quicker means of disposing of their problems.

> And therefore a general custom of simulation is a vice, rising either of a natural falseness or fearfulness, or of a mind that hath some main faults, which because a man must needs disguise, it making him practise simulation in other things, lest his hand should be out of use.[64]

Such criticism is rarely justified, because very few practical situations can be effectively reduced to such simple terms. Nevertheless, the process of building a simulation model is essentially a simple one, calling for clear thought rather than mathematical sophistication.

The far-sighted manager, confronted with a complex problem in his own business, would do well to ask himself, 'Can simulation help me?' He may be surprised to find out how often the answer is 'Yes'. In fact, with Cambridge research workers helping 'Neddy' with a model of the entire national economy, we may find our business affected by a computer simulation whether we like it or not.

INDUSTRIAL DYNAMICS

A group of research workers at the Massachusetts Institute of Technology under Forrester[66] is investigating some of the problems of very large business organizations with the aid of a

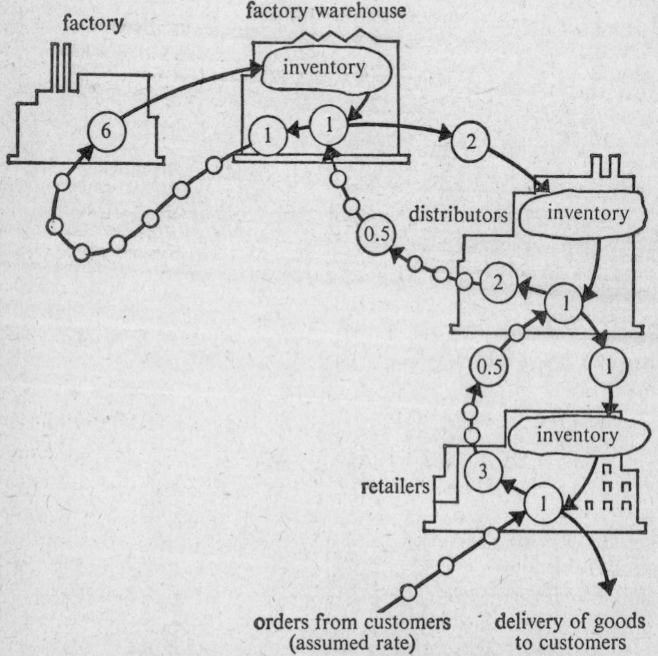

Fig. 7.9 The encircled figures give the time in weeks needed for the transfer or processing of goods and documents

simulation programme called 'Dynamo'. They call this study 'Industrial Dynamics' and have tended to concentrate on systems which are made up of chains such as factory–warehouse–distributor–retailer, (Figure 7.9) in which the relevant variables are either 'levels' or 'flows' controlled by managerial decisions at specified points. The simple flow diagram in Figure 7.9 is analysed into elements which contain these three factors: Figure 7.10 shows the first stage of the analysis. In

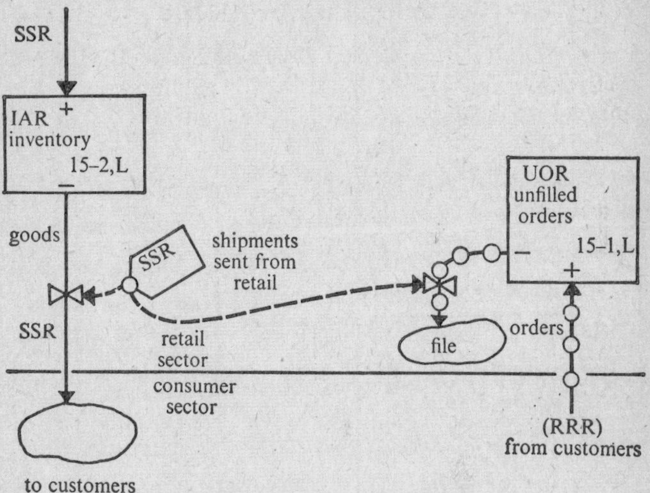

Fig. 7.10 Industrial Dynamics – Block Diagram

this diagram, the rectangle on the right shows unfulfilled orders and defines the mathematical symbol used to represent them, *UOR*, a coded reference number and an indication that this is a *level* (*L*).

Requisitions Received from Retail (*RRR*) add to this level, as the plus sign shows, and Shipments Sent from Retail (*SSR*) subtract from it: both these are *rates*. The functional relationship between the variables is expressed as an equation.

$$UOR.K = UOR.J + (DT)(RRR.JK - SSR.JK)$$

This is read as 'The Unfulfilled Orders at Retail at time *K*

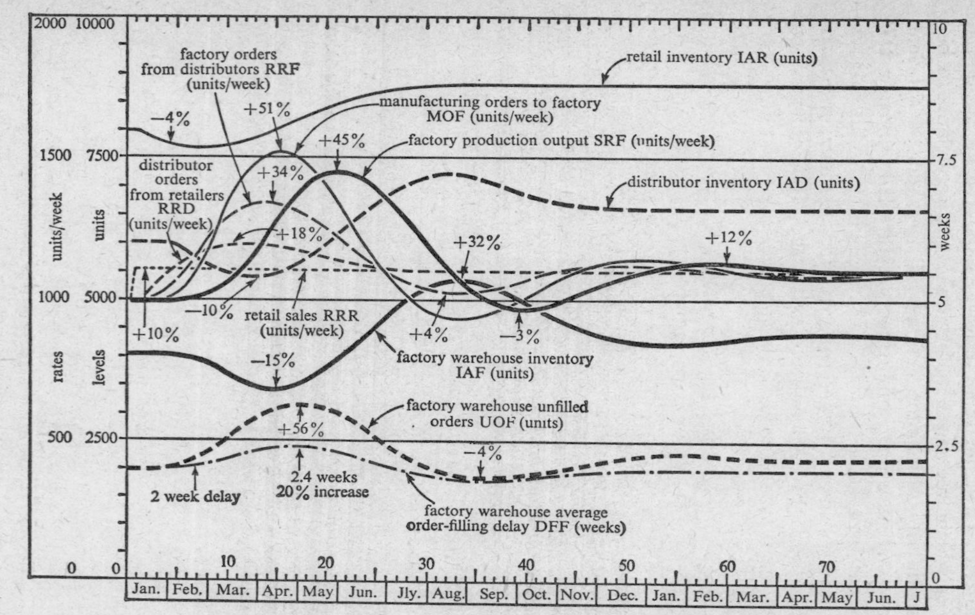

Fig. 7.11 Industrial Dynamics – Response Curves

equal the Unfulfilled Orders at Retail at time *J* plus an adjustment term. The adjustment term is the difference between the rate at which Requisitions Received from Retail flow in between times *J* and *K* and the rate at which Shipments Sent from Retail flow out, multiplied by the time interval *DT* between *J* and *K*.'

The whole structure of a production-distribution system may be built up in this way as a set of 73 equations which constitute a mathematical model of it. They are, in effect, written in an 'autocode' language which the Dynamo simulation programme will accept. The desired input, consisting of a set of starting conditions and specified pattern of sales (*RRR*) may then be fed in and the behaviour pattern studied. In one simulation, a sudden 10% increase in an otherwise steady rate of sales produced the response shown in Figure 7.11. Fifteen weeks after the sales increased, the rate of production at the factory had surged up to an increase of 45%; forty weeks later it had swung back in an over-correction, and only after about seventy weeks could it be considered to have completely adjusted itself to the new rate of sales.

Forrester has shown that violent oscillations of this sort can occur in organizations with a chain structure, even though the individual links in the chain may be managed according to rational rules. Since such chains occur in the national economy (Figure 7.12) which is known to have a boom–slump cycle, the potential importance of industrial dynamics is self-evident. One has only to read 'sales of motor-cars' for 'retailers' and 'the steel industry' for 'factory' to see how Britain's recent economic history might be explained, and its future productivity improved, by the application of industrial dynamics.

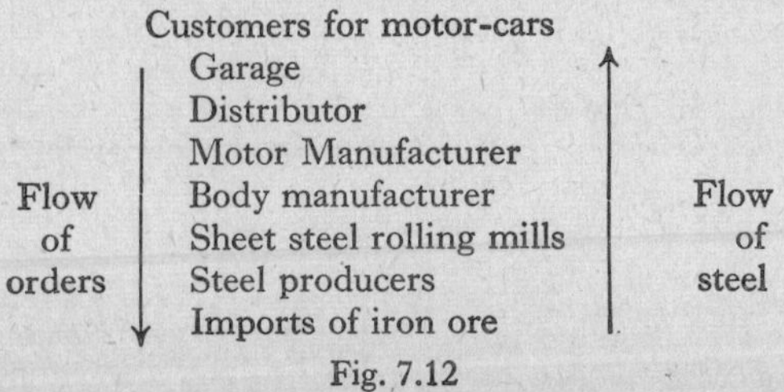

Fig. 7.12

7
Solutions to Exercises

Exercise 7.1

No, because the game has been completely defined by a logical flowsheet which calls for no human decision to be made.

Exercise 7.2

Are you quite sure that you have not tried to get too much detail into your diagram?

Exercise 7.3

Add all the state numbers together. If the answer is zero, all the bays must be occupied; if it is not zero, at least one bay is vacant.

NOTES AND REFERENCES

48 Jones, H. G., and Lee, A. M., *Monte Carlo Methods in Heavy Industry*, Operational Research Quarterly, September 1955, p. 108.

49 Thomas, G. W., Ramm, R. Q., and Rees, H. M., *Track Times and Soaking Pits*, Proceedings of the Second International Conference on Operational Research (1960), p. 336.

50 Lombaers, H. J. M., *Determining the One-Unloading Capacity of a Harbour Installation by Simulation on a Computer*, Proceedings of the Second International Conference on Operational Research (1960), p. 328.

51 McKee, P. R., Robinson, F. D., and Swan, A. W., *An Investigation into the Materials Handling System of a Fabrication Works*, Operational Research Quarterly, June 1962, p. 145.

52 Moody, L. A., *Production Allocation in the Beet Sugar Industry*, Proceedings of the Second International Conference on Operational Research (1960), p. 237.

53 Ventura, E., *Étude du roulage dans une mine par les méthodes de simulation*, Proceedings of the Second International Conference on Operational Research, p. 633.

54 Clapham, J. C. R., *A Monte Carlo Problem in Underground Communications*, Operational Research Quarterly, March 1958, p. 36.

55 Lathrop, J. B., *The Application of Operational Research Methods to Transport*, Proceedings of the Second International Conference on Operational Research (1960), p. 647.

56 Edwards, J. A., *Simulating traffic flow problems on a Computer*, Data Processing, July–September 1962, p. 192.
57 Adams, R. H., and Jenkins, J. L., *Simulation of Air Operations with the Air-Battle Model*, Operations Research, September–October 1960, p. 600.
58 Davies, O. L. (ed.), *The Design and Analysis of Industrial Experiments* (Oliver & Boyd).
59 Conway, R. W., Johnson, B. M., and Maxwell, W. L., *Some Problems of Digital Systems Simulation*, Management Science, October 1959, p. 92.
60 Harling, J., *Simulation Techniques in Operational Research*, Operational Research Quarterly, March 1958, p. 9.
61 Youle, P. V., Tocher, H. D., Jessop, W. N., and Musk, F. J., *Simulation Studies of Industrial Operations*, Journal of the Royal Statistical Society, Series A, 1959 (Part 4), p. 484.
62 Tocher, K. D., *The Role of Models in Operational Research*, Journal of the Royal Statistical Society, Series A, 1961 (Part 2), p. 121.
63 Malcolm, D. G., *Bibliography on the Use of Simulation in Management Analysis*, Operations Research, March–April 1961, p. 169.
64 Bacon, Francis (1561–1626), Essay *Of Simulation and Dissimulation.*
65 Tocher, K. D., *The Art of Simulation* (E.U.P., 1963), p. 73.
66 Forrester, J., *Industrial Dynamics* (Wiley, 1961).

8
Computers and Common Sense

> The tools of working out salvation
> By mere mechanic operation.
>
> SAMUEL BUTLER, *Hudibras*

INTRODUCTION

How does a manager set about using an electronic computer? Suppose he is a man with no great knowledge of mathematics, working for a company which has neither a computer nor the money to buy one: must he then banish the idea from his mind? So often he does, yet he need not. Let us see how he should go about it, taking as an example the aircraft maintenance project described in Chapter 2.

First he selects a computer service bureau. Then he asks whether they have a standard routine which will do the sort of work he wants. If they have, he sets out the problem in a standard form and selects the way in which he wants the answer printed. Then he gets his answer back; then he pays the bill.

We shall first look at this procedure in more detail; after that we shall see what happens when a standard routine is not available, and then we shall consider some of the wider implications.

FINDING A SERVICE BUREAU

How do you start? The answer may be right under your nose. So many companies have in their ranks a bright young man who has more spare time than the harassed manager, and whose natural curiosity and enthusiasm have led him into the professional circles where computers are talked about. Catch him before frustration drives him elsewhere, enlist his aid, and watch him flower. (If you cannot find such a man, perhaps you should transfer your own attention from computer applications to the wider issues of management succession in your firm.)

The nearest university or technical college would be the next source of information. Some of them have computers of their own, which they may run either independently or in collaboration with the manufacturers. You may, if you are lucky, get your work done for nothing. This is most likely to occur if you are willing to release the information for teaching or demonstration purposes afterwards. More probably, you will have to pay for the use of the machine at the same rates as the manufacturer himself would charge. What is quite certain is that any academic institution will do its utmost to give you helpful and unbiased advice.

Your search will most probably end in one of the service bureaux run by a manufacturer. If it does, you should realize at the outset that the manufacturer's main purpose is to sell or lease the machines he makes, and the service bureau is only a means to this end. However, this attitude is already changing; the idea of running a few very big computers as a public service has already taken root in the United States and may soon spread to Europe.

In the meantime, England has more computing service facilities, relative to its needs, than any other country, including the United States. One British manufacturer is even experimenting with a 'launderette' service where customers themselves will be allowed to operate the machines. Most of the bureaux are in London, but many have been established in provincial cities; lists of them are published from time to time in the computer journals.

The final selection of a bureau must inevitably depend on guesswork, friendly advice and the manager's native shrewdness. A big manufacturer may have a wider range of standard routines and plenty of expert help available (at an appropriate fee). A smaller one may, on the other hand, be able to offer more personal attention. The bureau chosen for the example in this chapter is not necessarily better or worse than the others.

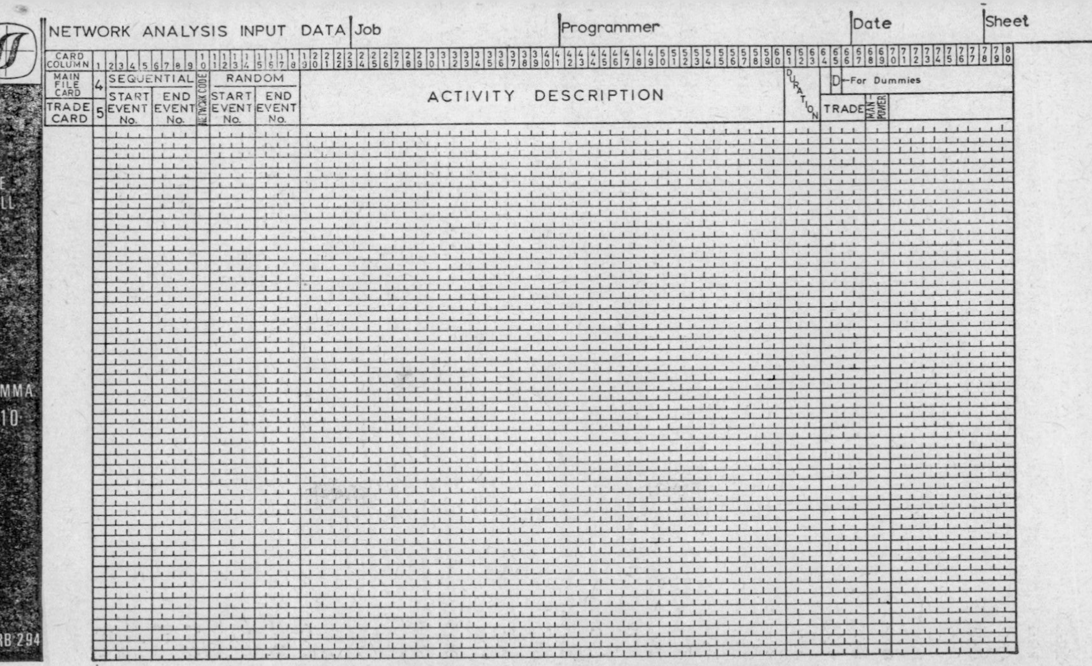

Fig. 8.1 Standard input form for network analysis

DE LA RUE BULL GAMMA 10 DLRB 294

NETWORK ANALYSIS INPUT DATA | Job SCHEDULE FOR AIRCRAFT OVERHAUL | Programmer C. S. KEHELA | Date 4/5/65 | Sheet 1

MAIN FILE CARD 4 — TRADE CARD 5 — D — For Dummies

Card	Sequential Start Event No.	Sequential End Event No.	Network Code	Random Start Event No.	Random End Event No.	Activity Description	Duration	Trade	Man-power
4	1	2				PREPARE FOR INSPECTION	1		
4	2	3				INSPECT AIRFRAME	10		
4	2	4				CLEAN & REMOVE WHEELS	4		
4	2	12				UNPANEL FOR LUBO ETC.	1		
4	2	15				UNPANEL ENGINES	3		
4	3	30				RECTIFY AIRFRAME	28		
4	4	5				INSPECT MAIN WHEELS	7		
4	4	6				INSPECT NOSE WHEEL	6		
4	5	7				RECTIFY MAIN WHEELS	9		
4	6	7				RECTIFY NOSE WHEEL	8		
4	7	10				TEST RETRACTION	1		
4	10	11				RECHARGE EMERGENCY SYSTEM	1		
4	10	30				RECTIFY RETRACTION	3		
4	11	30				DUMMY	0	D	
4	12	13				LUBRICATE	3		
4	12	14				CHECK INSTRUMENTS	18		
4	13	30				CHECK LUBRICATION	1		
4	14	30				RECTIFY INSTRUMENTS	24		
4	15	16				CLEAN PORT ENGINE	1		
4	15	20				CLEAN STARBOARD ENGINE	1		
4	16	17				INSPECT PORT ENGINE	24		
4	16	21				DUMMY	0	D	
4	17	30				RECTIFY PORT ENGINE	36		
4	20	21				DUMMY	0	D	
4	20	23				INSPECT STARBOARD ENGINE	20		
4	21	22				INSPECT FIRE EXTINGUISHERS	2		
4	22	30				RECTIFY FIRE EXTINGUISHERS	11		
4	23	30				RECTIFY STARBOARD ENGINE	30		
4	30	31				GENERAL CHECK	1		

Fig. 8.2 Completed input form

THE PROBLEM

The manager must know what his problem is, and must have reduced it to a calculation or a series of calculations. It is unreasonable to expect a computing service to analyse a practical situation in a business. In the example chosen, the arrow diagram for overhauling the aircraft must have already been drawn up by skilled men, and the durations estimated. It is only necessary to lay it out in the standard input form shown in Figure 8.1.

INPUT FORM

This form is arranged in columns, indicated by the short vertical strokes along each row. The two top rows ('Card Column') identify each column, the total number being 80 (to correspond with the standard punched card).

The method of entering the data is shown in Figure 8.2 and is obvious apart from one or two points. The letter 'I' has to be distinguishable from the figure '1' and zero is written as 'Ø', so as not to be confused with the letter 'O'. The entry '4' in the first column is a coding required by the computer, as are the *D*'s in column 65 wherever the row describes a dummy activity.

The manager will also be asked to supply some further information, such as the time units in which the data are expressed (in this case, hours), the amount of float which defines a sub-critical path (we have chosen 10 hours), and the way in which the output should be presented. As far as he is concerned, the work of preparing the input is now complete. The data are fed to the computer in a suitable form, and the output appears as shown in Figure 8.3. Compare it with Table 2.1: apart from minor differences in layout, they are identical.

The bill for this particular job was

Punching, verifying and sorting cards:	8s. 0d.
Computer time (Gamma 10 machine, 5 mins):	£1 5s. 0d.
Total:	£1 13s. 0d.

DE LA RUE BULL
Machines Limited

114 Southampton Row, London, W.C.1.
Area Offices in Birmingham, Bristol, Dublin,
Glasgow and Manchester.

The Gamma 10 is a computer designed primarily for commercial data processing: but it can also effectively handle technical and Management Science applications—including Scientific Inventory Management, Statistical Forecasting, Linear Programming, Simulation, Production Control and Network Analysis.

This Network Analysis Programme is a practical system for planning and controlling large projects involving construction, manufacture, research and development, etc. It uses the standard Critical Path Scheduling Technique but with a number of refinements and extensions.

It also exploits special features of the machine so as to produce a range of sophisticated analyses, including random numbering of events; calendar date output with allowance for holidays and weekends; scheduled start dates for individual activities; many sort routines; detailed work schedules for foremen; manpower aggregation and levelling; and cost forecasting and monitoring.

DATE: 040565 DE LA RUE BULL NETWORK ANALYSIS PROGRAMME GAMMA 10 PAGE 1

PROJECT: SCHEDULE FOR AIRCRFT OVERHAUL
FLOAT LIMIT: 10
C/P DURATION: 66
NUMBER OF EVENTS: 21

DIVISION: PLANNING
TIME UNIT: HOURS

NUMBER OF ACTIVITIES: 29

REPORT: ALL ACTIVITIES

CRITICAL	NEAR CRITICAL	START EVENT	END EVENT	NET-WORK CODE	ACTIVITY	TRADE	MAN-POWER	DURATION	START EARLIEST	START LATEST	END EARLIEST	END LATEST	TOTAL FLOAT
*	*	1	2		PREPARE FOR INSPECTION			1			1	1	
*	*	2	15		UNPANEL ENGINES			3	1	1	4	4	
*	*	15	16		CLEAN PORT ENGINE			1	4	4	5	5	
*	*	16	17		INSPECT PORT ENGINE			24	5	5	29	29	
*	*	17	30		RECTIFY PORT ENGINE			36	29	29	65	65	
*	*	30	31		GENERAL CHECK			1	65	65	66	66	
	*	15	20		CLEAN STARBOARD ENGINE			1	4	14	5	15	10
	*	20	23		INSPECT STARBOARD ENGINE			20	5	15	25	35	10
	*	23	30		RECTIFY STARBOARD ENGINE			30	25	35	55	65	10
		2	12		UNPANEL FOR LUB. ETC.			1	1	22	2	23	21
		12	14		CHECK INSTRUMENTS			18	2	23	20	41	21
		14	30		RECTIFY INSTRUMENTS			24	20	41	44	65	21
		2	3		INSPECT AIRFRAME			10	1	27	11	37	26
		3	30		RECTIFY AIRFRAME			28	11	37	39	65	26
		2	4		CLEAN, REMOVE WHEELS			4	1	41	5	45	40
		4	5		INSPECT MAIN WHEELS			7	5	45	12	52	40
		5	7		RECTIFY MAIN WHEELS			9	12	52	21	61	40
		7	10		TEST RETRACTION			1	21	61	22	62	40
		10	30		RECTIFY RETRACTION			3	22	62	25	65	40
		4	6		INSPECT NOSE WHEEL			6	5	47	11	53	42
		6	7		RECTIFY NOSE WHEEL			8	11	53	19	61	42
		10	11		RECHARGE EMERGENCY SYSTEM			1	22	64	23	65	42
		21	22		INSPECT FIRE EXTINGUISHERS			2	5	52	7	54	47
		22	30		RECTIFY FIRE EXTINGUISHERS			11	7	54	18	65	47
		12	13		LUBRICATE			3	2	61	5	64	59
		13	30		CHECK LUBRICATION			1	5	64	6	65	59

Fig. 8.3 Network analysis programme: schedule for aircraft overhaul

In practice, a minimum charge is applied. In this bureau it would have been £10, but for this sum one could obtain a similar analysis of a network of 200 jobs.

Let us now look at some of the items in this procedure in more detail, beginning with the computing routine itself.

STANDARD ROUTINES

Standard computing routines are always available for widely-used techniques such as network analysis or linear programming, and the range over which they extend is constantly widening. They are often referred to as 'library programs' or under the general term 'software'. In the early days of commercial computers, the makers put far too much emphasis on the machine itself – the hardware – and too little on the software, but this mistake is rapidly being corrected.

Programs in general will be discussed at greater length later: for the moment it is enough to understand that they turn the general-purpose computer into a machine which can carry out a specific calculation – in our example, finding a critical path. The calculation is always carried out within certain limits imposed either by the machine itself or the nature of the computing routine: they are set out in a Program Specification.

The specification sets out in detail what the program will do and what are its limitations. For example, a network analysis routine may only be able to accept networks of up to a certain size, as defined by the number of events or activities.

Some of the characteristics of the program we used may be seen by studying Figure 8.1. We could have dispensed with the $i\,j$ rule in numbering our original network, because this program can accept and analyse a randomly-numbered network: we have only to enter the event numbers into columns 11 to 18 instead of columns 2 to 9. Had we done so, the cost of computation would have been greater, because the machine would have re-numbered the network before analysing it.

The specification also tells us that we can suppress the printing of dummy activities in the output by entering the letter *D* in column 65, as we did on the input form. Other entries in columns 64 to 69 would enable us to enter the manpower requirements in various trade categories as input, and obtain aggregated figures for the manpower requirements at each stage of the project.

The specification sets out the limitations of the size of numbers: as is obvious from Figure 8.1, the largest permissible number for an event is 9999. The duration of an activity is limited to three digits, and the specification tells us the range of time units in which the duration can be expressed.

In some cases, the specification may contain a formula for calculating roughly how long the computer will take to complete the calculation. A preliminary estimate of the cost could then be made.

OUTPUT FACILITIES

Modern computer programs may offer a choice of various styles and layouts for the output which is usually called the 'print-out'. At one time, the output consisted of strings of figures and abbreviations which were difficult to decipher; then routines for tabulating the data were developed; now the computer can be made to present documents which are suitable for direct use by managers.

Figure 8.4 gives a good illustration of the versatility of computer routines and the wide range of output layouts, because it was produced by the same network analysis program which dealt with our aircraft overhaul. The complete network for launching a new product had been fed into the computer, with each individual activity coded to show the department ('trade') responsible for doing it. After analysing the network, the machine sorted the output into nine separate groups corresponding to the nine departments concerned and printed each group on a separate sheet. Figure 8.4 is the sheet corresponding to the Marketing Department (trade code M). A starting date was fed in with the input, and the event times were translated into calendar dates by one of the optional facilities of the routine. Only the earliest event times are printed out, and they are simply described as 'programmed

DE LA RUE BULL — NETWORK ANALYSIS PROGRAMME — TRADE SORT — GAMMA 10

DIVISION: RUN 1 — DEPARTMENT: MARKETING MANAGER

PROJECT: DREAMSWEET PRODUCT LAUNCH — DATE: 13 APR 65

PAGE 1

TRADE	START EVENT	END EVENT	DESCRIPTION	MP	DUR	PROGRAMMED START	ACTUAL START	PROGRAMMED FINISH	ACTUAL FINISH	REMARKS
M	3	4	PREPARE NEW PRODUCT MEMO NPM		8	18 MAY 65		21 MAY 65		
M	4	10	SEND NPM TO MARKET RESEARCH			21 MAY 65		21 MAY 65		
M	4	7	SEND NPM TO PRODUCTION			21 MAY 65		21 MAY 65		
M	4	5	SEND NPM TO RESEARCH			21 MAY 65		21 MAY 65		
M	4	11	SEND NPM TO ADVERTISING AGENCY			21 MAY 65		21 MAY 65		
M	4	6	SEND NPM TO BUYER			21 MAY 65		21 MAY 65		
M	17	21	FORECAST SALES		10	21 JUN 65		25 JUN 65		
M	21	30	BEGIN TO PREPARE NEW PRODUCT AUTHORITY NPA		10	28 JUN 65		2 JLY 65		
M	21	22	SEND SALES FORECAST TO PRODUCTION			25 JUN 65		25 JUN 65		
M	30	31	COMPLETE NPA		4	21 JLY 65		22 JLY 65		
M	31	43	SEND NPA TO MARKET RESEARCH			22 JLY 65		22 JLY 65		
M	31	45	PREPARE SALES CONFERENCE		60	23 JLY 65		2 SEP 65		
M	31	34	SEND NPA TO ADVERTISING AGENCY			22 JLY 65		22 JLY 65		
M	31	33	SEND NPA TO PRODUCTION			22 JLY 65		22 JLY 65		
M	31	32	SEND NPA TO BUYER			22 JLY 65		22 JLY 65		
M	45	46	RUN SALES CONFERENCE		4	4 OCT 65		5 OCT 65		

Fig. 8.4 Departmental schedule prepared by computer

start' and 'programmed finish'; the critical path and floats are described in a master print-out elsewhere but are suppressed in this part of the output, presumably on the grounds that the Marketing Department might adopt a dangerous '*laissez-faire*' attitude if it knew that some activities had large floats.

The output has also been made to include 'actual start', 'actual finish' and 'remarks', so that it can be filled in directly, returned as a progress report by the Marketing Manager, and used to prepare an amended input for re-scheduling the product launch if the given dates have not been met. (The cost of the complete analysis was about £5.)

PREPARING THE INPUT

How are the data in Figure 8.2 put into the computer? Most modern computers take in both the program and the figures as standard 80-column punched cards. Punch operators put the cards into a punching machine with a keyboard, by means of which they transcribe each figure (or letter) into a hole (or two holes), the position of which corresponds to the value of the corresponding digit.

Figure 8.5 shows the card for the first activity in the aircraft overhaul. Each column has ten positions, numbered from 0 to 9. The identification number of every second column is also printed in fine type between 0 and 1 and again between 8 and 9. This card has been prepared in a machine which also types the character corresponding to the punch-hole, so it is easy to see that the start event number '1' is represented by a hole in row 1 of column 5. Letters are represented by two holes in the same column.

Exercise 8.1

The letter 'F' in the word 'FOR' is represented by two holes. Where are they?

Great care is taken to ensure that cards are punched accurately. Two entirely separate operators prepare packs of cards corresponding to the same set of data, and these duplicated

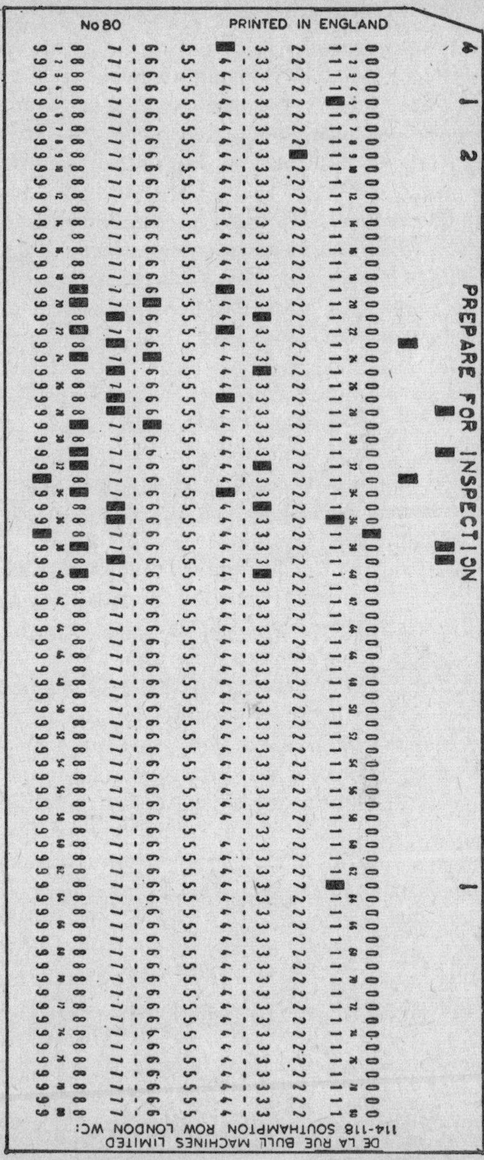

Fig. 8.5 Punched card for first activity

packs are then compared by a machine called a 'verifier'. If the cards in any identical pair fail to agree, the verifier indicates the error. Thus the only possibility of error in the input is for two operators to make exactly the same mistake, which is unlikely. Computers themselves also contain elaborate checking devices.

When the cards are fed into the machine, they pass through a card-reader which detects the holes and their positions with the aid of photo-electric cells. These cells generate electrical impulses corresponding to the appropriate numbers, which are fed into the computer.

The labour needed to punch tapes or cards has always presented a problem to the users of electronic computers. The 'mark-sensed' card is one of the means used to reduce the effort of preparing data; numbers are marked on a card in the appropriate columns with a pencil containing a magnetic 'lead'. A set of magnetic sensing devices then detects the location of each mark and converts it into electrical pulses.

The ideal input machine would be one which could read input directly from printed or even written documents, and some progress has been made in developing one. The Electronic Reading Automaton (E.R.A.) produced by Solartron uses photoelectric cells to detect the pattern of light and dark squares generated by superimposing a scanning grid on to printed numbers. Figure 8.6 shows how the light and dark squares are generated, and how they may be represented by digits, with '1' representing a shaded square and '0' an unshaded one. The machine has the ability to compare the sets of digits with standard patterns stored in it, and thus translate the patterns back into the original numbers. One such machine is in service with Montague Burton Ltd, 'reading', at a speed of 400 digits per second, the tally rolls from cash registers and producing punched cards from them. More modern machines such as the R.C.A. 'Videoscan' use scanning methods similar to those of television and can read up to 1,500 characters a second.

An alternative to optical scanning is to use characters printed in magnetic ink. The MICR system (Magnetic Ink Character Recognition) is mainly used by banks, and the specially designed characters are now becoming a familiar feature of our

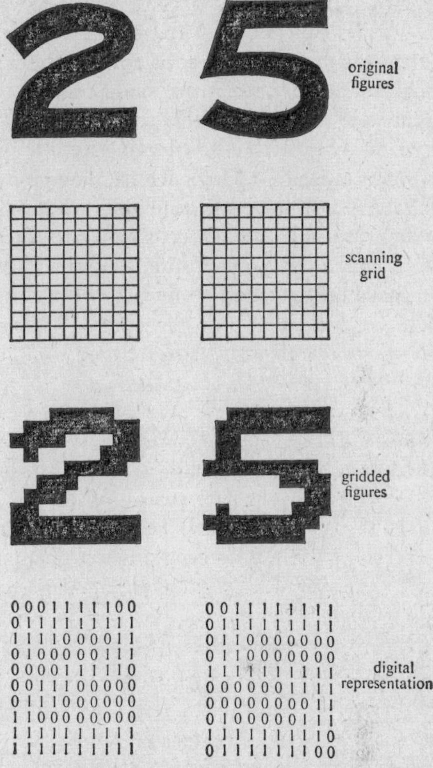

Fig. 8.6 Digital representation of figures

cheque-books. The digits are distorted into shapes which, when printed in magnetic ink, can be readily distinguished by magnetic reading heads while still recognizable by the human eye.

Difficulties in the field of mechanical perception are many – size and alignment of characters, similarities such as 5 and S or I and 1, and defective printing all constitute major problems – but a considerable research effort is being applied to them and it seems only a matter of time before computers will be taking their information direct from the printed page.

ORGANIZATION OF A COMPUTER

The detailed mechanisms which enable a computer to do its work so quickly and accurately are of little interest to the manager. They are often over-emphasized, so that the unfortunate layman is left with a bewildering jumble of impressions about binary arithmetic, logical switching circuits, transistors and the like, which are not really relevant.

It is, however, useful to know the broad areas into which an electronic computer is divided, if only to dispel some of the myths which have accumulated around these machines. They

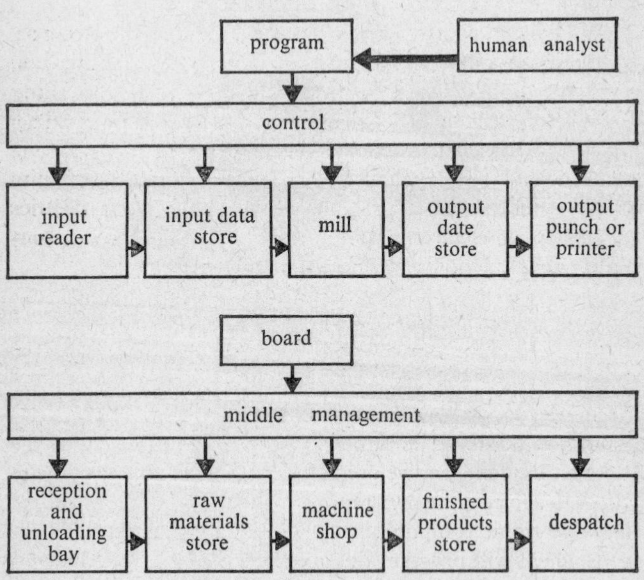

Fig. 8.7 Organizations of electronic computer and engineering factory

are illustrated in Figure 8.7, which also shows a factory organization for comparison.

The complex switching circuits which perform arithmetical and logical operations are the very heart of an electronic computer. It is they who do the 'processing' of the data which are fed to them, and in this sense they are similar to the machine shop of an engineering works or the weaving shed of a textile factory. The resemblance led Charles Babbage to coin the word 'mill' for this part of any calculating engine.

The rest of a computer is built around the mill in much the same way as a conventional factory. The input is taken in as already described, stored as 'raw material' until needed, then fed to the mill and processed; the 'finished' products – output data – are stored until needed and then sent to an output mechanism. All this needs a control – the middle 'management' of the computer – which is held in the internal circuits of the machine.

This built-in control carries out the routine tasks necessary to the efficient internal working of the machine. There is, however, a form of control at a still higher level, corresponding to the policy-making board of a manufacturing company. This is the program of instructions which dictates to the machine exactly what series of calculations it must perform. The ability to accept and act on a program is one of the characteristics which raise an electronic computer far above the level of conventional calculating machines; the other is its speed.

THE PROGRAM

When we use an ordinary desk calculator, we feed in one number to be stored, and then press either the '+' key or the '—' key. By doing so, we prepare or 'program' the machine to add or to subtract the next number to be fed in. The equivalent in an electronic computer is some internal switching arrangement which will program the machine to add. It will be constructed in such a way that a particular set of electrical impulses will operate it, and the set of impulses will correspond to the input of a certain code symbol. Thus, the letter A could mean 'add', the letter S, 'subtract' and the letter M, 'multiply.' The coded instruction, like the numbers themselves, will be fed in by a suitably punched card.

If we have a string of numbers to add on a desk-calculator, we have to keep on pushing the '+' key as each new number is fed in. The electronic computer, on the other hand, can accept and apply a whole sequence of instructions, such as

Read in the first number
Read in the second number
Add the two together to give a sub-total
Read in the third number
Subtract it from the sub-total
Print out the answer

This sequence, when written in the appropriate program code, might be expressed as:

R 1
R 2
A 1 & 2
R 3
S 3
P

This is a very simple form of computer programming, analogous to assembling a few parts in an engineering shop. The programmer has a much greater job of internal management to specify – getting data into and out of the machine, moving blocks of it around from one store to the other, even making such decisions as when to scrap information (which is what we do when we 'round off' a number). How does his work compare with that of managing a business?

In a real factory, the manager can rely to some extent on the training his men have already received. For instance instead of specifying the following operations in detail:

Pick up nut with left hand
Pick up bolt with right hand
Bring nut and bolt together
Align nut and bolt
Push nut on to end of bolt
Turn nut
Repeat turn until nut is tight
Release nut from left hand
Release bolt from right hand,

he can simply issue the overall instruction 'Assemble nut to bolt'. The detailed instructions are already stored as a sub-routine in the man's brain because they are needed so often. If the man were completely unskilled, the manager could still make life easier for himself by having a prepared card available with 'Assemble nut to bolt' as the heading and the program of instructions set out underneath. The man could then teach himself the job.

The computer programmer can organize his own work in a similar way. He can draw up a series of instructions such as

Put $y = 1$
Divide a by y
Add the quotient to y
Halve the sum and use it as a new value of y
Repeat all but the first instruction until further changes in y cannot be detected
Replace a by y

and, after translating them into machine language, punch them on to a set of cards entitled 'Replace a by its square root'.

Exercise 8.2

Putting $a = 100$, check that this series of instructions will replace it by its square root. Do not work to more than four decimal places.

Other sub-routines may deal with cube and higher roots, powers of numbers, logarithms and trigonometrical functions. They are usually written by the manufacturers' programming staff and assembled into a 'library' on punched cards. In this way, the standard computing routines already mentioned are built up.

Programming is not quite so simple as this brief description makes it sound. For one thing, every eventuality must be foreseen: suppose that a network contains a loop which has remained undetected because the events were numbered randomly. When the machine attempts to re-number the network sequentially, it will meet an impossible situation and may stop. On the other hand, it may go on trying over and over again. A good program will stop the machine; a better program may signal the nature of the fault, by printing out 'LOOP', an even better one may print out not only the type of fault, but its location also. The skill, forethought and ingenuity of the programmer play a great part in ensuring the efficiency and versatility of programs.

Commercial operations may also be reduced to standard routines: examples are converting decimals of a pound sterling to shillings and pence, or working out PAYE deductions for compiling payrolls.

Many computer manufacturers have formed users' associations, whose members contribute new standard routines to the library as well as exchanging more specialized programs amongst themselves.

To complete the picture, one must include the standard routines which are permanently built into a computer to deal with essential matters such as starting-up and testing. Unlike programs received through the input, they cannot be erased.

Finally there are the 'compiler' routines which make programming easier. When they are fed into the machine, they set it up so that it can accept instructions in a different 'language' from its normal code. Taking an earlier example, the series of instructions $R1$, $R2$, $A1$ and 2, $R3$, $S3$, P could be generated by a suitable compiler routine from the input $t = a + b - c$.

Compilers also help to make electronic computers interchangeable. The machines made by one manufacturer will have their own particular programming code and those of a second manufacturer will have a different one. If each manufacturer prepares a compiler routine which will translate instructions in some universal 'language' into a program in his own code, then programs written in the universal language can be run on any machine. Such universal languages already exist: they include FORTRAN (Formula Translator), COBOL (Common Business-Oriented Language) and ALGOL (Algebra-Oriented Language).

At one time it was hoped that compilers would become so simple that any layman could learn to program a machine in a few hours. To some extent this has been achieved, and many scientists can prepare simple programs to aid them in their calculations. In general, though, some skilled help will always be needed when a new computing routine is to be created. The problem is especially difficult for managers, since computers can only deal with *Q*-factors.

In general, applying an electronic computer to management problems takes place in two stages, systems analysis and machine coding. The second of these has already been described: the programmer knows at the outset what the calculation is, and has only to translate it into machine language. The other is the far more difficult job of reducing a business problem to a prescribed calculation: this is called Systems Analysis. Sometimes it is straightforward: in putting a payroll calculation on to a computer, the work is first broken down into sections such as basic rates, overtime, piecework rates, incentive bonus, PAYE deductions and so on. A sub-routine is written for each section and the complete program is then built up. A cynic has observed that a payroll calculation is always a good starting point for a new computer, because so many people can be relied on to check the output in great detail.

The work of a Systems Analyst will be more difficult when he comes to deal with business procedures which are not quite so clear-cut; for example, what is the set of rules which a despatcher uses in making up loads for vehicles and deciding their routes? Even the man himself does not know how he reaches his decisions, and methods for obtaining optimum solutions are not yet known. Empirical rules, trial-and-error and statistically designed experiments may all have to be called to the analyst's aid. Whatever the problem, he is almost certain to attack it by drawing up a logical flowsheet.

FLOWSHEETS

We have already met logical flowsheets in Chapter 7, so the example given in Figure 8.8 should look familiar. It represents a simple stock-checking routine; the sausage-shaped 'decision boxes' mark all those points in the system where the next part of the procedure depends upon a test of some numerical value. Box 5 tests whether the stock is at or below the Re-Ordering

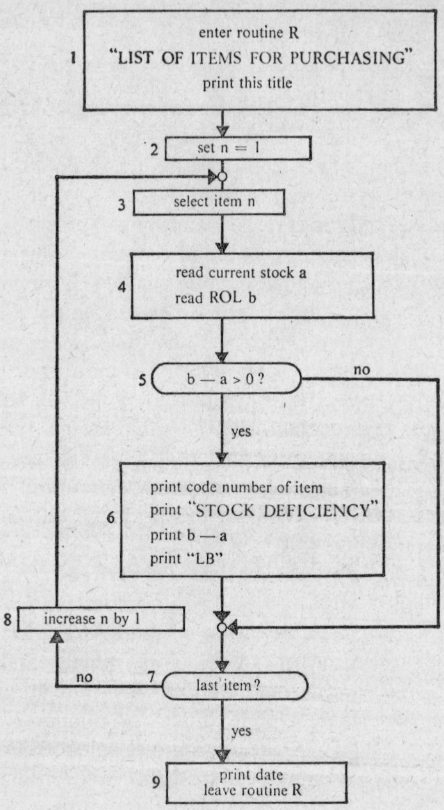

Fig. 8.8 Flowsheet for stock-checking routine

Level. If it is, the item goes into the list to be considered for purchasing (Box 6). If the stock is above the ROL, the item is passed over.

The loop is linked up between Box 7 and Box 3 with the aid of the counter *N*, and enables the same simple routine to examine a large number of items. The capacity to obey looped routines is one of the most powerful weapons in the programmer's hands, and flowsheets will often contain loops within loops. One must always make provision for getting out of loops as well as entering them; this is done by having a decision box – Box 7 in this example – which tests whether the routine should leave the loop or not. A counter is usually the subject of the test: here it is N. If we know the total number of stock items to be checked – call it M – then the test in Box 7 could be simply

$$N = M?$$

The need for Box 7 illustrates one of the weaknesses of computers which most programmers learn painfully through their initial mistakes. You cannot rely on the common sense of an electronic computer, for it has none. In this respect it is a moron, and must be told how to recognize the last item, and to stop when it is reached. Otherwise, it will go on trying to read non-existent data until something breaks down. Neither is it enough to instruct the machine to divide x by y: one must first test that y is not zero.

Exercise 8.3

Use the following list to work through the flowsheet of Figure 8.8 and produce an exception list.

Item No.	*Current Stock, lb.*	*ROL, lb.*
N	a	b
1	316	200
2	150	100
3	75	75
4	369	120
5	12	50
6	0	100

Exercise 8.4

Insert an extra test in Figure 8.8 so that Item No. 3 and others like it will be shown as being just on the Re-Ordering Level.

Exercise 8.5

The flowsheet (Figure 8.9) for finding a square root by the method described earlier is arranged to print out the answer as soon as successive estimates differ by less than 0.01. There is an error in the testing method. Can you detect and correct it? If not, try working through a specimen calculation for $a = 0{\cdot}5$.

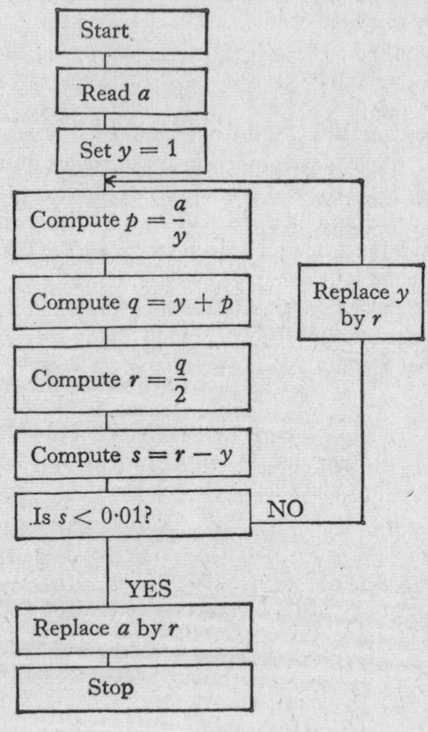

Fig. 8.9

COST OF PROGRAMMING

It must now be obvious that the operation known loosely as 'putting a job on to a computer' is neither easy nor cheap. The demand for computer programmers and systems analysts has grown at a faster rate than the supply, and the facilities for training such men are still inadequate. In consequence, their salaries are high. Detailed analysis of management systems always take longer than one expects, and computer programs do not always work properly the first time. They have to be checked and revised, in the procedure known as 'de-bugging'. The whole process may well consume several man-years of highly skilled work.

The initial cost of programming is therefore high: it can easily run into hundreds or thousands of pounds, even for a relatively simple job. Nevertheless, the situation is already much better than it was a few years ago, and is constantly improving. The advent of compiler routines has already been mentioned: simultaneously, some manufacturers have been developing 'building bricks'. In these, certain complex calculations (such as forecasting procedures) which constantly recur in business problems, are available in a form which can be readily 'slotted in' to bigger programs.

DECISION BOXES

The tests in the decision boxes are no more than traffic signals based on simple logical rules, but some of the consequences of this simple mechanism are far-reaching. It is not difficult to imagine an extension to the flowsheet in Figure 8.8 which would refer to a master file when stock was too low and then set in motion a sub-routine for producing a purchase order, even comparing suppliers' prices and selecting the lower if required to do so. Such procedures do in fact exist. This 'decision-making' power of a computer has given rise to some gross misconceptions. Imagine a personnel officer specifying that, for a particular job, a man should have a degree, an intelligence quotient greater than 120 and be not less than 5′ 8″ tall. A flow sheet can easily be drawn up for selecting the cards corresponding to suitable people from a file pack: this was done, even before computers were available, by the conventional punched card machinery of WOCCI, the War Office Central Card Index. How easy it is to misrepresent this as a machine making a decision about a human being's suitability for a job! This is misplaced anthropomorphism.

We have been warned, by Lorentz and others, not to attribute human emotions and qualities to animals whose behaviour resembles our own. The same warning needs to be repeated about electronic computers. Because electrical engineers have adopted certain jargon terms, such as 'memory' for a store of data; because the machine can be made to imitate learning by suitable programs; because irresponsible or ill-informed writers have labelled them 'electronic brains'; because they can be made to select alternative courses of action: because the finer details of their construction are beyond the comprehension of a layman, these machines have been credited with human or even superhuman attributes and elevated to the status of the businessman's bogy-man.

The computer will make all managers redundant....
The computer will be the next chess champion....
The computer will start the next nuclear war....
The computer says....

The computer says no more than it has been told to say. The most important difference between the two diagrams in Figure 8.7 is the heavy black arrow showing that the management of the machine is imposed on it by an outside agency and not generated spontaneously from within.

The real danger lies in ascribing to the output of computers a sanctity which it does not possess. The program under which it operates may have been drawn up by a man who knows all about the machine but nothing about the business. He may have written a program to calculate economic lot sizes and inserted his own value of that most important figure, the required return on capital. Or he may have devised a method for allocating routes to delivery vehicles which has never been tested in practice. It has truly been said of electronic computers that, whatever else they do, they will faithfully reproduce in their output all the errors of the input, and this applies as much to the logical structure of the program as it does to the numerical value of the data. And a computer cannot fire the first ICBM of a nuclear war unless some human fool wires it up to do so.

When it comes to chess, the situation is less clearly defined. Unless the programmer has a deep insight into the game he is unlikely to write a good set of instructions for winning. Nevertheless, he has at his command the power to evaluate hundreds or thousands of alternative moves in great detail and at high speed, as long as the evaluation follows rigidly prescribed rules. It is here that we see the computer at its most efficient, as an amplifier of the human brain. The combination of human insight and the mindless calculating ability of electronic machinery might well produce a new chess champion half flesh and blood, half wires and transistors, but the computer will never, never do it alone.

8

Solutions to Exercises

Exercise 8.1

In positions 6 and 8 of column 29.

Exercise 8.2

a	y	$\frac{a}{y}$	$\frac{a}{y}+y$
100	1·0000	100·0000	101·0000
	50·5000	1·9802	52·4802
	26·2401	3·8110	30·0511
	15·0256	6·6553	21·6809
	10·8404	9·2248	20·0652
	10·0326	9·9675	20·0001
	10·0000		

Exercise 8.3

LIST OF ITEMS FOR PURCHASING.

5 STOCK DEFICIENCY 38 LB.

6 STOCK DEFICIENCY 100 LB.

12 NOVEMBER 1965

Exercise 8.4

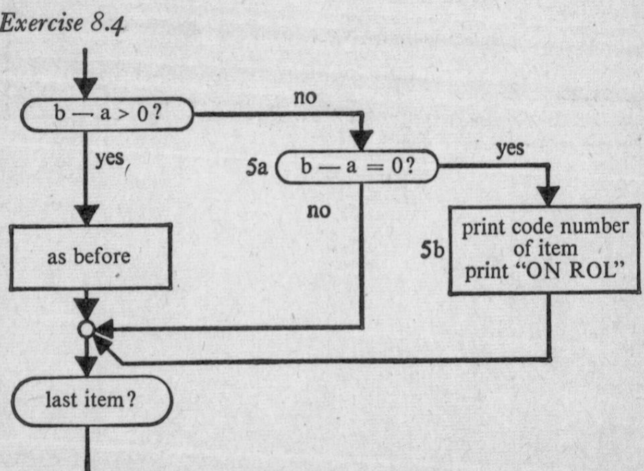

Exercise 8.5

$$a = 0{\cdot}5$$
$$y = 1$$
$$p = a/y = 0{\cdot}5$$
$$q = y + p = 1{\cdot}5$$
$$r = q/2 = 0{\cdot}75$$
$$s = r - y = -0{\cdot}25$$

Is $s < 0.01$? Yes, because s is preceded by a negative sign, and the calculation stops. We need to test the *absolute* value of s; one way of doing so is

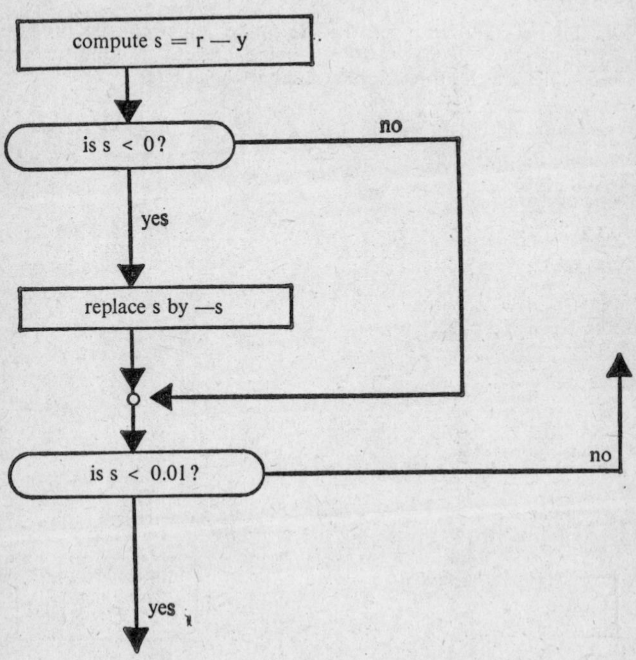

NOTES AND REFERENCES

67 Battersby, A., *Chemistry and Industry*, 15 November 1957, p. 1488.
68 Roach Pierson, D., *Data and Control*, November 1963, p. 27.
69 Kemeny, J. G., Schlaifer, Snell, and Thomson, *Finite Mathematics with Business Applications* (Prentice-Hall, 1962), p. 40.
70 Bowden, B. V., *Faster than Thought* (Pitman, 1963), chaps 1–5.
71 De Paris, J., *Data Processing for Management*, September 1963, p. 22.
72 Elmaghraby, S. E., *Management Science* (1964), p. 494.

ADDENDUM

As this book goes to press, the 'Scientific American' has produced its September 1966 issue which is entirely devoted to 'Information'; it contains much up-to-date news about computers.

9
Curves and Capital

I'm very well acquainted too with matters mathematical,
I understand equations, both the simple and quadratical.

W. S. GILBERT, *The Pirates of Penzance*

WE have seen how much can be accomplished with no more than simple linear functions, but inevitably we shall reach a stage where linear functions cannot adequately represent the true relationships between factors in the real world. The average temperature is not a linear function of the time of year, and neither are the sales of goods which depend on it, be they winter overcoats or beer; the amount of a chemical produced in a reaction may increase at a slower rate as the reaction proceeds; the rate of growth of demand for electricity follows a steepening curve, and so on.

Because linear relationships are so easy to handle mathematically, several methods of turning non-linear functions into linear ones are used in practice. One is to break up a curved line into a number of short straight ones: such a method has been described by Garvin[73] for dealing with the relationship between the amount of TEL (tetra-ethyl lead) added to motor spirit and the octane number which measures the anti-knock properties of the blend. The graph of the true curve is shown in Figure 9.1, the linear approximation in Figure 9.2. The TEL is divided into five imaginary types, with restrictions imposed so that all of 'Type 1' must be used before any 'Type 2' is added, and so on.

Another method is to 'transform' the data. Figure 9.3, shows the cost of binding, per book, plotted against the size of the order. Figure 9.4 shows the same relationship transformed into a straight line by plotting the total cost of the order instead of the cost per book.

This is our old acquaintance from Chapter 3,

$$y = mx + c \tag{9.1}$$

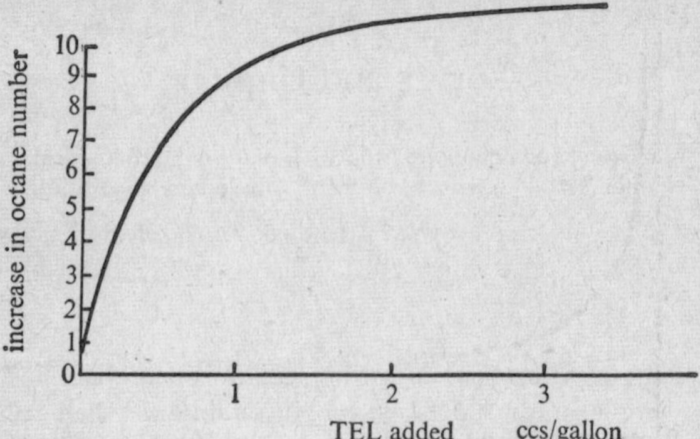

Fig. 9.1 True relationship between TEL and octane number

We can interpret this equation by saying that for any order there is a fixed cost c which does not depend on the size of the order: in Figure 9.4 it is £25. There is also a cost m, the variable cost per book, which *is* directly proportional to the size of the order.

The *total* cost per book (call it b) is m plus some share of the fixed cost c which must also be borne by the book. Expressed mathematically:

$$b = y/x = m + c/x \tag{9.2}$$

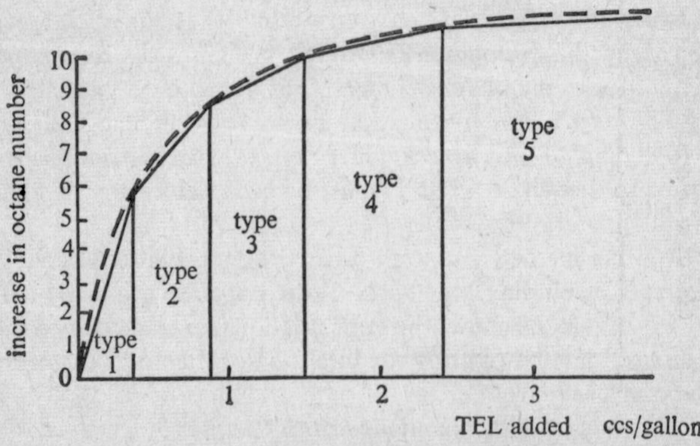

Fig. 9.2 Linear approximation to TEL/octane number graph

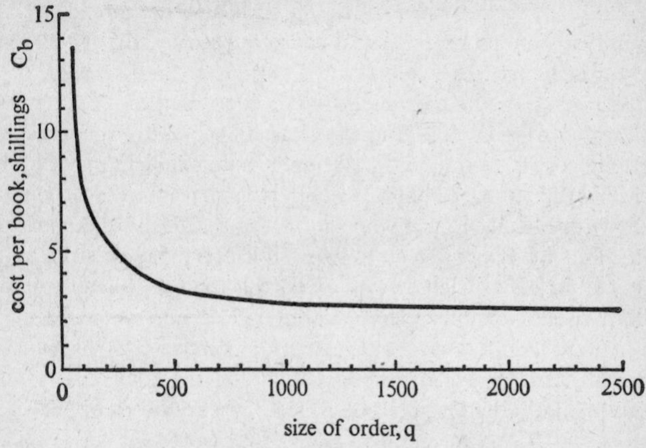

Fig. 9.3 Cost of binding books, per book

This is the equation of the curve in Figure 9.3, which is a hyperbola. Considering the process in reverse, we may say that by multiplying equation (9.2) by x throughout, we have transformed it into the linear equation (9.1).

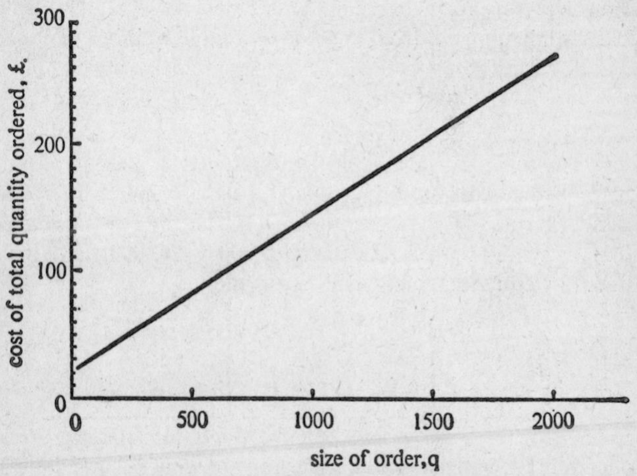

Fig. 9.4 Cost of binding books, total for order

Problems in which a fixed charge has to be spread over a number of items are frequently encountered by managers. The number bought or made may be varied at the discretion of a manager: thus the cost of setting up a production line may be allocated over the number of items subsequently made by it, or the cost of taxing and insuring a motor vehicle may be included in a mileage charge. (There is a story about an accountant with a Rolls-Royce who said, 'It is ruinously expensive to run, but I just *have* to go to work in it every day: it's the only way I can keep the cost down to less than half-a-crown a mile.') Both these examples were encountered as linear functions in Chapter 3, and Pascal's Pressings (Exercise 3.2) provide a useful starting point. The equation for the total cost y (in shillings) of a batch of spacing pieces was found to be

$$y = 0{\cdot}25x + 600 \tag{9.3}$$

in which x is the number of pieces ordered. The total cost per piece, b, is found by dividing both sides of the equation by x:

$$b = \frac{y}{x} = 0{\cdot}25 + \frac{600}{x} \tag{9.4}$$

Compare this equation with (9.2). Its graph, in Figure 9.5, gives a picture of the familiar 'economy of scale' which results from spreading the fixed costs over a large number of items.

Exercise 9.1

The cost of tax, insurance and hire purchase instalments for a motor-lorry in a single year is £1,200; petrol, oil and maintenance cost 1s. 6d. a mile and we assume there are no other charges. Draw a graph showing the total cost per mile for yearly mileages in the range 6,000 to 30,000, and write down its equation, using shillings as the unit.

CONFLICTING GOALS

Economies of scale – low costs through high output – are generally recognized as desirable aims for any business, but the other side of the picture is often neglected. There may be

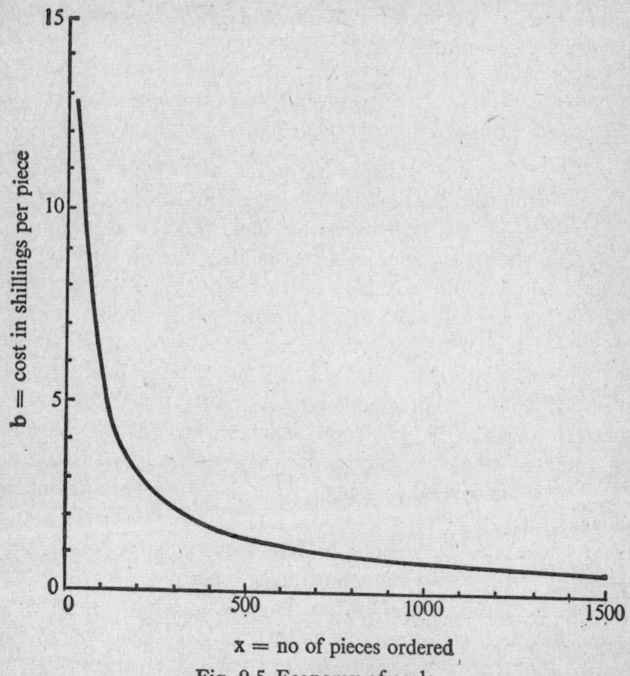

Fig. 9.5 Economy of scale

some costs which *increase* as the scale of manufacture increases, notably those connected with the financing of the business.

Suppose that Pascal's Pressings are in a situation differing only slightly from the one already described: we are no longer concerned with the cost of the initial tools, but rather with the preparations for manufacture of repeated batches. There are again certain fixed jobs (and therefore costs) which do not depend on the number to be made: issuing the authority to manufacture, drawing the tools from stores, fitting them to the machine and adjusting it, and so on; the sum of all these fixed costs is the setting-up cost, which amounts to £5 (100 shillings). Material and labour costs, together with services such as electricity and lubrication, come to 1s. for each part.

Then the cost per unit, in shillings, is given by equation 9.5, where x is the number in the batch.

$$c = 1 + \frac{100}{x} \tag{9.5}$$

The Production Manager has to decide how many to make in this batch, and has tentatively picked a figure of 10,000 (equal to the current yearly demand for these pieces). Equation 9.5 gives the cost per piece as 1·01 shillings. Assuming that the whole batch could be made quickly – within a week, let us say – then he will have to pay for materials, labour and services for all 10,000, which means an investment of 10,000 shillings or £500. This sum will, of course, be gradually repaid during the year as the goods are sold, but the average balance outstanding will be £250, on which the company's bankers will charge interest at, say, 8 per cent per annum, amounting to £20. This investment cost is one we have not previously considered.

If the batch were only half as big, the investment cost would be only £10 a year, but the cost per piece would go up to 1·02 shillings. We therefore have two conflicting goals to reconcile, because economy of scale is only achieved at the expense of a greater investment of capital. How do we reconcile them?

The mathematician will generalize the problem in the following way. Let the batch size which it is required to find be q items and the annual sales be s. Then

$$\text{Number of batches per year} = s/q$$

Let the fixed setting-up cost be f; multiplying this by the number of batches gives the total setting-up costs incurred in a year, which we shall call c. Then

$$c = \frac{fs}{q} \tag{9.6}$$

For Pascal's Pressings, $s = 10{,}000$ and $f = 100$ shillings so

$$c = \frac{1{,}000{,}000}{q}$$

The variable cost of an item is m; the initial investment for q items is mq and the average balance outstanding is half this. If the rate of interest is r (expressed as a fraction, i.e. 0·08 instead of 8%), then the annual cost of the investment, i, is given by

$$i = \frac{mrq}{2} \tag{9.7}$$

For Pascal's Pressings, with $m = 1$ and $r = 0{\cdot}08$

$$i = 0{\cdot}04q$$

The direct manufacturing cost per year, g, is given by a simple linear function which does not depend on the batch size:

$$g = ms \tag{9.8}$$

and by collecting together the costs in equations (9.6), (9.7) and (9.8) we arrive at a total annual cost C:

$$C = c + i + g = \frac{fs}{q} + \frac{mrq}{2} + ms \tag{9.9}$$

Exercise 9.2

Draw up a table of the following form for the case of Pascal's Pressings, using pounds sterling as the unit instead of shillings.

Number of Pieces in Batch q	*Annual Costs, £*			*Total Annual Cost £* C
	Setting Up c	*Investment* i	*Manufacturing* g	
1,000				

Use a range of batch sizes from 1,000 to 10,000 at intervals of 1,000 and set up an equation relating C and q, as an aid to calculation.

Exercise 9.3

If you were the Production Manager, which batch size would you choose and why?

ECONOMIC BATCH SIZE

Figure 9.6 shows how the various components of the total cost vary with the batch size: (it corresponds to the solution of Exercise 9.2). The direct manufacturing cost g has been included in the vertical scale on the right-hand side of the graph, but since it does not vary with the size of batch, only the total $c + i$ need be considered: it is shown on the left-hand scale. The lowest value of $c + i$ is £20, corresponding to

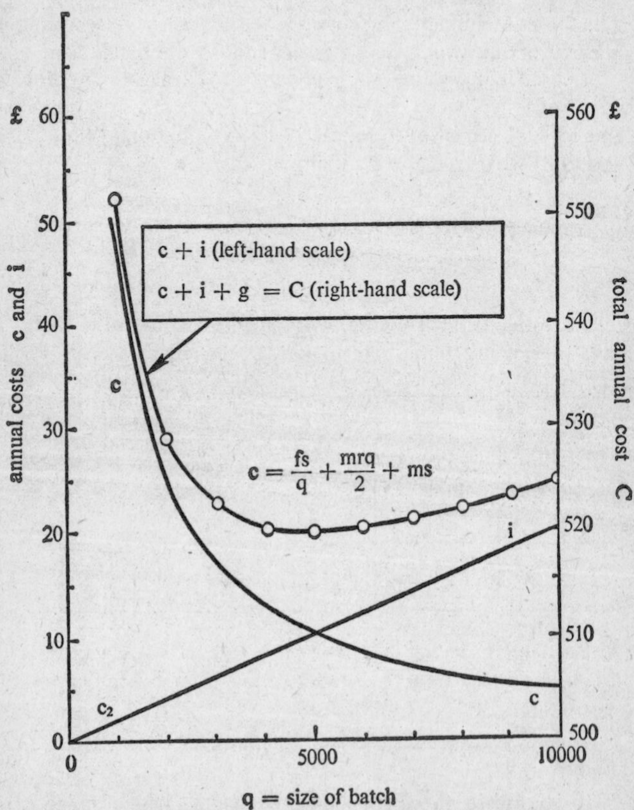

Fig. 9.6 Economic batch size

5,000 pieces: the latter is known as the 'economic batch size': it represents the best balance between the two conflicting goals of achieving economies of scale and keeping investment costs down.

The question now arises, 'Must we necessarily draw a graph to find the economic batch size – is there not an algebraic method of finding it?' There is such a method, but in order to understand it we shall need to look rather more closely at gradients of curves, which correspond to the rates at which one variable changes with respect to another.

Exercise 9.4

If the batch size q is increased by 1,000, to what extent do the setting-up cost c and the investment cost i change if the increase in batch size is from

(a) 1,000 to 2,000?
(b) 4,000 to 5,000?
(c) 9,000 to 10,000?

RATES OF CHANGE

One characteristic of a linear function is that the rate at which one variable changes with respect to another is always the same: this is the same as saying that the graph of such a function has a constant gradient. In Figure 9.7, the right-

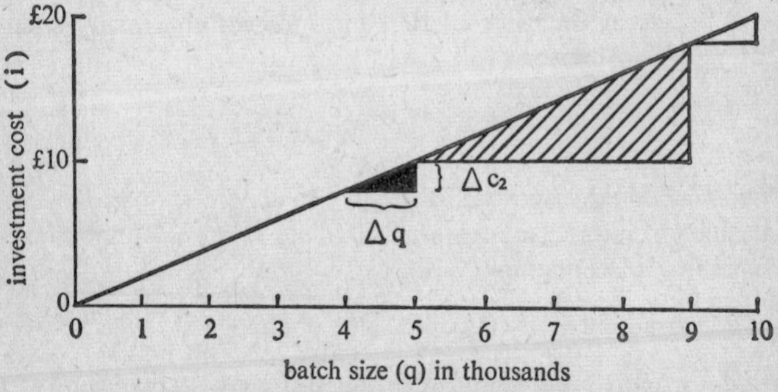

Fig. 9.7 Variation of investment cost with batch size

angled triangles will all have the same ratio between the vertical and horizontal sides. We called this the gradient m in Chapter 3, but here we shall describe it in a different way. The Greek letter delta (Δ) in Figure 9.7 does not represent a quantity, but is a sign which means 'the difference between two values of —'. In the black triangle, $\Delta\, i$ is the difference between £10 and £8, i.e. £2, (40 shillings); $\Delta\, q$ is the difference between 5,000 and 4,000, i.e. 1,000. The gradient m is given by

$$m = \frac{\Delta i}{\Delta q} = \frac{40}{1000} = 0{\cdot}04 \text{ shillings per piece}$$

and for a linear function it is the same no matter where we draw the triangle, and no matter how large it is: the big shaded triangle has

$$\Delta i = £18 - £10 = £8 = 160 \text{ shillings}$$

$$\Delta q = 9000 - 5000 = 4000 \text{ pieces}$$

$$m = \frac{\Delta i}{\Delta q} = \frac{160}{4000} = 0{\cdot}04 \text{ shillings per piece}$$

If we want to find the gradient at a point rather than over a range of values, we can reduce the size of the triangle until it becomes vanishingly small, knowing that the ratio $m = \dfrac{\Delta i}{\Delta q}$ will not change.

A different notation is used for such infinitesimally small triangles: we write

$$m = \frac{dc}{dq} \tag{9.10}$$

Once again, the symbol '*d*' does not denote a quantity, but means 'an infinitesimally small part of . . .': we cannot cancel out the *d*'s in equation (9.10).

The gradient $\dfrac{di}{dq}$ is called 'the rate of change of i with respect to q' or, more technically, 'the first differential coefficient of i with respect to q'.

DIFFERENTIAL COEFFICIENTS OF NON-LINEAR FUNCTIONS

A glance at Figure 9.8 will show that the gradient varies at different points along non-linear functions.

It follows that triangles of different sizes enclosing a point on the curve will give different estimates for the gradient at that point. Thus, the big unshaded triangle gives

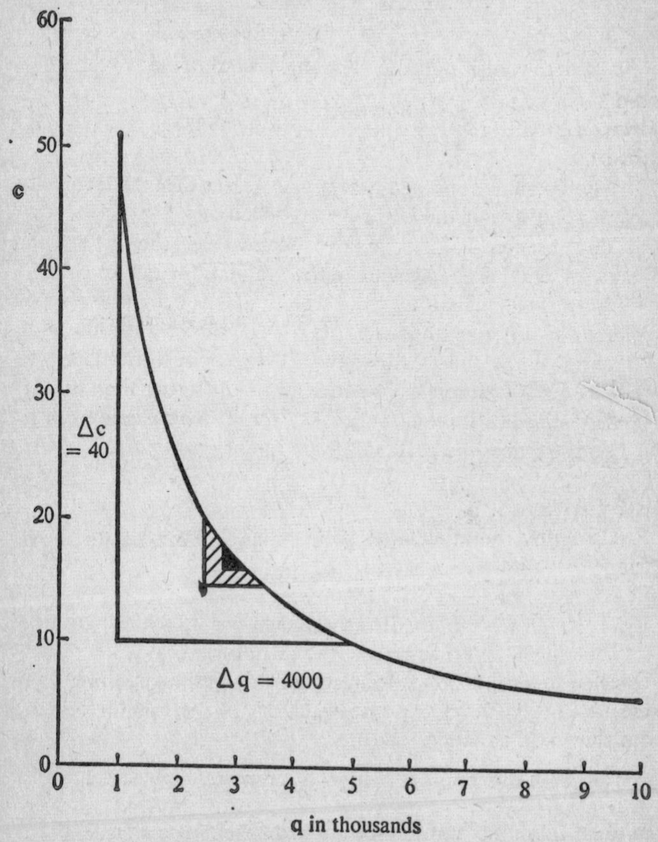

Fig. 9.8 Variation of setting-up cost with batch size

$$\frac{\Delta c}{\Delta q} = \frac{50 - 10}{1000 - 5000} = \frac{40}{-4000} = -0{\cdot}01$$

The shaded triangle gives

$$\frac{\Delta c}{\Delta q} = \frac{20 - 14{\cdot}3}{2500 - 3500} = \frac{6{\cdot}7}{1000} = -0{\cdot}067$$

The black triangle gives

$$\frac{\Delta c}{\Delta q} = \frac{17{,}857 - 15{,}625}{2800 - 3200} = \frac{2{\cdot}232}{-400} = -0{\cdot}0558$$

An almost vanishingly small triangle would give

$$\frac{\Delta c}{\Delta q} = \frac{-0{\cdot}0111}{2} = -0{\cdot}00555$$

These values approach nearer and nearer to some true value of the gradient at the point $q = 3{,}000$.

The branch of mathematics known as the differential calculus enables us to calculate the gradient (or rate of change) directly. To explain it in detail would take us beyond the scope of this book; it is sufficient to say here that it reproduces in algebraic form the calculations we have just carried out on Figure 9.8. (A simple explanation of the differential calculus is to be found in *Mathematician's Delight* (1943) by Sawyer.[74])

For instance, the gradient at any point on the graph of

$$i = 50{,}000/q$$

is shown by the calculus to be

$$di/dq = -50{,}000/q^2 \qquad (9.10)$$

from which we can confirm that when q is 3,000, the gradient is $-0{\cdot}00555$. In other words, the setting-up cost is decreasing at the rate of 0·00555 shillings for every extra part made.

Exercise 9.5

What is the rate of change of investment cost when the batch size is

(a) 5,000?
(b) 10,000?

The differential calculus has given us standard methods of calculating rates of change for simple equations, and some of them are given below:

If $y = a$ (constant) $\quad \frac{dy}{dx} = 0$ (9.11)

$y = x \quad \frac{dy}{dx} = 1$ (9.12)

$y = ax \quad \frac{dy}{dx} = a$ (9.13)

$y = x^2 \quad \frac{dy}{dx} = 2x$ (9.14)

$y = ax^2 \quad \frac{dy}{dx} = 2ax$ (9.15)

$y = \frac{a}{x} \quad \frac{dy}{dx} = \frac{-a}{x^2}$ (9.16)

There is also a useful rule that when a function contains two or more terms which are added (or subtracted), they may be differentiated separately and added (or subtracted).

For example,

if $y = x^2 + ax, \quad dy/dx = 2x + a.$

Exercise 9.6

Differentiate, i.e. find $\frac{dy}{dx}$ when y equals

(i) $3x$

(ii) 16

(iii) $3x + 16$

(iv) $\frac{1}{x}$

(v) $\frac{a}{x} + bx^2$

(vi) $\frac{a}{x} + bx + ms$

The final example in Exercise 9.6 is similar to equation (9.9). The last term in this equation is constant and its differential coefficient is equal to zero. Putting

$$a = fs \quad \text{and} \quad b = \frac{mr}{2},$$

$$\frac{dc}{dq} = -\frac{a}{q^2} + b$$

$$= -\frac{fs}{q^2} + \frac{mr}{2} \qquad (9.17)$$

MINIMA

Look at the top curve in Figure 9.6. At the point $q = 5{,}000$, $c = 520$ it reaches a lowest point. This is technically called a 'minimum' because the values of C rise on both sides of it.

The minimum corresponds to a point at which, since the curve is flat, its gradient $\frac{dc}{dq}$ is zero, so from equation (9.17) we have

$$-\frac{fs}{q^2} + \frac{mr}{2} = 0 \qquad (9.18)$$

i.e.

$$\frac{fs}{q^2} = \frac{mr}{2} \qquad (9.19)$$

from which it follows that

$$q^2 = \frac{2fs}{mr}$$

and

$$q = \sqrt{\frac{2fs}{mr}} \qquad (9.20)$$

Exercise 9.7

Substitute the values

$$f = £5$$
$$s = 10{,}000 \text{ per annum}$$
$$m = £0{\cdot}05$$
$$r = 0{\cdot}08 \text{ per annum}$$

in equation (9.20) and find q.

Exercise 9.8

Multiply both sides of equation (9.19) by q, and compare the result with equations (9.6) and (9.7). What conclusion do you reach?

SENSITIVITY

Common sense should never be far around the corner when mathematical methods are being used in management problems, and sensitivity checks are one way of applying it. The possible inaccuracies in the original data are measured and their effect on the final answer are deduced; we can then judge the sensitivity of the answer to such errors, assess its reliability and, if necessary, try to re-measure the original data with greater accuracy. For example, the economic batch size in this case is associated with a total annual cost of £520 (see Figure 9.6). Of this total, £500 is beyond our control, being fixed by the supplier, but the other £20 is the cost figure we can alter by varying the batch size. In this sense, a batch of 3,650 would cost £21, so a reduction of 27% in the batch size only increases the cost by 5%. A batch of 6,850, 37% greater than the economic batch size, also increases the cost by only 5%. The cost is not 'sensitive' to the batch size, and the latter may therefore be adjusted cheaply in cases where it may be convenient to depart slightly from the true economic level.

PROFITS, PRICES AND PARABOLAS

One view of maximum profit was put forward in the chapters on linear programming. An important assumption was made but not explicitly stated – prices and profit margins remained constant whatever the quantity of goods made and sold might be. Is such an assumption justified?

The classical economists argued otherwise. Under 'perfect' competition, they said, the 'rational entrepreneur' would always buy from the cheapest source, so a lower price would always cause greater sales. Putting this theory into the simplest terms – a linear function – we may write

$$q = a - ep \tag{9.21}$$

with

$$\begin{aligned} q &= \text{quantity sold} \\ a &= \text{constant} \\ e &= \text{gradient} \\ p &= \text{selling price} \end{aligned}$$

A linear function of this sort is not likely to be valid over a very wide range of *s*, and would usually be qualified by limits in the usual way

$$p_1 \leqq p \leqq p_2$$

with p_2 and p_1 representing the upper and lower limits of validity respectively.

The gradient *e* is, of course, the rate of change of quantity sold with price,

$$\frac{dq}{dp} = -e$$

and has a negative sign because it is reasonable to assume that sales will go up as the price goes down. The quantity 'e' is related to the economist's 'elasticity of demand'.

One should stop and think very carefully about this set of assumptions before charging ahead and applying them. On the one hand, the appeal to elasticity is evident in any retail outlet with price reductions, 'special offers' or trading stamps; it has given rise to the fierce arguments about Retail Price Maintenance and the dilemma of those supporters of a competitive economy who attempt to eliminate the effects of free competition. On the other hand, buying is a complex process of decision-making in which price is only one factor. The wary customer is suspicious of too low a price: one furniture manufacturer has told of a new type of chair, whose revolutionary design kept the cost, and therefore the price, extraordinarily low. 'We couldn't sell it until we put the price up – they just wouldn't believe there wasn't a catch somewhere'. The same phenomenon has been noticed in certain 'quality' newspapers, where an increase in price has led to higher sales.

Other manufacturers go out of their way to persuade people that they are not in a free market. Peas, petrol or pork-pies are assigned 'plus-values', the alleged differences from competitors' products making a direct comparison of prices impossible.

With this caveat, let us follow up the implications of elasticity. If the total sales revenue is R, then

$$R = pq \tag{9.22}$$

Substituting equation (9.21) gives

$$R = p(a - ep)$$

i.e.

$$R = ap - ep^2 \tag{9.23}$$

The total sales revenue is not a linear function of the price, but a *quadratic* one because it contains p^2.

Exercise 9.9

A supermarket sells peas at the normal market price of 1s. 8d. a tin, and disposes of 1,200 tins weekly. The manager estimates that for every penny by which the price is reduced, sales will increase by 120 tins a week. The lowest possible price is 1/–, which is what the supermarket pays the wholesaler.

(a) What are the values of a and e in the equation (9.21)?

(b) Draw up a table showing the weekly sales and sales revenue for a range of prices from 1/- to 1/8d. at intervals of 1d.

(c) Draw a graph of sales revenue against price.

Suppose that the spacing pieces made by Pascal's Pressings will sell at the rate of 6,000 a week when the price is sixpence (0.50 shillings) and at only 1,000 a week if the price is 1 shilling, with a linear relationship in between. Then

$$q = 11{,}000 - 10{,}000p \tag{9.24}$$

and

$$R = 11{,}000p - 10{,}000^2 \tag{9.25}$$

$$0{\cdot}050 \leqq p \leqq 1{\cdot}00$$

The graph of equation (9.25) is shown in Figure 9.9. It shows how sales revenue rises steeply as the price is lowered, reaches a maximum at a price of 0·55 shillings per piece and then begins to fall off. For prices below 0·55, the loss in profit outweighs the growth in sales, the reverse being the case for

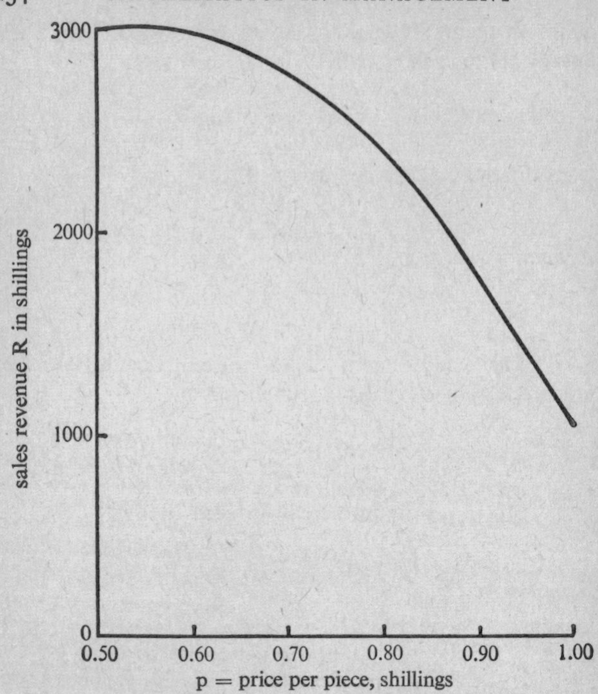

Fig. 9.9 Law of diminishing returns

prices above this figure. This is the 'Law of Diminishing Returns', which is in the mind of every Chancellor of the Exchequer before Budget Day. If he raises the tax on beer or cigarettes, can he be sure that the total revenue will increase?

The curve in Figure 9.9 is a *parabola*. The general equation of a parabola is

$$y = k + mx + nx^2 \qquad (9.26)$$

and in equation (9.25),

$$y = R, \qquad x = p,$$
$$k = 0, \qquad m = 11{,}000 \quad \text{and} \quad n = -10{,}000.$$

Every parabola has a point on it at which a maximum or

minimum occurs: if we differentiate equation (9.26) (see equations (9.11) to (9.16)) we find that

$$\frac{dy}{dx} = m + 2nx \qquad (9.27)$$

and the differential coefficient is zero when

$$m + 2nx = 0$$

i.e. when

$$x = \frac{-m}{2n} \qquad (9.28)$$

If x is to have a positive value, then m and n must have different signs.

For the minimum value of R in equation (9.25)

$$p = \frac{11{,}000}{20{,}000} = 0{\cdot}55$$

as Figure 9.9 shows.

Exercise 9.10

Calculate the price at which sales revenue is a maximum for the data in Exercise 9.9. Check your result against the graph.

We now know how to fix the price which will maximize sales revenue if (and it is a big 'if') we have some idea of the elasticity. This may well be too simple a view: maximum sales revenue only means maximum profit when costs are constant, whereas we know that increased sales may lead to economies of scale. In Exercise 3.2, we said that the spacing pieces made by Pascal's Pressings had the following cost function:

$$C = 600 + 0{\cdot}25q \qquad (9.29)$$

which is a special case of the more general equation:

$$C = f + vq \qquad (9.30)$$

in which f and v are the fixed and variable costs respectively. The gross profit B is given by

$$\begin{aligned} B &= R - C \\ &= (ap - ep^2) - f - v(a - ep) \end{aligned}$$

which simplifies to

$$B = -ep^2 + (a + ev)p - (av + f) \qquad (9.31)$$

Differentiating gives, for a maximum,

$$\frac{dB}{dp} = -2ep + (a + ev) = 0$$

and therefore

$$p = \frac{a + ev}{2e} \qquad (9.32)$$

It is interesting to note that the fixed cost f does not affect the price at which profit is maximized.

Exercise 9.11

Use equation (9.32) to calculate the 'optimum' price for spacing pieces made by Pascal's Pressings.

Exercise 9.12

Draw up a table of p, q, R, C and B for the spacing pieces, using values of p

(a) from 0·50 to 1·00 inclusive at intervals of 0·10.
(b) for any further values which the results might suggest.

How sensitive is the gross profit to changes in the price?

HOPF'S PARABOLAS

Harry Arthur Hopf formed one of the earliest management consultancy companies in the U.S.A., and propagated a good deal of sound business sense in his teachings. In mathematical analysis, he had a weakness for parabolas; he spent much of his time fitting them to observed data and calculating the corresponding 'optima'.[75] The weakness of Hopf's arguments lies in the fact that other curves (such as logarithmic ones) could have been fitted with equal validity, and would *not* have shown maxima or minima. Hopf's work is of historic interest to the student of management, but some of his conclusions should not be accepted too readily.

For example, in his work on insurance companies, he fitted a parabola to data for ten companies. The administrative expense as a percentage of actuarial net premiums was made the dependent variable y, and the average executive experience, in years, of the major executives was the independent variable x. Hopf fitted his parabola presumably by the method of least squares and found the equation to be

$$y = 19{\cdot}15 - 0{\cdot}5257x + 0{\cdot}014x^2 \tag{9.33}$$

He then went on to say that

> the turn of the curve is clearly defined at the point indicating an average of twenty years of executive experience.

The two exercises which follow show how tenuous this evidence is, and other criticisms may be directed at Hopf's approach. For instance, is it reasonable to assume that executive experience is the only assignable cause of variations in administrative expense?

Exercise 9.3

Comment on Hopf's deduction from his equation by differentiating it and finding the value of x for which y has a minimum value.

Exercise 9.4

Carry out a sensitivity test by calculating values of y corresponding to $x = 15$, 20 and 25. Bearing in mind that the estimate of administrative expense could easily be in error by 1 unit either way, would you attach much importance to executive experience as a factor which influenced it?

SUMMARY

We have seen in this chapter that some managerial problems need to be described in terms of hyperbolas or parabolas as well as straight lines. Logarithmic curves are also useful and so, in some special cases, are those of the simple trigonometrical functions. We rarely need to use more difficult equations than these, because usually our management information is not precise enough to make such elaborations worth while.

Finding maxima or minima by drawing graphs is simple but time-consuming, and the process of differentiating and equating to zero provides rapid solutions to problems of minimizing cost or maximizing profit. It follows that the elements of the differential calculus ought to be far more widely known among managers, accountants and other managerial advisers.

9
Solutions to Exercises

Exercise 9.1

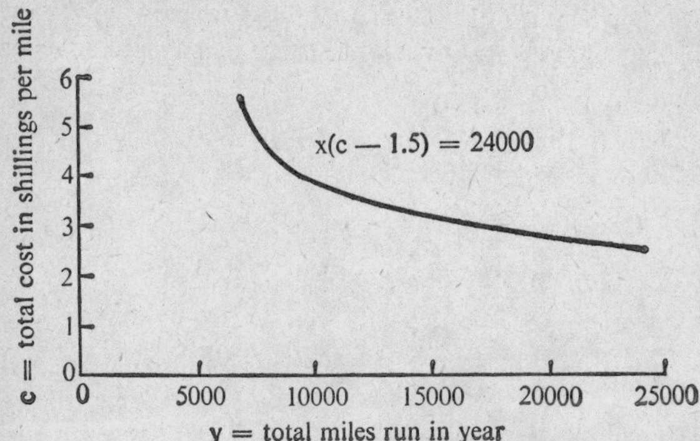

Exercise 9.2

Number of Pieces in Batch	*Annual Costs, £*			*Total Annual Cost*
	Setting up	*Investment*	*Manufacturing*	*£*
q	*c*	*i*	*g*	*C*
1,000	50	2	500	552
2,000	25	4	500	529
3,000	16·7	6	500	522·7
4,000	12·5	8	500	520·5
5,000	10·0	10	500	520
6,000	8·3	12	500	520·3
7,000	7·1	14	500	521·1
8,000	6·2	16	500	522·2
9,000	5·6	18	500	523·6
10,000	5·0	20	500	525

$$C = c + i + g$$

$$= \frac{50{,}000}{q} + 0{\cdot}002q + 500$$

Exercise 9.3

Presumably you would choose a batch size of 5,000 because the total cost would then be at its lowest.

Exercise 9.4

Change in batch size		*Change in cost of*	
from	*to*	*Setting up*	*Investment*
1,000	2,000	−£25	+£2
4,000	5,000	−£2·5	+£2
9,000	10,000	−£0·6	+£2

Exercise 9.5

$$\text{(a)}\ -\frac{50{,}000}{(5{,}000)^2} = -0{\cdot}0020$$

$$\text{(b)}\ -\frac{50{,}000}{(10{,}000)^2} = -0{\cdot}0005$$

Exercise 9.6

(i) 3

(ii) 0

(iii) 3

$$\text{(iv)}\ -\frac{1}{x^2}$$

$$\text{(v)}\ -\frac{a}{x^2} + 2bx$$

$$\text{(vi)}\ -\frac{a}{x^2} + b$$

Exercise 9.7

$$q = \sqrt{\frac{2 \times 5 \times 10{,}000}{0{\cdot}05 \times 0{\cdot}08}} = 5{,}000 \text{ (refer back to Ex. 9.3)}$$

Exercise 9.8

$$\frac{fs}{q} = \frac{mrq}{2}$$

i.e. $c=i$

The conclusion reached is that the annual investment and setting-up costs are equal when the batch size has the value which gives minimum total cost. Check that this is so by studying Figure 9.6.

Exercise 9.9

(a)

$$e = 120 \text{ tins per penny reduction.}$$
$$\text{therefore } q = a - 120p, \qquad 12 \leqq p \leqq 20$$
$$\text{and } a = q + 120p$$
$$\text{When } p = 20, \qquad q = 1200$$
$$a = 1200 + 120 \times 20 = 3600.$$

(b)

Price (pence) p	*Sales (tins)* q	*Revenue (pence)* pq
20	1,200	24,000
19	1,320	25,080
18	1,440	25,920
17	1,560	26,520
16	1,680	26,880
15	1,800	27,000
14	1,920	26,880
13	2,040	26,520
12	2,160	25,920

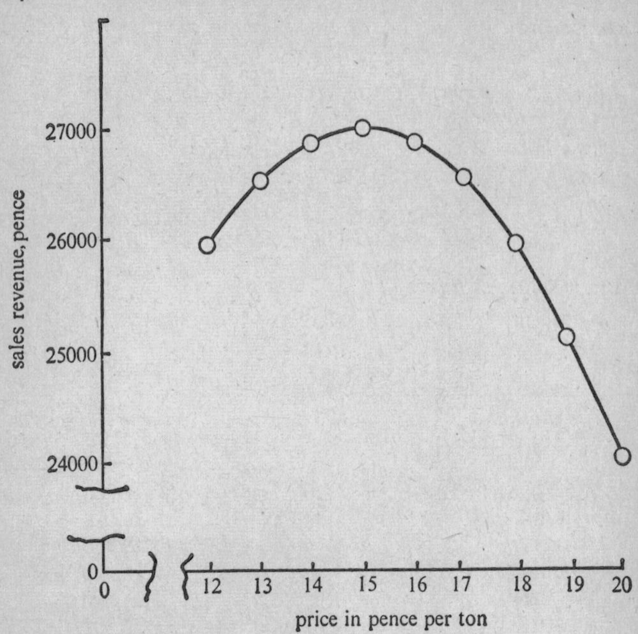

Exercise 9.10

$$R = 3{,}600p - 120p^2$$

$$\frac{dR}{dp} = 3{,}600 - 240p = 0$$

$$\therefore p = \frac{3{,}600}{240} = 15$$

This value of p corresponds to the maximum revenue (27,000) in Exercise 9.9.

Exercise 9.11

$$a = 11{,}000$$
$$e = 10{,}000$$
$$v = 0{\cdot}25$$
$$\therefore \quad p = 0{\cdot}675 \text{ shillings.}$$

Exercise 9.12

p	q	R	C	B
0·50	6,000	3,000	2,100	900
0·60	5,000	3,000	1,850	1,150
0·70	4,000	2,800	1,600	1,200
0·80	3,000	2,400	1,350	1,050
0·90	2,000	1,800	1,100	700
1·00	1,000	1,000	850	150

Further values of p give

0·65	4,500	2,925	1,725	1,200
0·66	4,400	2,904	1,700	1,204
0·67	4,300	2,881	1,675	1,206
0·68	4,200	2,856	1,650	1,206
0·69	4,100	2,829	1,625	1,204
0·675	4,250	2,868·75	1,662·50	1,206·25

A change of 0·005 in the price, up or down, makes a difference of 0·25 shillings in the gross profit: this is trivially small.

Exercise 9.13

$$y = 19{\cdot}15 - 0{\cdot}5257x + 0{\cdot}014x^2$$

$$\frac{dy}{dx} = \quad - 0{\cdot}5257 + 0{\cdot}028x = 0$$

for a minimum

$$\therefore \quad x = \frac{0{\cdot}5257}{0{\cdot}028} = 19 \text{ years.}$$

Hopf has obviously rounded off this result to obtain his figure of 20 years.

Exercise 9.14

$$x = 15, \qquad y = 14{\cdot}4$$
$$x = 20, \qquad y = 15{\cdot}2$$
$$x = 25, \qquad y = 14{\cdot}8$$

It is obvious that y is not very sensitive to changes in x.

NOTES AND REFERENCES

73 Garvin, W. W., Crandall, H. W., John, J. B., and Spellman, R. A., *Management Science* (1957), p. 407.

74 Sawyer, W. W., *Mathematician's Delight* (Penguin Books Ltd, 1943).

75 Hopf, H. A., *Management and the Optimum* (6th International Congress for Scientific Management, 1935). Quoted in Nerill, H. F., *Classics in Management* (1960), p. 355 (American Management Association).

10

Statistics and Sundries

> Lest men suspect your tale to be untrue,
> Keep probability – some say – in view.
>
> ROBERT GRAVES, *The Devil's Advice to Story-Tellers*

STATISTICAL METHODS[76]

The preceding chapters have surveyed some of the mathematical procedures which can help the modern manager to solve his problems, but they have necessarily omitted many others. Foremost among the omissions are the methods of mathematical statistics which have been derived from the theory of probability. Some mathematicians will argue that 'statistics is not included in mathematics' and imply that there is something rather disreputable about the whole basis of probability theory. Perhaps this is another aspect of the Snobbery of Purity, for of the practical value of statistical methods there can be no doubt. They have led to improvements in many fields where human welfare is affected (medicine, agriculture, psychology and sociology among them) and where random effects obtrude. The highly variable conditions of real life make it difficult for investigators to detect the effects of new drugs, new fertilizers and new methods of treatment as soon as they move outside the carefully controlled conditions of the laboratory: no two patients are exactly alike in their response to a drug, no two fields have the same soil. A crop growing in a field treated with a new fertilizer may have different weather from a 'control' crop without it, and so on. Statistical methods help the investigator to decide, in spite of the fog of uncertainty, whether the new drug or fertilizer really is effective. The old saying, 'You can prove anything by statistics', is wrong, for no statistician can ever produce a hard and fast proof of anything. He deals with the balance of probabilities, and his 'proof' will take some such form as, 'Either this new drug works, or you have a freak result with odds of 250 to one against a repetition'.

So also in management, for the man who works in industry is constantly beset by outside interference. How, for example, can a food manufacturer assess the state of his market? Each individual customer is a creature of whims and fancies: if he himself does not know which foods he means to buy next week, how can the manufacturer predict his behaviour? He can only do so in the vaguest terms, but it is a remarkable fact that the behaviour of large numbers of people is much more predictable than that of the individuals themselves. The Ministry of Food in Britain during the Second World War was able to predict the food requirements of the whole population within narrow limits, and plan not only a basic food ration but also a 'points' system which would enable each consumer to adjust his personal intake.

MARKET RESEARCH[77]

Aggregate effects of this sort begin to appear when the 'large numbers' are still relatively small. Six hundred is a large number of people, but it is still only 0·001% of a total population of sixty million. Nevertheless, by studying the behaviour, characteristics, or opinions of this small fraction, a researcher can often draw useful conclusions about the corresponding factors in the whole population. This is the basic idea of market research, and statistical methods can help in assessing the limits of reliability of the results. By the skilful use of such methods, the sample can be chosen so that the limits are as narrow as is possible for the size of the survey – in other words, so that the sample is 'representative'.

STOCK CONTROL[78]

Another important application of statistical methods is in controlling stocks of materials during manufacture and distribution. A manufacturer may find that, although his sales in any one month are not perfectly predictable, a statistical analysis of his previous sales over several months will yield useful data. An 'expected value' of next month's sales can then be deduced and will enable him to prepare his manufacturing programme. The limits of confidence which accompany this figure will be used for calculating the level of reserve stock which he must carry in order to cope with a reasonable range of variation. Some managers have been able, by the use of simple statistical techniques, to reduce the capital tied up in stocks by as much as 40%, with no loss of efficiency or customer service. Moreover, questions such as 'what do we mean by a *reasonable* range of variation?' can lead to profound inquiries into the general management policy of a company.

QUALITY CONTROL[79]

Statistical control of the quality of manufactured goods has been applied in this country for a quarter of a century, but many companies still remain in ignorance of its advantages. Variations in some measure of quality, such as dimensions or the proportion of flawed items, also obey statistical laws; by studying and applying them we can take steps to avoid unnecessary expenditure on inspection, machine supervision, or replacing rejected material; we can also ensure that quality is specified at levels which are a reasonable compromise between what is needed to satisfy the customer and what can be produced at a price he is prepared to pay.

The mathematical theories of statistics may appear complicated to the layman, but this is no excuse for avoiding them. The fundamental concepts, as distinct from their detailed interpretation, are not difficult to understand, and often make an immediate appeal to our common sense or intuition. Tables, special graph papers and rapid statistical methods have taken much of the sting out of the calculations and, of course, the electronic computer can take care of the drudgery of calculation once the methods of working have been decided.

FORECASTING[80]

The art of business forecasting has also been greatly advanced by the work of statisticians. The nineteenth-century biologist Galton developed a method of fitting curves to observed data when he was investigating the relationship between the heights of fathers and their sons. He called it 'regression analysis' and it is now the most widely used method of scientific forecasting. The curves may be linear or may follow some of the curves described in Chapter 9, and the method of analysis permits us not only to project them into the future as expected values but also to work out the limits within which the forecast may be reasonably expected to lie. Simple transformations are often used, as when the sales of a commodity are believed to be increasing by a constant percentage r each year, but with random variations. The latter may make it difficult to estimate the value of r which will give us the best projection of past data. The method is to start with a 'base year' which we call year O, we denote the sales in that year by s_o. Then the sales in the next year, s_1, will be given by

$$s_1 = s_o(1 + \frac{r}{100}) \tag{10.1}$$

and the sales in any subsequent year n will be s_n, where

$$s_n = s_o(1 + \frac{r}{100})^n \tag{10.2}$$

This is the same equation, incidentally, as the one which is used for compound interest, s_o being the initial sum invested and s_n its value after n years at r per cent interest. To say that sales increase by five per cent every year is the same as saying that they are multiplied by a factor of 1·05, and by using this approach we get a simpler equation. In general terms, we say that the rate of interest, r, is transformed into the multiplier R by the equation

$$R = 1 + \frac{r}{100} \tag{10.3}$$

which gives, by substitution in (10.2),

$$s_n = s_o R^n \qquad (10.4)$$

We still have the awkward problem of R^n to deal with. Once again we can transform the variables, using that most useful invention, the logarithm. You may remember that if

$$R = 10^c,$$

c is the logarithm of R and, from reasoning which can be found in any elementary textbook,

$$\log R^n = n \log R$$

and this rule indicates how the variables in equation should be transformed.

Taking logarithms throughout gives

$$\begin{aligned} \log s_n &= \log s_o + \log (R^n) \\ &= \log s_o + n\log R \qquad (10.5) \end{aligned}$$

Since s_o is constant, its logarithm is also constant, so we put $\log s_o = c$. We also believe r to have a constant value, so $\log R$ is also constant and we make it equal to m. The independent variable with which we are concerned is n, so let $n = x$. Then the dependent variable, which we shall call Y_n, is defined by the transformation $Y_n = \log s_n$ and we have, by substitution,

$$Y_n = mx + c \qquad (10.6)$$

which is the general equation to a straight line. This bit of mathematical reasoning shows why we so often use semi-log graph paper for projecting sales. An example is given in Figure 10.1, which is a graph showing the rate of growth of the consumption of alkali in Britain, taken over the last sixty years and projected forward to the year 2000. Alkali is a widely used industrial commodity, and it is of interest to compare its average rate of growth ($r = 3{\cdot}25\%$) with current 'Neddy' targets for the economy as a whole.

There are even more advanced techniques of statistical forecasting, such as 'multiple regression' by which we can relate a dependent variable (for example, sales) not only to a single independent variable, time, but to several of them, such as weather or population.[81] The equations which are used for this

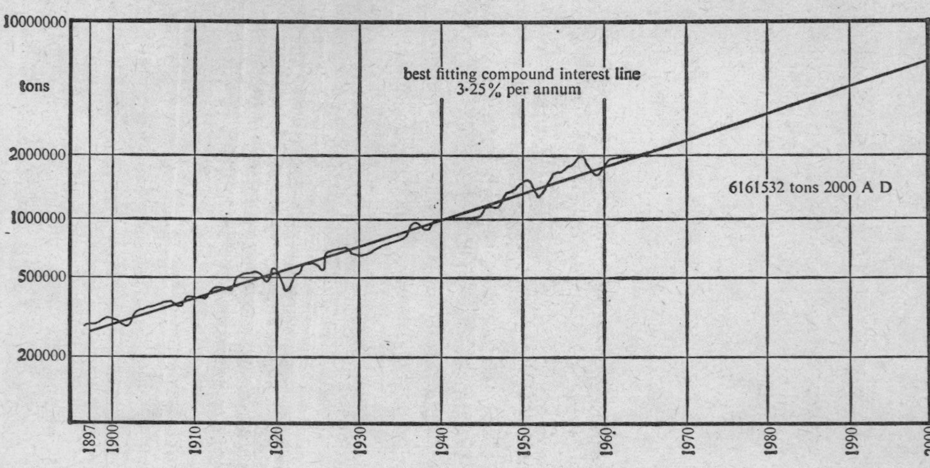

Fig. 10.1 Rate of growth of alkali consumption *Reproduced by courtesy of I.C.I. Ltd.*

purpose are very like that which described the multi-factor bonus scheme (see Figure 3.6 and equation 3.16).

BRAND LOYALTY AND MARKET SHARES

An even more recent advance has been the use of 'matrices of transition probabilities' for forecasting changes in market shares.[82] A simple matrix for three branded products is shown in Table 10.1, the probabilities having been deduced from observation of a small representative panel. In this simple case, we can easily calculate the market share which each brand would have when an equilibrium was reached.

If the market shares of Plankton, Seaweed and Kelp are p, s, and k respectively, then p, s and k will all have constant values when the market is in equilibrium, that is, when all market shares are stable.

For their next purchase, 0·7 of the previous buyers of Plankton will again buy Plankton, 0·1 of the buyers of S will switch to Plankton, and so will 0·2 of the Kelp addicts. A little thought will show that because p remains unchanged,

$$p = 0{\cdot}7p + 0{\cdot}1s + 0{\cdot}2k \qquad (10.6)$$

which gives

$$-0{\cdot}3p + 0{\cdot}1s + 0{\cdot}2k = 0 \qquad (10.7)$$

A similar operation on s gives

$$0{\cdot}2p - 0{\cdot}5s + 0{\cdot}2k = 0 \qquad (10.8)$$

Having tacitly assumed that the three commodities share the whole of the particular market which is being surveyed, we can also write

$$p + s + k = 1 \qquad (10.9)$$

We now have three simultaneous equations, which, when solved give

$p = 0{\cdot}343$ (34·3% of the market)
$s = 0{\cdot}286$ (28·6% „ „ „)
$k = 0{\cdot}371$ (37·1% „ „ „)

1·000

TABLE 10.1

Brand Loyalty: Matrix of Transition Probabilities

If the customer's last purchase was A, then the probability that his next purchase will be B is given in the various cells.

		B (Next purchase)		
		Pythagoras' Processed Plankton	*Socrates' Shredded Seaweed*	*Keltic Kelp Kakes*
A (Last purchase)	Pythagoras' Processed Plankton	0·7	0·2	0·1
	Socrates' Shredded Seaweed	0·1	0·5	0·4
	Keltic Kelp Kakes	0·2	0·2	0·6

The result is rather surprising, because the highest 'brand loyalty' is towards Pythagoras' Plankton (see the entry 0·7 in Table 10.1), and yet this is not enough to ensure it the highest market share. To some extent, this is due to the seaweed-eaters, who tend to turn to kelp rather than plankton when they switch brands. Here is a way of predicting how market shares may change, instead of having to wait for the results of market audits.

Why have so few manufacturers tried it out? Either because, lacking mathematicians to advise them, they do not know of it – or if they do, the dreadful words 'matrix of transition probabilities' or 'Markov chains' (and the symbols which accompany them) have frightened them away.

COMMUNICATION AND MENTAL WORK

The study of mental work has interested many scientists, from Charles Babbage[83] to the modern workers in cybernetics. The current trend is to use the mathematical theory of communication, developed in the 1930s by Shannon[84,85]. This theory is built up from the idea that the amount of information in a signal depends upon its rarity. You can see this by imagining two incomplete messages in Morse code:

(a) PLEASE SEND ME A R———
(b) PLEASE SEND ME A X———

In the first of these, *R*, being a commonly used letter is said to be a signal with a low information content, and so the message as a whole will have a lower information content than (b) because X is a rarer letter.

The concept of rarity is closely allied to that of probability, and by applying statistical reasoning, Shannon and Weaver succeeded in building up a measure of information. Some rather crude attempts have been made to apply their system of measurement to mental work, which may be defined as the reception, storage and transmission of information. The attempts have been limited by the lack of distinction between information which has *meaning* or *relevance* and that which has not. Recent developments of the theory have interpreted the meaning of the signals in terms of the action which they initiate. (In case (b), one might send off a xylophone and a xerographic machine accompanied by a xenophobe and stand a reasonable chance of having interpreted the meaning correctly.) Devising and applying a numerical measure of 'meaningfulness' may well be one of the great new contributions of mathematics to management in the next decade.

INSPECTION AND INFORMATION

The theory of information has been applied to inspectors looking for faults in glass bottles.[86] Each inspector was looked on as a communication channel with a limited capacity to handle information. The input signals were the flaws detected by the inspector, and his output was the action taken to separate faulty bottles from good ones. For a given frequency of defects, the rate at which information flowed through the 'channel' was obviously proportional to the rate at which the bottles passed along the inspection line. If the information capacity of the channel, that is, the inspector, were exceeded, his *apparent* output would rise because he would appear to inspect more bottles. His *true* output would, however, remain constant because he would make a greater number of mistakes by rejecting good bottles or passing bad ones. Similar work has been done on airline pilots and radar operators.

THE OVERLOADED CONTROLLER

One of the most remarkable applications of statistics to management problems has been described by Lee.[87] His team tackled the problem of the Departures Controller at London Airport, who was thought to be carrying too heavy a load of work. The Controller's job was to keep in touch with more than 20 people who collectively supervised the preparation of an aircraft for take-off: he received their messages, made decisions and passed on instructions. In other words, he worked with his brain rather than his muscles.

A team of investigators from British European Airways built up a measure of the mental work load (not quite the same as Shannon's) and used it to divide up the Departure Controller's job when it became obvious that it took two men to handle it. The obvious division was to allocate the work according to the existing organization, that is, domestic flights to one man and foreign flights to another. The measurements showed that this proposal was inequitable, and a better alternative was found. The work tended to build up into a peak near the scheduled take-off time, and in fact half the total work for each aircraft was concentrated into the last twenty minutes.

The method which was finally devised called for the first Controller to handle each aircraft until twenty minutes before its departure, at which time he handed it over to the second. Lee said of this:

> The division of responsibility would be quite even, because the more serious, because more urgent, snags occur near flight

departure. Although Controller A would be dealing with as many as 40 flights at one time, whereas Controller B would not be concerned with more than about 8, the actual number of calls handled per minute and the number of topics being stored by each in his memory, would be almost the same, and both well below the respective critical levels.

SUMMING UP

This book is presented as a 'shop-window' of mathematical methods and concepts which can be of immediate, practical use to managers. The price they have to pay is the effort to break down the barrier of communication between themselves and the mathematicians. If the simplified descriptions in the preceding chapters have helped to breach this barrier, they will have achieved their objective. And if you, the manager, like the look of what is in the window, why not come inside and see the whole stock? Or if you, the mathematician, find the manager a more interesting and demanding customer than you first thought, why not try serving behind the counter for a while?

NOTES AND REFERENCES

76 Freund, J. E., and Williams, F. J., *Modern Business Statistics* (Pitman, 1959).
77 Schreier, F. T., *Modern Marketing Research,* Wadsworth Publishing Co. Inc., Belmont, Calif., U.S.A. (1963).
1962).
78 Battersby, A., *A Guide to Stock Control* (Pitman, 1962).
79 Juran, J. M., *Quality Control Handbook* (2nd edn., McGraw-Hill, 1962).
80 Brown, R. G., *Statistical Forecasting for Inventory Control* (McGraw-Hill, 1959)
81 Snedecor, G. W., *Statistical Methods* (4th edn, p. 133, Iowa State College Press, 1946).
82 Styan, G. P. H., and Smith, H. Jr, *Journal of Marketing Research* (Feb. 1964), p. 50
83 Morrison, P., and Morrison, E. (eds), *Charles Babbage and his Calculating Engines*, Part II, chapter VI, (Dover, 1961).
84 Shannon, C., and Weaver, W., *The Mathematical Theory of Communication* (University of Illinois Press, 1949).
85 Ashby, W. R., *An Introduction to Cybernetics* (Chapman and Hall, 1957).

NOTES AND REFERENCES *cont'd*

86 Broadbent, S. R., *Journal of the Royal Statistical Society, Series B* (1958), vol. 20, p. 111.

87 Lee, A. M., *Operational Research Quarterly* (1959), vol. 10, No. 4, p. 206.